Nature Walks

D1430390

Other books by Cathy Johnson

Nature

The Nocturnal Naturalist
On Becoming Lost: A Naturalist's Search for Meaning
A Naturalist's Cabin: Constructing a Dream
The Naturalist's Path: Beginning the Study of Nature
One Square Mile: A Naturalist's Journal of America

Art

Drawing and Painting from Nature
Painting Nature's Details in Watercolor
The Sierra Club Guide to Sketching in Nature
Watercolor Tricks and Techniques
Creating Texture in Watercolor

Nature Walks

Insight and Advice for Observant Ramblers

Cathy Johnson

STACKPOLE
BOOKS

Copyright © 1994 by Stackpole Books

Published by
STACKPOLE BOOKS
5067 Ritter Road
Mechanicsburg, PA 17055

All rights reserved, including the right to reproduce this book or
portions thereof in any form or by any means, electronic or mechanical,
including photocopying, recording, or by any information storage and
retrieval system, without permission in writing from the publisher.
All inquiries should be addressed to Stackpole Books, 5067 Ritter Road,
Mechanicsburg, PA 17055.

Printed in the United States of America

10 9 8 7 6 5 4 3 2 1

First edition

Cover design by Tracy Patterson
Cover illustration by Cathy Johnson

A few pieces of the material contained in this book appeared in different form
in *Country Living* and *Sierra* magazines. Our thanks to them for their
cooperation.

Library of Congress Cataloging-in-Publication Data

Johnson, Cathy A. (Cathy A.)
    Nature walks : insight and advice for observant ramblers / Cathy
Johnson. — 1st ed.
        p.   cm.
    Includes bibliographical references.
    ISBN 0-8117-2561-8
    1. Walking — North America.   2. Nature trails — North America.
I. Title.
GV199.44.N67J64   1994
796.5'2'097 — dc20   93-34104
                                                             CIP

To Harris,
who is always beside me—
in mind and spirit
if not in body.

Table of Contents

Preface

A SLOW RAMBLE ON FOOT—shank's mare—is conducive to both observation and contemplation. Locomotion by long muscles and willpower beats the exhaust-fumed rumble of a car any day. Driving requires a constant coordination of hand and eye and steering wheel (with brakes and gearshift thrown into the equation). Other cars on the road, the patchwork of traffic signs, and the arterial branching of streets, roads, and highways combine to render all attempts at clear-headed noticing stillborn. Even a bicycle requires us to shift gears and thread our way through the distractions of traffic and balance and mechanical coordination. It's impossible to lose ourselves in thought—or free ourselves for observation—when we must stay so firmly grounded in the necessities of getting from here to there.

Walking, on the other hand, is nearly as natural as breathing. Most of us don't remember learning how—it's just something that happens. And when it does—one foot in front of the other, one foot in front of the other—thoughts are free to go skipping over the landscape like thistledown on the wind.

The steady rhythm of breath and footfall, the elastic expansion and contraction of thigh muscles, the inaudible metronome of heartbeats are conducive to a kind of open-ended reflection; the slow pace is perfect for stops often and immediate, governed by the spontaneous.

A new dimension opens before the serious walker—not the race walker or the backpacker loaded down with seventy pounds of gear, just the one who finds feet a delightful mode of casual travel. Perceptions alter with the changing perspective. A lifelong dependence on the sense of sight merges with a baroque tapestry of scent and sound and touch.

A thousand subtle perfumes caress my face and I follow the dominant one to its source—flower or fungi or simply the nose-tickling scent of frost forming on dry midnight grass. I catch the flavor of my neighbor's fire on the air and know that he is burning the prunings from his apple orchard; the perfume is unmistakable. The sharp tang of walnut scents the earth itself. Dig a hole near one of these trees and you will find that pungent aroma infuses the soil as though earth were a vast extension of tree. It's defensive; the walnut protects itself from competition for light and nutrients by emitting a strong chemical that discourages other growth nearby.

The hedge apples that squirrels have harvested from my Osage orange trees are also aromatic; you can tell where the brush-tailed rodents have had their feast by scent alone. It's not something you'd catch from your car window.

Sounds are no longer a half-noticed jumble, but a complex, symphonic score when we enter the arpeggio afoot. Cars roar and clank, and bikes set up their own competing counter-rhythm, a mechanical hum of chain links and the hiss of tires against the road; the symphony then is by Bartok. Only the whisper of footsteps—stilled the instant I am—is quiet enough to allow me to hear each subtlety of note and breath.

The far-off yammering of migrating geese, almost too faint to decipher woven into the wind, nonetheless raises the hair on my arms when I pick it out among the other instruments. It's a sound that seldom fails to touch us with a delicious unease as though we, too, needed to be somewhere other than here—like the sound of a train whistle down the corridors of memory. The insistent, repeated entreaty of a whippoorwill recalls me to my own past in a small, heartland town. These big-mouthed members of the goatsucker clan have been known to call over 2,000 times without a rest.

On an autumn night, the snare-drum-and-wire-brush whisper of woolly-bear caterpillars in the dead leaves is barely audible; they are intent on their own downward migration into the rapidly chilling soil. I try to imagine a winter spent snug underground, locked away from the rigors of fire tending and ice storms—and know for a certainty that I wouldn't change a thing. A midwinter walk is a brush with the immense, precipitous edge of life itself, a tightrope between survival and death; we are never more fully alive. The edge between heat exhaustion and sanity on a hot midwestern afternoon is as real, as equally invisible.

Landscape, at this pace, is as variable as clouds on a midsummer day. Afoot, microclimes of temperature and humidity change from warm to cool in the space of a hundred feet. Habitat modifications are immediate, as edges give way to open savannas, and forests close in again a few yards down the path. Vertical explorations—uphill, upcountry—multiply change to the tenth power. Boredom is impossible.

Walking segues almost without effort into stalking, if necessary. The sudden sight of a green heron requires only freezing in place, perhaps kneeling to disguise our two-leggedness, and watching for the opportunity to move closer. No need for brakes and slamming car doors. On foot, I may be able to approach a band of feeding deer if I move only when they do; spotting a herd framed in the windshield can't touch the feeling. Last summer I stepped aside like a matador on the narrow woods path to allow a frightened fawn to race past me, full throttle. Had I been in my car, he would have been roadkill. Instead, he was heart-pounding delight.

Not everything I stalk is animate—although some would assert that the wily morel is indeed sentient, and as sneaky as they come. On a May morning, Ed Wilde and Gary Willnauer—a teacher and an attorney in their everyday clothing—accompanied me on a trek near historic Fort Osage to search for the delectable mushroom. The men carried their muskets and dressed in period attire while I clambored over deadfalls and slid down inclines slick with leaf litter, filling my botanist's collecting tin with the stuff of a mycologist's dreams. I slipped into the past as easily as falling down those inclines, only wishing for knee breeches to replace my petticoats and apron; beyond that the sense of the past entwined with the present was palpable. The fort's oak log buildings, barely visible through the forest, were lovely and welcoming, and I could have believed my naturalist's rambles had somehow found a door to the early years of white discovery in Missouri Territory. Michael J. Fox can go back to the future if he likes; the age of exploration on the frontier is far more fascinating to me. The morels, fried on the hearth in the factory's kitchen, were shared among reenactors and public alike, tying us all together in fact as well as in imagination.

The expended energy of such a trek is therapy; when I am wound tight and ready to explode, a brisk walk cranks back the tension a few notches. If only temporarily, I forget what it was that had my pressure valves overloaded and find myself transfixed by something satisfyingly other. When I am sad or depressed, the steady pace that carries me far from my black mood delivers me back at my doorstep ready to pick up the thread again—and far more able.

Walking is far more than mere therapy for a neurotic mind, of course; it's a way to enter the equation, to rejoice in life—my life, the larger life around me. It's a way to lose myself in what I see and hear and feel.

It's easy to see what's what at a snail's pace, impossible at fifty-five mph, encased in steel and rubber. On shank's mare I can move to a rhythm all my own, a rhythm more synchronous with the slow turning of the earth and the unfolding of life before me.

Acknowledgments

EVERY BOOK IS A GROUP EFFORT; no one works totally alone in a garret, pecking away at an old typewriter. Libraries and librarians offer assistance, resident experts in many fields answer questions, friends and family support and encourage. This book is no exception.

William E. Pittman, Curator of Archaeological Collections at the Colonial Williamsburg Foundation, was extremely helpful in offering a view of archaeology that I could relate to natural history. Kevin Morgan, an amateur archaeologist in the truest sense of the word *amateur*—he loves what he does—helped me understand and recognize the significance of my finds among the flint.

Pete Rucker, DVM, and Robert Buzard, GP, were my medical experts for wildlife and humans respectively; George Hiser, agent for the Missouri Department of Conservation, was also helpful in answering questions and sharing impressions.

Dr. John MacDougal and Chris Dietrich of the Missouri Botanical Gardens sent reams of information, as did the Konza Prairie Research Project in Kansas.

As always, the women at Mid-Continent Library in Excelsior Springs were a constant help, especially at the last minute—

and especially Marian Hurtubise; they're used to me, but still patient. Friends Grady and Terri Manus, Ed and C. J. Wilde, Steve Wilson, Scott Sturgeon, Duke Drury, Rob Stone, and Bishop David Jones offered a glimpse of the past and shared their combined lifetimes of research into history and historical natural history with me, aiming me toward sources archaic and modern. My sister, Yvonne Busey, and her husband, Richard, offered their home, their car, and their Nevada for my research.

My editor at Stackpole Books, Judith Schnell, was invariably helpful and supportive, believing in the project from the beginning and being patient to the end. My other editors, including those at *Country Living*, *The Artist's Magazine*, *Sports Afield*, and *Family Adventures*, were patient with conflicting deadlines and juggled schedules while this book was in the making.

And as always, my husband Harris saw me through a difficult birth in the form of a book that outgrew its original intent.

Introduction

I ALWAYS IMAGINE, when I see something in nature that strikes a particularly resonant emotional or intellectual chord—or stirs my curiosity—that *this* walk, *this* day, will stand out among all the others, that I will remember it forever. I do not. My short-term memory synapses shut down in minutes; there's simply too much data to save. Static claims a goodly amount. In order to access long-term memory, I employ written notes and field sketches; it's a way of creating my own visual aids. Even left-brained people (which I am not) benefit by using these keys to memory and learning; don't corporate reports utilize pie charts? When you make your own visuals, taking time to fully absorb, choosing just what to include and how to annotate your findings, the benefit is much enhanced.

What is interesting to me is that keeping this kind of annotated journal has a side effect I hadn't anticipated: It increases my powers of observation. As I stop, look closely, and decide on what to sketch, I am seeing far more than ever before. If I can maintain a broad enough focus, peripheral vision picks up still more; then I can zero in on whatever it was that piqued my interest.

I may take a camera along to record quick impressions, and

that's fine. But a camera's eye opens only for a fraction of a second before it's ready to move on. It has no memory whatsoever (beyond its own negative image), and though the tangible results of what it "sees" may act as triggers to my memory, unless I have taken the time to really look at what I've photographed, it is as though I am merely a technical adjunct to the lens—a casual observer at best.

This is not true of professional nature photographers, of course. If you wait half a day for the perfect shot (which I do not), then you obviously have the opportunity to observe in depth; to absorb in plenty. But for me the hand-eye coordination and emotional investment of a sketch is the key.

A sketch takes time—that precious commodity that we hate to waste and seem, these days, to have so little of. But it is a commodity with curiously elastic properties. When we spend it wisely it expands to encompass more than the increments ticked off on a digital watch; it becomes the milieu in which we swim, the air we breathe, the beating of our hearts. A sketch may take thirty seconds, three minutes, an hour—in that time I am exposed to the whole ecosystem that surrounds my subject. I am a receiver. My audio system is fully operational. My visual gears are engaged. Skin cells record the most subtle of passing sensual stimuli. My powers of observation have increased tenfold.

When I remember the early naturalists who explored my neck of the woods, like Lewis and Clark, who first noted the Osage orange whose rough fruit I hold in my hand, I am tied to the past with the bonds of discovery and delight. Clark sketched his finds in his journal as I do today.

I try to build time to sketch into my walks. I allow an open-ended arrival-and-departure schedule that would drive an airline to bankruptcy in a month. I go prepared to ramble.

What you choose to take along as sketching tools or a field notebook is up to you. My advice—hard earned, hard learned—is to keep it simple, keep it lightweight, and keep it accessible. I use a hardbound book that will withstand the rigors of a ramble that may include a climb up a limestone bluff or a leap across an icy stream; I've dropped my journals down many an incline and dented many a corner in the process, so I know that they survive. So do I.

A #2 pencil with an eraser is a good choice, and accessible to anyone. An HB mechanical pencil, .5 to .7 mm, obviates the need for a sharpener (they usually come with erasers, as well). If you like crisp images and easily read notes, try a fiber-tipped pen; Micron Pigma makes a waterproof one—the better to sketch in the rain, my dear.

And don't be concerned if you are not an artist—if you "can't draw a straight line." These pages are _your own_ place; no need to share them with anyone unless you want to. Sketch if you like; take rubbings; use written notes alone—it's the act of taking time to observe, fully and carefully, that counts.

What you choose to include is up to you, but I find it helpful to include the date, journal-style, and a few weather notes. At one time I carefully recorded highs and lows, rainfall, and river stage, a fine way to know what's happening upstream. If you like, a rough note or sketch as to overall habitat or area will remind you of where you found your subject. Distance walked can be noted, as well as walking conditions. It's up to you; whatever you choose to include will act as memory jogs and keys.

There are thousands of sources out there to help you decipher your hieroglyphs. If you find your journals pose more questions than they answer, rejoice. The world—_your_ world— is still not so known and mapped as to prove too boring to explore. You can still plant your flag on a bump of knowledge, if only one _you_ were unaware of. That's the joy of learning.

Check your findings with the library's data banks. A university library is often a mine of information not necessarily available to the casual seeker. Find experts in that same university to give you their personal insights; they are usually more than willing to share their knowledge if you are sincerely interested.

It's a two-pronged approach. Walking allows me to go out where I can observe. The siren call to get out there and see what's what, to make notes and sketches, gets me out the front door, walking shoes on and journal in hand. The fact that there are so many habitats to explore, that there is such a seasonal variety, so much delicious difference between night and day, all that is sheer gravy. Boredom has no place in my vocabulary.

I chose to do this book as a way to explore; an excuse for discovery. It has been that. No matter what I imagine I will find, or how much preliminary research I've done, there's always something of the unexpected in the world outside my door. No amount of browsing through field guides can prepare me for the reality. Like the blind men describing an elephant, when I've only *read* what constitutes a prairie, a forest, or a marsh—or even a time of day—I can describe only a distorted picture of reality.

My intent was to explore and sketch and annotate these walks, *then* to add a bit of research to the picture. It's how I work best; it's how I share best.

And in the end, what we do with these sketches and notes is as individual as we are. Mine may provide me with raw information to compare with known facts; may help me identify a flower or insect I've found but do not recognize; may become the framework on which I hang the words of a book or article. They also act as a record of my days; an annotated journal; an observed life. They are learning tools and discipline and play, all at the same time.

• **One** •

Setting Out

BEYOND MY DOOR the world rolls endlessly away in all directions. Miles of possibility lie in undulating landswells embroidered with a tapestry of silvery creeks and blue-sky lakes, a magic carpet inviting me to step aboard. I almost hesitate to take that first step—where will it take me? Where will it lead? But the call of the natural is more insistent than Odysseus' sirens and resistance is not an option.

There is a subdued excitement in preparation; anticipation is a worthy response to embarking into the world. It matters not whether I've set aside this time, planned an excursion, and mapped out my route. I don't care. Any walk, any time, brings its share of satisfaction. Whether I've packed the car with provisions to last for a week or head out on a spontaneous walk around the neighborhood, I've always found something of note. Even when my preparations are as simple as stepping out the door, catching up my journal and a pencil as I go, there's a small flame of excitement.

We are no Magellans, exploring the New World; much of what is out there is known, written down in someone's book, cataloged and neatly filed away. But known to science is not known to me, known intellectually is not known viscerally. Discovery for myself, *by* myself, is the irresistible draw.

And it's not all so known as it might seem. Even science is baffled by everyday wonders. This summer I arrived—afoot—at my walnut grove and looked up to see a strange sight. The rough bark of the trees, normally dark and a dull gray in color, shone in the sun as though polished. I stood for several minutes, just staring, realizing *something* was not right, but not being able to fathom what it was. The place was different, as though under a spell. But instead of a dark spell, this one was light-filled and lovely.

At first I thought I simply had never noticed how many pale-branched sycamores there were—but though these trees were pale as sycamores, they were shiny, not dull and chalky. And they were everywhere, surrounding me with light. There was something unsettling about these pale glistening limbs reaching up to gather the sun. As I walked around the grove, looking up at the trees from all angles, I was astounded at their shine, gold as the morning light itself.

Upon closer inspection I could see filaments of white tying root to crown—not many, but enough. I knew that whatever had tied that fine macrame must also have created the upper limbs' odd polish.

How odd wasn't apparent until a few days later. A violent windstorm combed through the trees overnight, pulling dead-wood down to a jackstraw jumble of limbs. A long ribbon of pale stuff lay draped over a limb, and from a distance I guessed it to be a snake's shed skin to add to my collection. It was not. Instead, a long streamer had ripped loose from the limb it had wrapped so tightly, amazingly strong and reaching from trunk to twig. It was insect webbing, plastic and close-woven and utterly astounding. Now that I could see at first hand what it was that wrapped all the walnut trees from fifteen feet or so off the ground, I could not believe it. This was not the work of only a few insects; not even this two-inch by six-foot strip I held in my hand could have been that. This had to be the labor of a small army, multiplied by the webs that encased the rest of the

walnut
tree's
upper
limbs
all
shing
with
webs

fallen limb—times every walnut tree in the grove and squared to just this side of infinity.

I called Jerry Montraselli, the forester with the Missouri Department of Conservation at Burr Oak Woods, who was as nonplused as I. No, that's not quite right—at least he had the advantage of knowing my woods were not an isolated case. He'd gotten dozens of calls in the past few days from puzzled people whose trees were suddenly wrapped tight like last night's leftovers.

"We're working on it; we're calling it the Walnut Waxer," he told me. "Call back in a few days."

I hung up and looked out over the walnut grove. The glistening tourniquets were strong; I could barely break off the strip I'd investigated earlier. Would this kill the trees? Would they die of lack of light or air? Would the horde of invisible insects denude the canopy of leaves? Already I could detect a thinning of shade, open sky where none had been before. Two years of drought had stressed this area badly, and with this blow—and such a severe insect infestation had to be a blow—I could picture a landscape of skeletons reaching upward above my head.

When I called the state agriculture department, I became more puzzled still. "Webs in the trees? Sounds like fall webworm," the entomologist told me.

"But there aren't any loose hammocky webs," I replied. "This is a tight, shiny coating on the limbs."

"Well, then it sounds like an infestation of aphids. They get pretty bad, you know, and exude a honeydew that covers the limbs. We've seen it so extreme that there's literally a wet spot under the trees."

"But it's not that. It's a glossy webbing that actually wraps the limbs; it's almost like they were shrink-wrapped in plastic." I described the tough gray-white streamer I had picked up, but it was no use.

"I guess you've got me," he said. "Better talk to your local forester with the Conservation Department."

I waited a few more days and called Montraselli again, but a few days wasn't enough. He had called everyone he could think of that might have a clue—no one did. "We're still working on it."

Time passed and the rains came. Over a period of weeks the tight wrapping developed holes, then runs, then eventually it was no longer there. I had almost forgotten about it until one day I wondered if the mystery had been solved. Deep in winter I talked to Montraselli again. "Any luck with finding the identity of the Walnut Waxer?"

"Not yet. We collected larvae and we're cultivating them till spring to see what hatches. The problem around here is that by the time we noticed them they had finished feeding and we couldn't find any live ones; we had to go up north."

"But it seemed to have happened overnight," I said. "First the trees were normal, and in the space of a few days they were coated!"

"It just seemed that way; it was just that we hadn't noticed. By the way, my name didn't stick; we're not calling it the Walnut Waxer anymore—it's the Pantyhose Stripper!"

"Well, that's apropos," I laughed. "Who came up with that one?"

"Our female pathologist. I guess from a distance it looked like the trees had been waxed, but when you're holding them, the strips look just like pantyhose."

And so they do—support hose, given their strength and close weave. The Department of Conservation has sent samples to the Universities of Kansas and Missouri to incubate; the puzzle remains uncracked until spring, at least, and I am pleased to know that there is still mystery about. The unknown is in my woods and there's still plenty to discover.

Even those things I think I know—the blooming cycles of plants, the habits of mammals I've observed since childhood—can still surprise me. Violets may bloom in November. Last year a single branch of my forsythia took a notion to flower out of season, and put out yellow blossoms in the fall; who knows how it got its signals mixed?

This day I had taken a walk to see the Dutchman's breeches; they were almost in bloom, and there was a pale blush across the creek. The fact that the weather had been warm enough to call the first morels up from the soil wasn't exactly a deterrent, either. The rangy yellow pup that had half adopted me had come for a visit and joined me eagerly on my walk. He seemed agitated; his hackles were up, and I heard Ugly and Teeka, my neighbor's dogs, barking excitedly in the woods nearby. I wondered if their racket was what had the pup so alert. I went to investigate, and Ugly and Teeka ran off as though they were guilty of some mischief. In the flurry of movement I noticed a furtive shape that ducked behind the trunk of the tree about ten feet off the ground. It was too big for a squirrel, too bullet-headed for a cat. I crossed the creek and looked behind the tree to find an extremely frightened woodchuck, halfway up the small tree.

It is not the first time I've seen a woodchuck up a tree—but it is only the second after a lifetime of rambling through woods and meadows. The first time, I thought I was crazy, or that the woodchuck was. But the Conservation agent I called to question about the event said it was rare but certainly not unheard of. Woodchucks climb to escape predators—or perhaps to secure a particularly tasty morsel like a ripe pawpaw. This one appeared to have been taking refuge from Ugly and Teeka.

The pup—inexperienced or just stupid—didn't see him there, although he obviously scented something, hackles still spiked at attention. It was a perfect opportunity for field sketching, but I'd left my journal behind. I counted on the woodchuck's remaining immobile, frozen in place by fear, and hotfooted it back for the book. As I figured, when I returned the chuck was just where I had left him.

The pup didn't have a clue, though he snuffled around nearby, a patch of hair on his nape still erect. Each time he got too near the woodchuck's tree I distracted him, sketching the huddled form as quickly as possible. The chuck shut its eyes, unwilling or unable to look at our threatening presences below him.

After finishing my sketches and returning to the cabin, I remembered I had also brought my camera to the cabin with me, a rare occurrence—and a picture is worth more words than I had time to pen. (Besides, with a sketch I could be accused of imagining things or making up my picture with an artist's license to create.) I returned to the tree one more time and shot three or four photos from several angles.

But all this attention focused in one place was too much. Something was too obviously up, and it was a woodchuck. Suddenly groundhog eyes met dog eyes and the tension that had held for the last twenty minutes snapped like a rope. The silly animal broke and skittered down the tree and away through the woods with the pup in wild pursuit.

"Damn," I swore to myself, fearing that my curiosity and my inveterate desire to document may have cost the groundhog its life. The young hound's hunting instinct was fully aroused. He was totally, completely focused. He took off after the chuck, nose inches from the rodent's tail. The noise was horrendous, a series of yips and barks and howls and growls—some from the pup, some from the woodchuck.

They barreled through the underbrush at top speed, with me in their wake. I yelled and whistled at the pup, trying to break his concentration until the chuck could find its hole. Pushing through the mud and weeds after them, I hardly noticed the scratches and the need for gumboots.

There was a series of skirmishes as the chuck first turned to face his tormenter, then made a frantic break, then turned again to snarl at the dog before racing on a few yards farther.

At last, after a few hundred yards of this start-and-stop melee, we were almost to the big slump block in the creek, the big chuck desperately silent, the pup yammering, and me still whistling and calling. I caught the young dog's attention, at last, for the split second it took for the groundhog to gain the fallen rocks behind the block, and the pup looked back at me, accusingly or just for the hell of it, I had no way of knowing. I called him and cajoled him, and like the innocent he is, he turned with me and bumbled across the creek, stepping on the tipping rocks or splashing into the water and not caring, apparently, which one. Now he lay on the deck in the sun, dozing lightly, nose twitching, dreaming—perhaps—of woodchucks that climb trees.

Common sense—native intelligence, my husband, Harris, calls it—is a fine thing; it's not only Scouts who should be prepared. There are certain things I plan to carry if I am taking more than a simple turn around the neighborhood. Depending on my purpose and how long I intend to be gone, I try to plan accordingly. An afternoon's ramble in the summer mandates a source of drinking water, even if it is only a small canteen holding less than a pint. The one hanging handy at my shoulder is unbreakable tin, a reproduction of an historic model—a fine alternative to plastic.

My husband swears by deet, given chiggers and mosquitoes and the possibility of tick bite and Lyme disease (not to mention Rocky Mountain spotted fever), though I admit to forgetting to use it as often as not. If I am to be long in the sun, a sunscreen prevents regrets, and sensible, seasonal clothing allows me to stay as long as I want in the outdoors.

A longer trek involves carrying food; how much depends on the duration and object of the stay. My friends Ed Wilde, Gary Willnauer, Steve Wilson, and Duke Drury, who trek living-history style, swear by the lightweight staples of another era. For a weekend (or longer) journey, they carry venison jerky, a bit of bacon or salt pork, cornmeal, and brick tea of the type the colonists used. Dried apples or other dried fruit provide quick sugar energy and light weight. I borrow from their experience or take along an apple and some peanut-butter crackers.

Ed has cataloged for me the contents of his winter knapsack, haversack, and bedroll. This somewhat daunting list includes his food stores, fire-starting kit and tinderbox, folding skillet and corn boiler, knife, spoon, and fork, candles, extra moccasins and socks, compass, sewing kit for emergency repairs, journal, ink and quill. He assures me that the entire kit—including his hand-woven blanket—weighs no more than

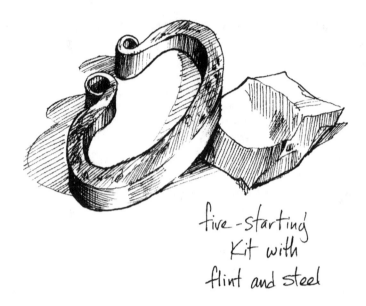

five-starting
Kit with
flint and steel

twenty pounds and that he could live in the woods for a week or more with its contents. Duke adds an essential I fully endorse: chocolate. He chews willow bark to stand in for aspirin, and why not? That's where the common drug came from in the first place.

The things they carry are documented to our country's past, things that served our forebears well and kept them alive. Daniel Boone, who lived the end of his long life in my state, carried a similar load. These survival tools have proven their worth. They also feel good in the hand—basic, uncontrived, and most decidedly non-high tech.

I pick and choose among yesterday and today for my own essentials on a solitary trek through the woods. My field journal and a pen or pencil are first on my list. A small pair of binoculars with wonderful magnification capabilities weighs only a few ounces; if I've remembered it, a pocket microscope brings the micro-environment to my attention. I carry deet, but I also take flint and steel and the turkey call Steve carved from a gobbler's wingbone. My expertise at calling up a turkey to observe or sketch is nil, but the neighborhood hounds think I'm fascinating.

It isn't necessary to always set forth alone, though I find I am more observant when my attention is not divided by two. When I am with someone—my husband, a friend—I look at them, I talk to them. And while that in itself is pleasurable, walking alone is conducive to a deeper kind of experience.

Either way, there are advantages and disadvantages. When I am with someone, I am twice myself. Two pairs of eyes may find things one misses. Two pairs of ears hear not twice as much but more, perhaps, unless idle chatter intervenes. I am safer with a partner—whether in the woods or in a more urban setting, walking on the buddy system is a fine thing if one becomes injured, ill, or harassed.

It all depends on the end in mind; if what I want is to plumb experience fully, to take my time, to let myself feel and think and notice—then a walk alone is the ticket. If exercise or fun or companionship is the goal, then a partner is as welcome as sunlight after a long, wet season. When a group of friends goes on a trek it is an entirely different thing, hilarious and bonding. Walking encompasses almost any goal; the aim is up to you.

Today when I step out the door there is no telling what I will see, what everyday wonders will unfold. There's an *overall* sense of common expectation, it's true—in spring I will see nesting birds and tender, ground-hugging flowers, in autumn a brilliant patchwork of leaves, in winter a delicate tracery of dark limbs. I know what to expect, what to look for. But beyond knowing, beyond expectation, there is no telling.

It is a fair morning, wrapped with pale, high mare's tails of clouds. The wind at 50,000 feet and higher above terra firma has combed them into images of itself. Who has seen the wind? I have, written in the clouds.

It is still cold in these early hours, though it is now spring. The scent of new life prickles in my nose like spice. I can't get enough and breathe deeply until I am dizzy, then sit quickly, grinning.

I have escaped. It is an odd sensation shared by many of us who love the outdoors. However loved, however pleasant one's home, still to get away, to be outdoors, is—there's no other word—to escape. No matter how happily married we are, what good friends we have, how satisfying our jobs are, we are like children again, bursting out the door and running for all we're worth. I don't care where I'm going. I don't harbor expectations; I'm open to suggestion. And I'm gone.

There's a luxury in this kind of freedom, however fleeting. To be by myself, to answer to no one, to be under no constraints other than those I put upon myself is to be rich indeed. Voluntary incarceration is not my style; I won't lock myself up without good cause.

"Aren't you afraid?" "Is it safe?" "Will there be other people around?" "Are you armed?" These are some of the questions I am most often asked about my work in the outdoors—

even when that work is as simple as taking a walk and sketching what I see. Gender aside, these are questions that affect us all these days. What used to be unthinkable is now an everyday occurrence in big cities, an occasional horror in small towns.

No, it is not safe. If I were looking for safe I'd lock myself in a room with deadbolts and barred windows, burglar-alarmed to my eyebrows. It is not safe; it never was, really. There have always been deadfalls, quicksand, poisonous snakes, lightning strikes. And there's always been the possibility of injury, of hypothermia or heatstroke. I practice ordinary precautions—against natural disasters or man-made ones—and take my chances with the rest.

We imagine the problem Out There to be an increase in crime against persons, forgetting that there's a lot more to be concerned with than what another human being can do to us—forgetting that common sense can overcome a lot of dangerous situations, and that educating ourselves about the dangers prevents many a disaster. And, finally, that it's worth it. It's all worth it.

Suggested Reading:

Baron, Robert C., and Elizabeth Darby Junkin (editors), *Of Discovery and Destiny*, Fulcrum, Inc., Golden, Colorado, 1986.

Kals, W. S., *Land Navigation Handbook: The Sierra Club Guide to Map and Compass*, Sierra Club Books, San Francisco, 1983.

Strickland, Ron (editor), *Shank's Mare: A Compendium of Remarkable Walks*, Paragon House Publishers, New York, 1988.

Thoreau, Henry David, *Walden*, any edition.

• **T w o** •

Walking Through Time

Stones and Bones

Bones lie scattered on the ground as though exhumed haphazardly by someone in a hurry; as though some ghoul had rushed through his grisly business and moved on. Here is a shoulder blade, bleached to a ghostly luminescence; there, a pelvis now cradles only air, not life.

It's a jigsaw puzzle of random pieces that once meant flesh and blood. Now, it's hard to tell what this creature might have been, and where the rest of it has gotten to. Cryptic gray-white shapes as hard as the limestone that beds them, the bones pose inevitable questions and hint at their own answers. The sense of the picture is still present in the pieces. This was once a sentient being, identifiable in whatever state; all it takes is a certain forensic knowledge. If I encounter a strange creature's bones in the woods, I sleuth out the answers from my books—and indulgent experts.

I pick up a bone as big as my shin bone and sniff it, trying to guess its age. I notice the fine tracing of tooth marks—some small mammal has found sustenance in the calcareous remains. We're good for something, all of us animals, even when it's too late to care.

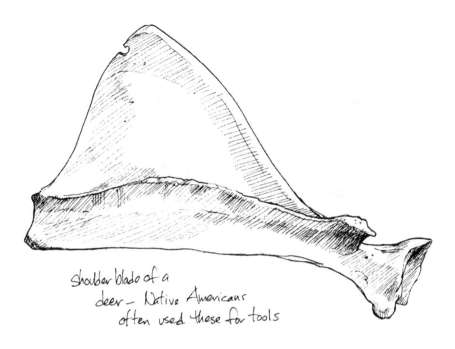

Shoulder blade of a
deer — Native Americans
often used these for tools

Here and there they lie as they died, strung bone on bone, vertebra on vertebra like a biology lab skeleton. These are easier to identify; if there's a skull it's even better. I look for these especially, pouncing on them as though I'd found a diamond, tucking them carefully into my knapsack to draw or to key out later at the cabin if mystery still remains. As a naturalist, bone hunting is part of my stock in trade, a kind of clue I can't afford to overlook; squeamishness has no place here. Mammals are secretive, many of them nocturnal and as seldom seen as Ed Abbey's favorite monkeywrencher. If it weren't for the mute evidence of bones, I'd have no idea of the diversity of life that shares this crazy quilt landscape of overlapping territories.

My worn copy of Schwartz's *Wild Mammals of Missouri* is invaluable for the work of keying bones, with silvery pencil drawings of skulls from every angle and close-ups of teeth and other details. Sometimes all that's left is a bit of jawbone, a snout that's lost everything but a V of teeth. Still, from their shape, placement, and number in the dental arcade, I can often tell an eastern spotted skunk from a mink; a raccoon, with its hard palate extending way beyond the molars, from a young coyote.

Possums—alligators with fur, carrying fifty piano teeth in their long snouts—waddle by in the dark, whether I see them or not; the bones say so. Successful in their ungainly homeliness and their marsupial lifestyle, their form hasn't changed in eons. Pugnacious badgers never observed in the fur populate these woods; testimony resides in bony remnants grinning side by side on my cabin shelf.

Similarities jump out in the observation. Curved, rust-striped front teeth attest that the eastern gray squirrel and the beaver both belong to the order Rodentia, though these rodents belong to different families—squirrels are Sciuridae, beavers, Castoridae.

The teeth of beavers are many times the size of those of squirrels. It's as if the squirrel's teeth were made as scale models: Once that's right, go on to the real thing. It's not hard to imagine trees being felled in a few hours by these strong cutting tools, sharp as German steel. Beavers are capable of amazing damage overnight, and trees are piled everywhere like a giant's game of jackstraws. A small and selective hurricane might have passed.

The lower incisors are immense, maybe an inch and a half long, big around as a finger and as sharp as though honed with Carborundum. The uppers nip them closely with a powerful cutting action; the neatly sliced limbs look as though they were severed with a garden pruner in a single, efficient cut.

I've found no beaver skulls on my land; the creek is too small and too seasonal to attract them, though once I did find several sticks with distinctive toothmarks whittled at their ends. I could discover no further evidence of beaver activity than these few cryptic limbs, none larger than half an inch in diameter. There were no felled trees, no dams, no bank dens—and certainly no huge, splayed footprints in the soft mud. I concluded that the limbs must have washed downstream with high water.

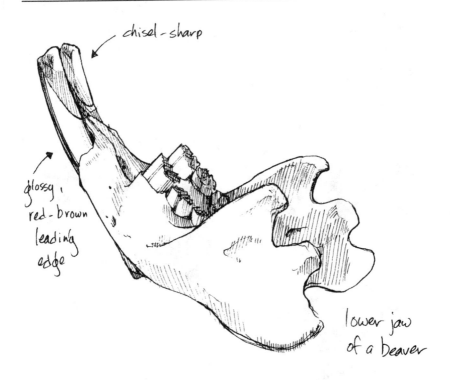

chisel-sharp

glossy,
red-brown
leading
edge

lower jaw
of a beaver

It takes a particular habitat to appeal to beavers. Here in Missouri they often make no dams at all, or dam only the head-waters and shallow channels—most streams are too deep or too subject to the fluctuations of flood.

That is not to say we don't have our share of beavers—they simply make bank dens instead of the characteristic domes, with living chambers snug and dry above the high-water mark. Here, they store food supplies and bear their young in safety.

To cut a tree, a beaver stands on its hind legs and has at it with those big chisel-like incisors. The animal cuts a notch at a convenient height, then cuts another a short distance below the first. Then bark and wood chips are chiseled away with the lower incisors while the big animal braces itself with its uppers. The beaver will work its way clear around a trunk in this man-ner, particularly on a larger tree.

How can the beaver know how a tree will fall? It doesn't plan cut and notch like a lumberjack, but it does apparently

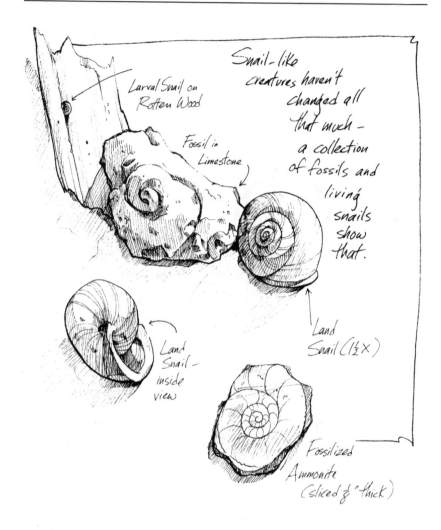

Larval Snail on Rotten Wood

Fossil in Limestone

Snail-like creatures haven't changed all that much — a collection of fossils and living snails show that.

Land Snail ($1\frac{1}{2}$X)

Land Snail — inside view

Fossilized Ammonite (sliced $\frac{3}{8}$" thick)

recognize that trees near creeks often lean toward water—or perhaps it's just easier to get at the leaning side to begin the deepest cut. The success rate at dropping the tree just where it does the beaver the most good is quite high.

Though beavers usually cut trees between two and eight inches in diameter, the late Charles Schwartz told of a record tree of five feet, seven inches going down to a family of rodents. I run my finger along the strong chisel edge of the skull's incisors and am not a bit surprised.

Older by far than the skulls I find on my rambles are the remains of fossils in the rocks and in the riverbeds nearby. Folded into the bone-colored limestone are clamshells 300 million years old. Chaetetes coral colonies have recrystallized into powdery ghosts, flaking away each time I touch them, leaving starshine on my fingertips. Blind trilobytes stare sightlessly from their eternal present—they stud the limestone matrix formed by even smaller creatures that lived and died in the inland sea when Missouri was an equatorial "X" on nobody's map. You are here—but where is everybody else?

A few miles away in the sandbars of the Kaw River in the neighboring state of Kansas, fossil hunters find colossal skulls and whole bones that tell the tale of a somewhat later time—a mere 1.5 million years ago at the close of the last Ice Age. The upper leg bone or humerus of a giant short-faced bear was found there recently, the largest of its kind found in the world. This bear would have been over eight feet high at the shoulder, a daunting sight had anyone been there to see it. These bears roamed the continent from Alaska to Mexico, preying on great herds of extinct grazing animals.

The calcium-bearing limestone that underlies much of my area affects the land in ways subtle and profound. The creekbed slashes through the valley, a jumble of rocks of all sizes that slow the progress of the water or crash into the meanders in high water, jackhammering the banks into ever-changing shapes like a restless sculptor who can't seem to quit his creation and call it finished. Each time the water rises, the landscape changes, subtly or dramatically, and new fossils are exposed as great boulders are upended by the force of water.

Silently beneath the soil, the rocks leach nutrients that nourish a mixed colony of wildflowers. Spring Dutchman's breeches, trillium, and pale corydalis grow in the limestone glade; clammy cuphea, sticky stemmed but not sweet, lines the path through September woods. Dr. Richard Gentile, a geologist at the University of Missouri in Kansas City, tells me that prickly pear cactus is often found in conjunction with Bethany Falls limestone, that rocky member that appears throughout the layers of midwestern rock like a bookmark; there's something compatible there.

My friend Linda Ellis, botanical illustrator and past president of the Missouri Native Plant Society, says you can tell a lot about what goes on under the soil by what grows *in* it. Different plant colonies put down roots where they'll do the most good—in a hospitable habitat where conditions for growth are met. The Dutchman's breeches don't grow in the same spots as the black-eyed Susans, but both grow in Missouri in abundance.

The rocks and boulders that are sorted with each high-water flood are habitat to any number of creatures. They provide cracks and crevices for hiding, den sites for more permanence, sunning opportunities in plenty. I may see a skink dash between the stones, or a family of raccoons appear from a hollow under the largest boulder. As I walked beside the creek in the warming spring air, I discovered the long loops of a dark brown snake, soaking up the sunshine. Its head was shiny as though polished, but the body was dull colored. Along its graceful body I could see a slight mottled pattern, and its head was somewhat wedge-shaped, though I could see no pits to identify it as a poisonous pit viper. Thinking it might still be a Massasauga rattler, an endangered species only recently found in my part of the state, I waited until I was finished sketching and found a long stick. I nudged the snake gently, hoping to get it to move enough so I could see its tail. If there were rattles there, perhaps it was a Massasauga; if not, I didn't know *what* it was.

There was not a sign of a rattle as the snake's tail disappeared into the crevice in the rocks. When I returned to the cabin I could not find the snake in *Amphibians and Reptiles of Missouri* in either the poisonous or the non-poisonous section. I called George Hiser, our local conservation agent, to describe the reptile to him. It was impossible to identify the snake over the phone, of course, but he thought perhaps it might have been a prairie king snake.

"It wasn't a bullsnake; we don't see them around here."

Large, dark-colored snake with very subtle markings — I have no idea what he is.

He did clear up the mystery of the shiny head and dull body, though.

"It has probably just emerged from hibernation," he said. "It's wearing last year's skin, and it's just ready to shed."

A snake's skin gets dull just before the creature shimmies out of it, a natural result of the separation between this old covering and the new. If I had waited a bit longer I might have seen the skin split the length of the body, and watched as the snake used the rough limestone rocks as traction to scrape away the old, dry cuticle.

Beside the creek to the east is a four-foot wall of rubble, rocks and gravel piled together carelessly as though a bulldozer had pushed them there. It was a blade of water, not steel. The ridge of mixed stones and earth runs for a hundred feet and more along the creekbed; the flood must have been enormous, and I look anxiously to see its height—where is the high-water mark? How near to the cabin's foundation, the height that had seemed so far distant when I laid its lines for digging?

Scrambling up the face of the rubble wall, I find another of those odd bits of knapped flint that hint at purpose, and wonder if it could be a prehistoric scraper. I test it in my hand to feel

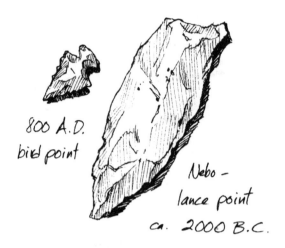

800 A.D. bird point

Nebo – lance point ca. 2000 B.C.

the usefulness of this primitive tool. It is sharp enough to cut flesh; a fine line of red is proof of that.

Artifact hunting is a common activity when rains expose surface flint in the fields. Kevin Morgan, a friend who documents his finds and gives talks on the culture that predates ours by many centuries, is my best source when I want to know what's what.

"We've got evidence of occupation that goes back as far as the Archaic Period," Kevin told me. "That's generally accepted as about 2000 B.C., but it's hard to pin down. You have to have organic remains to use carbon dating. They've found one hearth that they were able to date back to 2400 B.C. with that method.

"Then we have the Woodland Period, about A.D. 1, then the Mississippian; we've probably even got Paleo, too, if we could get up on the hills and excavate. I never did find anything I could positively identify as an *historic* artifact. That's funny, since the Iowas were all over this area."

"The Osage, too," I reminded him. "They mostly lived down near the Osage River, but when Fort Osage opened in 1808, they moved here to be near government protection and trading." They stayed a relatively short time—until 1827—but they lived and hunted in the vicinity long enough to have left clues.

sharp edge

Small granite
Celt - like
a hand-axe

Kevin has found a wide variety of tools and other artifacts: spearpoints, knives, arrowheads, scrapers, drills, axes, metates, or mortars, and manos, or grinding stones. He keeps careful records of each find and its locale.

"I've never found a banner stone, though a lot of other people have," he said.

"What *is* a banner stone? I've seen one, but what is it?" I asked.

"Well, they used to think it was just something the Native Americans hung outside their lodge—maybe as a ceremonial thing. But now they believe the stones may also have been counterweights for atlatls or throwing sticks. Banner stones make a point go a lot farther—and with a lot more accuracy. With greater velocity, too. I'll bet that's mostly what hunters used to bring down larger game; an arrowhead or spearpoint alone just doesn't have the force.

"I know a guy who reproduces these; he's sixty-five years old, and he can throw with fantastic accuracy and distance using an atlatl and counterweight. It's not like he has to do this to eat, so if *he* can do it, imagine what somebody that got his food that way could do.

"It's odd, but banner stones are consistent in weight, even though they're different sizes and shapes, depending on what kind of stone they're made of. The hunters knew the weight they needed."

I am always alert, on these walks through habitat, for signs of human life as well as wildlife, mindful of the fact that we have lived here for thousands of years. The first week I owned my place in the country I discovered a square nail on the pale, broad forehead of stone that gleams beside the creek crossing. Ever on the lookout for meaning—for clues—I pondered the nail and wondered if it meant there had been a house nearby. The old maps of this county, from an 1876 atlas, show nothing of a homestead, though on the hill a collapsed, stone-lined hole suggests a well or cellar.

The older timeline is marked with those arrowheads and spearpoints, drills and metates. Kevin spends long hours walking near these midwestern rivers, looking for prehistoric camp-sites with an archaeologist's focused interest. He has found several, six within the city limits of my small town. The original occupants were at home here long before we settled in and hooked up cable.

French trappers and traders worked these waters as early as 1680, and a busy trading post was set up beside the river only twenty miles from my home. It was remarked upon by Lewis and Clark when they began their journey in 1804.

So was the future site of Fort Clark, later known as Fort Osage in honor of the people it was intended to protect and serve; it was the second fort in the new Louisiana Purchase, and the westernmost outpost of the United States government until

1818. The fort was built under the direct supervision of William Clark, by then Superintendent of Indian Affairs, and was rebuilt using original documents and Clark's own design still on file at the War Department in Washington, D.C. An archaeological dig conducted in 1939 unearthed the original foundation, and the place has been reconstructed on these old stones. It offers insight into early frontier history—and produces an odd, prickly sensation when I look out over the river to see a land much changed since 1804.

Eagles, though not populous, still find these loess bluffs fine for winter hunting. Pelicans settle in on their migration on the lee side of wing dams. Geese still follow the river, spring and fall, as always; though much is changed, much remains timeless.

Wild greens still provide a source of food at the edge of the woods; I pick a wooden bucketful to share with the reenactors. My friend Terri Manus uses them later in the season in her dye pot.

During a recent living history weekend at the fort, I walked beside the river with a friend, and looked back up the bluff at the reconstructed log buildings. Gulls cried overhead and the scent of river mud was a constant—and suddenly the high, sweet sound of "Shenandoah" played on a pennywhistle drifted down on the summer wind. It could have been nearly two hundred years ago; it was yesterday.

Always looking for clues to the natural history as well as the human history of our recent past, I was delighted to discover that two expeditions upriver in 1811 included the naturalists John Bradbury and Thomas Nuttall, who covered the same ground where I now live. Lewis and Clark were themselves naturalists. In 1804, they were charged by Thomas Jefferson to record the plants and animals new to science. They were also given the task of noting the weather, geology, and ethnology of the region. Osage orange, a tree now widely found in America, was one of the first discoveries when the explorers left St. Louis on their search for a route to the Pacific. I'm delighted to note that they were also asked to watch for a living woolly mammoth or mastodon, since bones of these prehistoric mammals had been discovered in the East and presented to Jefferson. Science believed they might still wander these western hills, hidden in the unknown reaches of America.

These names—Nuttall, Bradbury, Lewis, Clark—all have found their way into the taxonomy of the natural world, as did Audubon's, a few years later. Their discoveries are written in my field guides, encoded in the Latin names of birds and plants that I have known since childhood. I like to imagine their sense of discovery—and the aching newness of all that is now familiar to me.

History is not so far past for us; it still seems fresh in our minds. The "raw frontier" retains some of its flavor. There are burial mounds, strange petroglyphs, ceremonial caves where Native Americans met beyond memory. In Kansas City, I'm told, there is a stone with runes that resemble Viking symbols; I'll find that as well, one day, if I can.

Fossil or arrowhead, bird or mammal or bumblebee, these things stop me. I give myself permission to wander with a child's sense of curiosity, and I stop to explore the infinite in the infinitesimal. At a walker's pace the world slows for discovery.

There's a ledge of ice here, cantilevered over the receding waters of the creek. Four inches now above the moving stream, the shelf slowly disappears, drip by cadenced drip. Bits of grass and leaves are frozen into its surface, sunken into their own minuscule craters; their darker color hoards the sun's thin warmth and melts the ice around them. The sun on my shoulders, penetrating, comforting, gathering between my shoulder blades, is like a banked fire, and I bless the dark jacket I've worn for collecting it there. The ice itself chills fingers to a stinging numbness, but I can't resist tracing my hand across the polished surface that looks at once smooth and rugged. The crystal veneer melts almost imperceptibly under my touch, accelerating spring thaw by a heartbeat.

Bright as a pomegranate's fleshy seeds, the red fruits of

jack-in-the-pulpit stand out against the dark, half-frozen mud by the creek. Each shriveled scarlet drupe bears its hard seed inside. I pick off a few and step them into the ground where I find them, planting the next generation, and take the rest with me. So far I've found none of these deep-forest wildflowers near the cabin; the remaining seeds will be dropped at random in the woods nearby, planted as casually as a squirrel would.

I'm looking for the remains of the moonshiner's cabin my neighbor Donny tells me is back here, a joss-stick pile of logs and moss-covered debris, but so far have found only an abandoned garden far from the road, where the green, frozen spikes of bunching onions huddle as if for warmth among the bleached outer leaves.

Signs of human life among the hills seem oddly out of place, oddly welcome. Again, I've let the edgy bustle of town drive me to a walk alone, and find myself inexplicably pleased to discover that this hilly backwater has felt the touch of someone's hoe. Bunching onions are hardy perennials, coming up year after year in the same place. There's no way to tell if these were planted last year or ten years ago—or more. With no one to harvest them, they could continue indefinitely here alone in the woods; I nibble on vegetative eternity and wonder whose forgotten bounty feeds me. The strong onion flavor fills my senses like memory, an anonymous legacy I will remember in the spring; the soup pot will be the better for it.

The old trace road across from my cabin leads to the creekside garden; it is that trace where I often walk (clear as a highway here, there lost among the saplings) that leads to the moonshiner's cabin. I have looked to find it on the brittle, yellowing maps in the county offices, but there is nothing there.

A glint of white catches my eye through the woods; it is a frozen waterfall that cascades in stasis down the face of a limestone bluff across the creek. A gargoyle's grin of icicles edges the bottom, and bubbles move amoebically behind the ice wall's translucent face. There is a continuous drip into the tiny catch-pool as the sun hits ice full on, a sound that at home

augers its way into my consciousness and pushes everything
else aside. Here it suggests a life beyond the human, as living
water chuckles to itself in the profound privacy of the woods.

One huge limestone slump block nearby is bearded with
walking ferns, *Asplenium rhizophyllum.* The long tongue-like
fronds are shriveled in the dry cold, matted over thick cushions
of moss, but with renewed moisture they will become fresh,
acid green, springy. The mature blades are lanceolate, tapering
to a narrow filiform tip from which tiny plantlets may form, a
kind of simple self-propagation. Some blades are twelve inches
long, with furry brown spore cases on the back like the chrysa-
lis cases of tiny insects. *A Field Guide to Missouri Ferns* says
this particular fern is not found in my corner of the state, and I
wonder if I've found something rare—or simply misidentified
the evergreen plant.

There is a new compost of leaves in the gulch, and signs
of a woodcutter's wasted work, stove lengths of walnut abandoned and rotting on the forest floor. A section of broken bone,
stubby and thick, gleams white beside a log. Small, gnawing
mammals have incised it with a scrimshaw of tooth marks, hungry for minerals; I add it to my collection.

I find another large bone, a shoulder blade this time, just
down from the big pool where the dogs wade. It's at the base of
the bluff, caught in the clinging roots of trees. My own shoulders flex ruefully in discomfort as I think of its weight added to
the collection I'm already carrying. Juggling an armload of
bones and other small treasures while climbing is not conducive
to good balance.

But these calcium remains tell me what shares this small
sector of Missouri with me. I found the bones of a full-grown
deer here last year, scattered along a dry run of the creek as if
the animal had disintegrated in flight, the skull still pointed
toward water. I gathered as much as I could in my arms and
lugged it back to the cabin with me.

Eastern skunks, woodchucks, turtles, turkey vultures, and
squirrels have also left their remains, an ivory endowment to
teach me the names of my neighbors—but the squirrels are

everywhere on my land. I need no forensic evidence to prove their occupancy. Fox squirrels and grays coexist, if not peacefully, then under a lasting cease-fire. They join forces to curse me from the trees, scatter-shot invective like shrapnel on my bare head. Still, when I find a tiny skull with those distinctive in-curving teeth, I tuck it in my pocket to sketch.

The creek is more of a collector than I am. On its long sweep to the Gulf of Mexico, it picks up every bit of Styrofoam, every beer can, every discarded washing machine in the county. The beautiful woodland stream with its waterfalls and deep, clear pools is also a dump. Trash punctuates the banks every few feet, impossible to ignore. Looking for the white flash of bone among the rocks, I see every torn foam cup, every skull-shaped bleach jug instead, a goose chase of garbage. Is it a curiously midwestern quirk to fill every available ravine with our junk? The next good rain carries it to the creek, and "out of sight, out of mind" works only if you stay indoors.

We have an endless supply of detritus. Waste is a part of us; things, in this culture, are eminently disposable. Boom or bust, the only thing that changes is the quantity. Study our midden to know our lives; in this last half of the twentieth century, our lives consist of polystyrene cups and bleach jugs, oil filters and the colorful artifacts from the local fast-food joint.

The midden of our throwaway culture is an ugly sort of reminder—but in fact it's the quality of the trash that's objectionable. When I search for arrowheads or history, it's midden I find. The trash of another era is my reward for an hour spent head down and wandering.

My husband, trained in an earlier era than I, saves everything. Empty pill bottles, jars, socks with holes, torn trousers, food long fossilized in the refrigerator. "Don't throw it away; it could be useful." I hear his mother's voice within his thought patterns, and when he was young it was true. "Use it up, wear it out, make it do or do without . . ." Fine advice, when you were speaking of goods that could be repaired and reused easily, and at home. Socks could be darned; worn clothing metamorphosed into colorful quilts. Jars—good, strong pickle or jam jars—became canning jars and were used from year to year until they were broken and discarded at last. Furniture was repaired—or turned to firewood. Food was used to the last scrap and the slops were fed to the chickens or pigs, or composted. Even things well worn had a threadbare dignity; kept long enough, they became antiques, and patina can be lovely.

Polystyrene never acquires patina. A bird feeder or flour scoop made from a bleach jug is still an ugly thing. Disposable culture has led to overflowing landfills, itinerant garbage barges looking for a home, and trainloads of other people's detritus shipped to the Midwest from the coasts. "Not in my backyard" is part of everyone's vocabulary.

"Not in my ancestral burial grounds" is the rallying cry of the remnants of the Iowa peoples who once populated these lands. Near my home, the push-and-pull debate between landfill opponents and proponents has raged for four years. The latest round of hearings has filled the local newspaper for months, and territorial considerations are as real as ever. People who moved to the country for the quiet and the wildlife are appalled at the thought of heavy trucks and blowing trash, not to mention the infiltration of chemicals or heavy metals into streams and groundwater. Proponents of the landfill cite the rapid filling of other sites nearby and the need for more space. And the last of the Iowas have reason to believe the proposed site is on ancestral lands; they don't want their dead disturbed, as who does—and there's no easy answer.

Recycling at home—first-person and immediate—is no longer possible, except for those things that were always reusable—the sturdy glass jars, the quilt pieces, the makings of a stockpot or compost pile. I wait today for the trash men to pick up my waste and hide my face in shame. A blizzard of paper enters this house each week. We are inundated by junk mail, magazines, newspapers—and at this writing, only the newspapers can be reused by a reluctant local recycler. In truth, they are being warehoused somewhere, waiting for a bullish market on once-read news.

Our recycling bin at the local discount store was abused by

the same people who cared enough to package up their recyclables, put them in the car, and drive them there. Piles of trash mounded around its base when it was too full, and I wondered where they thought the truck that came to trade the huge iron bin for an empty one was going to put the overflow. "Oh, they can load it into the new bin when it arrives," I could imagine the thought process went—but that wasn't in the job description of the truck driver. It's the job description of people who care enough to recycle.

Often enough, all it would have taken was to walk around to the back side of the bin; there was usually room there. On rainy days, those too lazy to investigate those portals left paper bags of cans and plastic to absorb the rain and fall apart in the parking lot, creating a new problem for someone else. I suppose they went away feeling virtuous for making the effort.

I could see it coming. Inevitably, the big chain store— which is, after all, in business to make money, not points with environmentalists—did away with the bin to reclaim a clean parking lot and their employees' time. Now, we scurry to find new places to rid ourselves of our mountains of junk. I notice an increase of trash along my country road and in the parks; at home the garbage truck takes it away to someone else's backyard. For now.

But I wonder, will today's trash be a great delight to some future archaeologist as evidence of a Woodland Indian's camp is to me today? I imagine this future archaeologist's conclusions, and wish they did not apply so uncomfortably to me.

There's a new word for the scientists who probe these more recent middens: garbologists. They dig through trash from decades rather than centuries past to find that even biodegradable paper—when kept in anaerobic conditions away from light and water (at the heart of a landfill, say, and in a plastic trash bag)— can last virtually forever. And that a hot dog, likewise buried, looks the same after twenty years as it did the day it was discarded. That says something about the quality of our preservatives, if not our recycling efforts.

Even if the landfill is left for a century and more, surely it can't be as fascinating as the trash middens of the past. Our conclusions are as different as the way we live our lives. As I walk through the woods that reclaimed a cluster of homes and outbuildings some seventy years ago, I find history hidden in a collapsed root cellar and join in my casual way the work of archaeologists from Stonehenge to Williamsburg. Here are thick, blue jars that held the hope of survival. A few are still intact, and I know that tomatoes and peaches were on the menu on cold winter days, as they are today. A rusty file is tucked beneath the rafters, a pocketknife's pearly handle gleams from the dirt floor like a mussel shell on the beach.

The stones themselves are tightly laid; still strong, and except for the fallen roof, they maintain the integrity of form the stonemason had planned. Here in the back woods, someone knew what he was doing. I compare these tightly laid stones to my own sorry attempts at wall-building and admire the skill of the mason.

What's amazing to me is that this probably was not a professional stonemason—not here, not then. This ability to lay mortarless stone upon stone to last a century or more must have been common knowledge to nearly every householder. Now only a few retain the knack, and we wait months for their services. I remember John Jerome's book, *Stonework*, in which he taught himself the art of laying a stone wall (or perhaps the stones themselves imparted the knowledge), and I vow to add this to my list of future projects. If Jerome could learn by doing, so can I.

It's trash that tells us about ourselves—how we lived, what we owned, how our technology developed. When excavating a historical site, the trash midden is Mecca. Find that, and you've hit pay dirt.

C. J. Wilde, a friend and professional weaver, told me excitedly of the research she had done on her blankets. She had come to know the thread count, fibers, and color of the blankets that kept our forebears warm in their unheated bedrooms. It's archaeology of the truest sort, and I am reminded of the bits of papyrus and linen cloth in an Egyptian tomb—a long way from the hot dogs and disposable diapers in our modern-day landfills, if only in what it reveals about the quality of our lives and expectations of endurance and durability.

William E. Pittman, curator of Archaeological Collections at Colonial Williamsburg, tells me of the importance of well fills to the discovery and interpretation of artifacts. Once a well went dry or the stone lining started to crumble, or it became contaminated for some reason, the owners usually filled it in with household refuse.

"We can associate these wells with specific, documented households, and date them that way," said Pittman. "Usually, there's a kind of stratified time capsule over a relatively short period of time—a year or two. Often, we know who owned or rented the property (and the well) at a specific period and by that we can know when these things were discarded within a very narrow range. It's episodic filling, over a fairly short period.

"We find larger things in a well than in an open, shallow trash pit: perhaps whole bottles or plates, rather than fragments, because when they hit mud or water they were less likely to break. Anaerobic conditions, like those you find in a filled well, preserve artifacts better, particularly leather and textiles that are almost never found otherwise. We even found boxwood shrubbery prunings, still green after 200 years. Wells and other similar pits are the only place organic things really survive—it's the lack of oxygen.

"At the John Custis home, the well was filled post-1760, apparently after a major housecleaning—there were whole dinner plates, a tin cup, and the remains of food. When such things (organic artifacts, especially) come to the surface, they must be immediately treated or they begin to deteriorate.

"We date these artifacts by *terminus post quem*—that means by the latest thing found in the dig. We mark out a square, usually one meter, and, using the natural layering of the soil as a measure, give every artifact found a number. Then identification is done by the most recent thing there. For instance, creamware was introduced by Wedgwood in 1762

(Wedgwood was a prominent china supplier and one of the first real marketers of his product in a mass-production way). Pearlware didn't come in until 1775, so if there is pearlware it's at least 1775," Pittman continued.

"How did it happen that there were so many whole artifacts down the wells?" I asked. "I thought the people would be much more saving than that—use it up or wear it out, as my grandmother always said."

"There was some handing down of items," Pittman agreed, "especially nice pieces, which might have been passed down through the generations. More common things were given, perhaps, from master to slave. But if items passed out of current fashion, they were often simply thrown away.

"At that period in our history—in the eighteenth century— we were largely tied up with conspicuous consumption, as we are today. People are always surprised when I tell them that, but our forebears were very concerned with who they were, and with their status in the community. It started in the late seventeenth century, with the beginnings of the Industrial Revolution, when more things became available; in the eighteenth century they become more attainable as well."

Ravines, deep trash pits, and wells are our best sources of intact or nearly intact artifacts, but sheet refuse is by far in the vast majority. These sheet refuse "fans" were a broad, flat plane, a living surface that people walked on. Anything that was thrown out and remained whole didn't stay that way long. They tell us a lot not only about what tools and utensils people used, but what foods—cultivated and otherwise—were available to them. In others words, a lot about the natural history of the past.

"Seventeenth-century domestic sites are much cleaner than those of the eighteenth century," Pittman continued. "It was more rural, there were more small towns, more space. People dug a hole and put their trash down it, then filled it in and dug another. As towns grew, the topography changed. There wasn't as much space and there was less and less reliance on individual trash pits. People just opened the door or window and threw things out, or tossed them beside the walkways."

That's a picture I hadn't imagined; it doesn't fit my memories of my grandmother nor my idea of Harris's mother, carefully saving things for later use—though he does tell me tales of small-town refuse stashes of liquor bottles beneath a shed floor in dry, dry Kansas. "Out of sight. . . ."

"It's amazing that any of our ancestors survived to majority," Pittman told me. "At one of the Williamsburg taverns the backyard space between the tavern proper and the smokehouse, backhouse, and other outbuildings was *filled* with sheet refuse.

"In fact, the owner was known to own large stone rollers that were used to roll all the stuff into the topsoil. In July and August, given the sheer volume of refuse generated by a tavern or publick house, this could not have smelled very good. In a domestic situation there were smaller amounts, but still there were 'shatters' of sheet refuse on a smaller scale."

My short course in archaeology better prepares me to understand what I see, and to know where and how to look; it's a skill I will use on my rambles. Even the animals that populate these Missouri woods leave their digs and middens. The levels at which things are found tell me much about how old the site is, how long it has been in use, and if it is active now or has long been abandoned. I can discover what type of creature has used the den by what is left there, and speculate on our resemblance to these other animals.

As I enter the ravine that leads to the big cave, the deep chill in the air signals a change of location; the cold breath of the stone itself blows on my cheeks. The large tumbled rocks in the dry streambed teeter as if to trip me up, as if the place were booby trapped against intruders—a mine field of the imagination. The thick leaf fall makes firm footing impossible, and I lurch and stagger like a drunk—but just seeing the big toothless grin of the open rock cave from this vantage point is never enough. I want to stand in its mouth and look out, an unspoken word. Mine field or no, I stagger on up the hill to the grail of the silent cave.

There has been a camp fire under the long, rocky ledge since the last time I was here, just a few feet from the back wall; it is the perfect place. The amphitheater of stone would reflect a well-laid fire back to its maker, warming from both sides at once. This is the kind of cave that the Osage and Iowa peoples would have used for camping or hunting or ceremonial purposes. In the past I had thought to find the evidence of their fires in a blackened area on the cave's overhang or petroglyphs scratched into the stone, but had no success. The cave keeps its secrets well.

These more contemporary ashes are long cold; a deer has left its mark in the old fire, a perfect hoofprint preserved in gray-white ashes as though in plaster of paris. Was it a hunter's fire? If so, the deer lived to write its story in the dead coals. All other tracks are gone but my own, and the forest will soon erase these as well.

I had thought that the only human sign was the ashes, but I was wrong. As I explore, I find human excrement in one corner of the cave, and nearby a melted butane cigarette lighter, a cryptic reminder of stupidity—disaster averted, but barely. Some of these cheap lighters have proven as dangerous as Molotov cocktails; more so—they explode without warning or intent. Imagining its load of fuel spent and throwing the lighter into the coals is an invitation to a firestorm.

There's another sign of potential disaster, empirical irresponsibility. As I leave the cave I see that the fire builder has thrown charred logs down into the deeply carpeted ravine to disperse his fire. If that mattress of leaves, years deep, had kindled and caught this dry winter, the woods would have burned like Yellowstone. Judging by the crisp, tan carpet that fills the shallow cave's grin from ear to ear, the fire builder might have had a moment of panic if the leaves caught. If the smoke had blown from the east it would have filled the cave, and I'd have had other bones to find.

Suggested Reading:

Cvancara, Alan M., *A Field Manual for the Amateur Geologist*, Prentice-Hall, Inc., Englewood Cliffs, New Jersey, 1985.

Eisley, Loren, *The Immense Journey*, Vintage Books, New York, 1957.

Gould, Stephen Jay, *Wonderful Life: The Burgess Shale and the Nature of History*, Norton, New York, 1989.

Jerome, John, *Stonework: Reflections on Serious Play and Other Aspects of Country Life*, Viking, New York, 1989.

Lapidus, Dorothy Farris, *Geology and Geophysics*, Facts on File, Inc., New York, 1987.

Mitchell, John Hanson, *Ceremonial Time*, Anchor Press/Doubleday, Garden City, New York, 1984.

———, *Living at the End of Time*, Houghton Mifflin, Boston, 1990.

• Three •

Walking Through Weather

Summer Storm

There was nothing to announce the storm, no low growls and threats of saber-rattling thunder—at least none that I could hear from my post at the keyboard. It was as though the front had arrived by catapult—sudden, violent, and explosive. The opening volley was fired less than a mile away, if the lapse between flash and sound was to be believed. The next, fast on its heels, was closer still. The next exploded almost in my face. I turned off the computer and went to the porch to listen and watch.

The rain came straight down in hard rows. Then, as the wind picked up, blinding, blowing curtains of sound made a rush and roar that filled my ears and stirred something like a call to battle.

Between the heavy curtains, in the moments between gusts, I could see the far hill glowering above the river. The wind buffeted the trees' heavy foliage in waves; they writhed and tossed furiously. The thunder's artillery barrage was peppered with occasional sharp *cracks* as dead limbs gave before the power of the wind; I could hear nothing beyond that but the sustained roar of the storm.

It was frightening, but irresistible. I was alone at home;

there was no one to tell me nay, no one to worry about me, no one to offer the sensible advice: Get inside. Close the door.

The idea to walk into the storm grew in my mind and would not be put down. I paced around the house, caged and agitated; stepped onto the porch to survey the progress, then back inside, then out again. The storm was more exciting than ever, the wind louder, the lightning coming in bursts like fireworks. I had to see what it was like to be in the thick of it—in the belly of the beast.

I am no thrill seeker, usually. I don't skydive; I don't bungee-jump nor play chicken on the highway. There's no death wish lurking in my psyche. But this was something else, this urge to be a part of the storm. This was elemental. I had to know what it was like. I threw on my poncho and boots and hurried to meet the moment.

Just crossing the small state highway was a feat; all the water from the bluffs above my house poured down and across the road. Traffic slowed to a crawl; there was little enough of it out in the storm—most people were more circumspect. My street, a tributary that fed this larger stream, was suddenly a white water raceway full from curb to curb with churning brown water and the loose debris from all the houses on the hill. Pop bottles and beer cans rolled down the street; a raft of twigs and small limbs chased them, and stones and bricks rumbled down the hill.

There was a sense of urgency in my going, beyond the unsettling combination of anxiety and excitement the weather had stirred. I *had* to make it to the woods before the storm abated. It was an odd imperative I couldn't seem to ignore, and I hurried on past sodden streets and shuttered houses.

The river had already begun to rise—not out of its banks, not yet, but a wide coffee torrent stirred itself here and there to a mucky white water. Stiff collars of Elizabethan lace stood up around each obstruction, unmistakable visual aids to the water's direction and force. I hurried on across the bridge and down the road through the park. The arch of trees that normally make this stretch of road a peaceful and inviting vista tossed violently overhead, creating a fun-house tunnel that I walked with trepidation.

A quarter of a mile down the road, a tiny path turned aside into the deep woods of a Missouri Natural Area, a mixed forest of oak and hickory that was my destination. Water poured down the steep path, and above the shouts of the storm I could hear the little wash that drains the hillside, now a waterfall that buffeted the rocks and beat down on the road below. Its normal chuckle was raised to a roar that managed to compete, decibel for decibel, with the thunder itself—and win. The gale, finding the smallest interstices between the limbs, made giant wind instruments of the trees, and a great bagpipe drone echoed through the wood.

Once I was into the forest itself, the sound was deafening. I wondered where the birds and mammals were that normally accompanied my walks through the natural area; the entrance of the bee tree was deserted, the sounds I am accustomed to silenced or lost in the roar.

To say it was exciting to be there purposely and alone in the heart of the storm would be understating the case. It was terrifying, wonderful—outside of anything I'd ever done before. Giant trees I'd known as solid, upstanding citizens, normally motionless except for their uppermost limbs, now swayed almost to their roots. I laid my hand on a big oak and felt the vibration in its fibers; leaned against another and felt the movement of the tree against my back. I knew it was crazy to be there, insane to take such a chance. If my husband—ever cautious—could have seen me, I would never have heard the end of it.

I shouted just to discover if my voice would be audible against the storm; it was not. The old conundrum about the sound a tree makes falling in the forest when there's no one to hear took on a new twist: If a woman shouts into a storm and cannot hear her own voice, is she really there?

At that instant a *crack* echoed through the forest, ricochetting off the hills. A tree had fallen not hundred feet from where I stood, and I felt the impact through the soles of my feet. I *was* there, audible or not, and crazy as a loon.

It was enough. I turned tail and scuttled out of the trees as fast as I could, half laughing, tears on my cheeks, fully alive and loving every minute of it.

I've always been stirred by storms. When I was young, I watched a storm advance like General Price across a wide southern river valley. The sunny blue sky was swallowed by a wall of churning, purple clouds; the shadow of the storm fell on the patchwork of land below. When the wind finally reached the bluff where I stood, leaves blew straight up in front of my face like a curtain rising on an ancient Greek drama. I wanted, suddenly, to applaud. Fear would have been the sensible response; prudent retreat the wise action. Instead I stood there, allowing the wind to engulf me, waiting for the storm.

Prudence is indeed a virtue when it comes to this kind of power. A single limb torn from a tree could brain a human in an instant. A bolt of lightning contains up to 100 million volts and can strip an entire tree of its bark. More people are killed by lightning in a year than by tornadoes, those feared and destructive storms that bedevil the Midwest. Negative and positive charges must overcome the insulating resistance of the air to find a path to the ground in order to form a lightning bolt; that path can be a tree, a building—or a human being standing alone in the storm. (And yet each time I drive by the local golf course in a thunderstorm, some few stubborn souls are still about, choosing a wood over an iron and letting rip.)

There are oddities connected with lightning; it's a phenomenon at least as strange as a tornado. Ball lightning has been known to enter a house through a chimney and roll through the rooms until it finds an exit. My husband tells of a man walking by a barbed wire fence in an electrical storm when lightning hit the wire. It jumped from the fence to the metal clasps on the man's galoshes and appeared like bright laces, jumping from one to the next without ever hurting their wearer. The insulating rubber had saved him—though he was more than a little shaken up. People have had the shapes of their belt buckles burned into their flesh; their glasses melted on their faces; their hair singed off—and lived to tell about it. Ben Franklin had nothing on them.

I would never suggest someone walk into an electrical storm as I did. It was crazy; I could hear all the warnings about not standing under a tree in a thunderstorm or the power of wind echoing in my head. It wasn't that I didn't know of the danger; I did. I chose, on that one occasion, to ignore it—and lived to tell the tale.

Walking through weather and doing it relatively pleasantly, not to mention safely, is largely a matter of using your head, dressing sensibly, and taking it easy. You should also know your limitations and understand the physics of the body's adaptations to its environment.

When walking in a thunderstorm—a rare enough occurrence—I make sure my shoes have rubber soles. If I feel the kind of hair-tingling charge that presages a lightning strike, I hunker close to the ground—away from either a lone tree or the tallest tree around—and make of myself the smallest target I can. I carry nothing metal; if I have something in hand that could act as a lightning rod, I drop it, pronto.

I wear a hat in winter. An unsettling percentage of the body's heat escapes through the head as though the body were a chimney—which it is. Wool and silk are good choices for winter wear, my friend Ed Wilde reminds me; they both hold in the body's heat, and wool will keep you warm even when it's wet.

Ed knows whereof he speaks; on an early February trek in northeast Missouri, the thermometer dropped to six degrees above zero. Ed dressed in late eighteenth-century style in five woolen layers—three lightweight wool shirts, a waistcoat, and a heavy overshirt ("almost blanket weight"), cotton knee socks and two pairs of woolen socks, extra large moose-hide moccasins with a liner, and a pair of woolen knee britches. With his silk scarf pulled up to protect his face and a wool hat pulled low, he slept through a night on the frigid ground and woke refreshed.

It's the layers as much as the natural fibers that keep me

warm on a winter walk. It's essential to trap the body's heat and allow it to warm itself; layers of clothing accomplish that. It performs the same function as the hollow hairs of a deer's winter coat, or the down on a goose's breast, where tiny, loosely arranged filaments trap the air close to the body, warming the creature even on the coldest nights. This natural layering is further augmented by the outer layer of closely spaced, waterproof feathers—a system not overlooked by the makers of down-filled ski wear. A distinct advantage of layering is that if I exercise enough to get *too* warm, I can shed a layer or two until I am comfortable, then add them again when I begin to chill.

My warm ragg mittens let my fingers warm each other. Gloves make it every man for himself, although a lightweight pair worn *under* my rather oversized mittens is a good plan for frigid-weather walks. A wool knit scarf doubles as a shawl or balaclava, a wool tam warms my head and can be pulled low to keep ears covered; socks and heavy boots and an old quilted coat to cover the rest allow me to enjoy walks through the coldest weather. I've yet to have a real problem.

You can lose a great deal of body heat even when the weather is not that extreme. High humidity coupled with wind chill can drive the body's core heat down with frightening speed. Keep an eye on your comfort level; be aware that walking with the wind is much warmer than walking into it. If you've gone too far, it's a long way back with the wind in your face. Take along a snack for quick energy; peanut-butter crackers are a standby in my pack.

If you find yourself getting clumsy or confused, find a place to warm up. Build a fire (Ed carries flint and steel, but a packet of matches in a waterproof container works as well) and sit close to it, with your back to a tree or big rock to reflect the heat. If you have a poncho or blanket, this can act as a reflector, as well. Blend technologies old and new, and carry a friction-activated handwarmer.

And if you suspect frostbite, *don't* rub the affected part with snow. Warm it up slowly, with lukewarm (not hot) water, and seek medical help as soon as possible.

If you get wet, you will chill more easily, even in relatively mild weather; try to keep a lightweight poncho in your pack. The discount stores carry these for only a few dollars, or you can go top-of-the-line and buy one that will last forever. My friend Ed, again, has solved the problem eighteenth-century style; his poncho is of lightweight waxed fabric and works as well as Gore-Tex—as long as he stays away from the fire. He'd go up like a candle.

Summer poses a different set of problems. Heat exhaustion and heatstroke can become a problem in the Midwest and the South, where humidity is high and temperatures soar into triple digits. The desert Southwest can be as deadly. I take my precautions low-tech style and dress in lightweight cotton. When the heat is murderous, a dampened cloth around my neck keeps me more comfortable. I've also been known to wade in the creek like a kid, then wear my wet clothes as an air conditioner.

I take it easy on these hot-weather rambles. There's no need to break a speed record. A slow walk in summer weather allows me to take the time to see what's there—and it's infinitely safer.

I carry a lightweight canteen of water on any walk longer than a few blocks. Salt tablets are no longer recommended; when you lose moisture through perspiration, the salt already in your body can concentrate—you don't need to add more. It's the water that needs replenishing.

And when I feel myself getting dizzy or clumsy, I stop—in the shade—and let the core temperature drop.

A Walk Through Summer

In the heat of summer, the rains had stopped as though they would never start again. The dirt trails that were mud or snow for half a year dried rock hard; cracks reached deep into the earth. Here and there a half-inch pool of dust was marked with the graffiti of bird tracks and the evidence of hard use of these deep-dish dust baths. They're fine stuff for ridding feathers of itchy pests and parasites.

Of these there are plenty in the summer, and they bother us as much as they do the birds. Here in the Midwest we are dev-

iled by mosquitoes near any source of water at all (and that
source can be as inconspicuous as a pool of stagnant water in an
abandoned tire or as small as the tablespoonful held in a brome-
liad's leaf). Chiggers, tiny red mites that bite painlessly at any
spot where clothing is tight and the dining area private, leave
itching red welts that last for days. Fleas proliferate, and in their
wake—as part of a stage in their life cycle—leave animals in-
fested with tapeworms. Ticks find warm-blooded creatures (humans included) to be fine habitat for their feeding cycle.

It's hard to imagine the heat of summer being hospitable to
anything. In a drought year, especially, annual plants that de-
pend on a single year's growth from seed-sprout to root system
to sustain them are stunted and limp. Tall bellflower, normally
four to six feet tall, may grow to less than two. Leaves are sparse,
and flowers, normally a rich calico in my part of the country,
may be few and far between.

Fallen leaves and grass are tinder dry; the ground is hard
and uneven as though it were cement, set up as it was poured.
Worms are hard put to drill their way to the surface, and find the
last vestiges of moisture far below. We suffered through over
two years of drought, a few years ago, and it was as though it
would never rain again. Clouds would build to fantastic heights,
threatening mayhem, only to dissipate with a sullen rumble of
thunder—lying in their teeth.

My walks became slower, shorter; the effort it took to scale
the dry hills in the blue air of a midwestern summer was in
precarious equation with my need to see what's what. At least
there's not much competition for territory—or quiet—on these
deep-summer walks. Most sensible souls hover in the shade
clutching cold drinks, dive into swimming pools, or sequester
themselves by the air conditioner. Many of my normal walking
places, sociable most of the year, were deserted, wilderness by
way of hot weather. It was irresistible.

The creek kept up its bubbling song, though more subdued
each day. The tiny cold-water spring that rises from beneath a
ledge of rock slowed and stopped running. The creek itself gave
up all idea of motion to become a series of stagnating pools,

widely spaced beads on a rough, dry string. Daily these pools shrank in size, skimmed over with pollen and algae and the floating seeds of dandelion. Desultory water striders oared the pool in slow motion and still there was no rain. Huge, gray-green tadpoles that had been so numerous before the rains stopped began to thin out; the voices of adult frogs were heard less and less frequently. The small, shining fish were agitated, bunched tightly together in nervous formation; their anxious

milling was contagious, and I scanned the sky for any sign of rain.

There was none. Now, there was nothing left of the creek for miles but two rapidly disappearing pools. Finally the big pool below the limestone slump block had shrunk to little more than eighteen inches across, and the muddy expanse of new bank was a dense mosaic of raccoon prints.

Nature runs a tight economy. I had wondered what would happen to the fish and tadpoles when I saw their summer-swollen numbers, knowing food would run short with such brisk competition; if the creek stopped running, oxygen itself would be in short supply. But the raccoons are never oblivious to the laws of supply and demand. I had seen their tracks with increasing frequency in the last few days, and knew that they had found the crowded bounty of the pools. Each day there were fewer and fewer flashing silver bodies until at last I wondered if there would be fish or tadpoles or water itself by the next day.

And finally one night it rained. It began gently enough; where we live in town it seemed to stay that way, and I doubted the thirsty earth would have parted with a drop of water that fell on it. I expected it to absorb the rain like a sponge. But at the creek a few miles from my home, three and three-quarter inches fell, and by the time I returned, slogging happily through the woods, I could hear the whisper of the falls before I ever got to the clearing.

Water there was, and plenty, but it came too late for most of the fish and incipient frogs. The pools were nearly empty except for the sculling water striders and an occasional whirligig beetle, three minnows, and a single tiny frog that had escaped the hunger of the resident raccoons.

Winter Walk

Tracks are everywhere in the blue-shadowed snow cover; the game paths I keep open spring and summer with the scythe— and with my own feet—are still used by their original engineers. It is graphic proof that my co-occupancy of their territory has not substantially altered the world in any significant way—I am just another mammal on the path.

These smaller trails are as active as ever, it would seem. The animals that share this acreage ignore the tractor road that is our driveway; I seldom find tracks there, other than the right-angled skeins of passage across, not down. Only the neighborhood dogs, as domestic as I in their habits, make use of this path of least resistance.

In the woods, the star-like tracks of squirrels lead me to the walnut grove; rabbits' comical commas overlay them, and dogs or foxes or coyotes have followed along, nose to ground to pick up a mulligatawny of scents I can't begin to detect. We're not equipped. Canines have forty times as many smell receptors in their brains as we do; they can detect odors from literally miles away. That's why they are most excellent detectors of drugs or explosives, why they can track escaped prisoners from the days-old scent of discarded clothing.

Animal behaviorist Ian Dunbar states that if one gram of butyric acid (the ingredient in human sweat that makes it offensive) were dissolved in the air of a ten-story office building, a dog could detect it—outside the building—300 feet away and camouflaged with all the braided scents of a modern city. The wet noses of dogs and other predators aid them in collecting scent molecules; the genetic hunger for meat sharpens their ability to differentiate odors, to tell the age of these signs and the identity of their makers. This feral sense gives their world a richer texture than we can discern. I try to awaken my own senses, sniffing at the cold, clear air; stooping to smell the tracks beside my own; wondering if my prehistoric ancestors were better equipped than I. I can find no clue in the tiny tracks, only a more intense scent of earth and mycelium. There is nothing to tell me of musk or gender or time elapsed; any self-respecting coyote could tell these basics at first sniff. The family dog would find it a snap.

Such a fine evolutionary line; have we lost so much? Our skin is nearly hairless; our eyes have compromised their ability to pierce the darkness. They are too used to artificial lights, and not only in the city—every farmstead in the formerly transparent darkness now sports its own streetlight, dusk to dawn an island of opaque light. Our ability to sort out the subtleties of sound is often inundated among the sensory bombardment of modern life. Sense of smell is deadened by the myriad artificial odors we surround ourselves with—but still there are latent abilities just beneath the edge of consciousness.

What would awaken them, jump-start them into a semblance of what they once were? Would it take as long (slow evolutionary loops reaching forward to some half-wild awareness) to regain these skills as it did to lose them?

There are those whose tracking skills make mine look invisible. Practice and care and more patience than I can muster have given some the ability to stalk deer, to approach and touch their glossy flanks without scaring them, and to read the stories in the snow. It's a return to a different time, not just on the linear scale that arrows backward a hundred years or so (or a thousand, or a million) to a time when we were *all* more closely attuned—and less calloused by the blitz of sensory stimuli that surrounds us. It's parallel time as well; we could as easily step sideways to enter. It's that side door I look for today, walking slowly in the snow.

Some strange creature has left a line of flower-like tracks up the west hill. It seems to have toes arrayed around a central pad like petals around a daisy's center. I bend close to puzzle them out, and laugh when at last I realize what I see; this bizarre new creature is a cat, stepping delicately in its own tracks in the snow, a curiously feline habit. The marks overlap one another in time—it's both coming and going, there and back again. My own tracks left from yesterday lead away down the hill, and I try to step in them, cat-like, each foot in yesterday's marks. But yesterday I wore different shoes, and the trail no longer fits my stride. How was this odd gait comfortable—or even possible? I give it up, no longer living in the past but accommodating my pace to today.

The tracks of creatures that inhabit this land lead me along after them, avid as a canine. The snow that covers the hard-frozen waters of the little creek reveals this as the path of least resistance—small creatures have also used the ice-bound stream as a thoroughfare as smooth and hard as macadam. The tracks are cuneiform signs in a language I can't quite decipher—but for some reason need to. It is as if their message means something beyond the merely directional, a hidden code bearing the power of suggestion.

Dogs have come from the north road using the flat white ice as a thoroughfare, and deer have crossed its narrow expanse at intervals. Again there are the tiny handprints of squirrels, now plaited with the impossibly small tracks of some creature, a bird or mouse whose delicate quarter-inch feather-stitches decorate the smooth blanket of the snow. The wind has erased the identity of their maker, and no amount of squinting at them can aid in translation.

The tracks of a cottontail rabbit catch my attention, slow me down, make me, finally, see. Rather than proceeding purposefully up the creek or down it as they had on the land paths, the prints now stop at creek's edge and shuffle sideways, like someone in line at a cafeteria—which is, of course, the case.

When the marks shuffled in a tight two-step beside the clumps of folded grass, the signs were cryptic and confusing. The scruffy vegetation, tawny with winter but showing a few green blades, was already broken, or bent, or torn; impossible to tell if the cause was teeth or time or high water. But up the creek, just beyond a point where the ice is no longer dance-floor flat but inclined in a kind of creaking hammock, wild rose canes are nipped as neatly as though last summer's flowers had been cut for a bouquet. I kneel to inspect them more closely and find the ends sliced in a clean diagonal, usually just this side of a thorn.

Had the rabbit been able to avoid these needle-like daggers entirely? There is no medieval weapon as well armored as the common wild rose, no inch of cane without its thorn. Perhaps the mammal's strong teeth were simply able to chew them beyond harm. A rabbit's incisors are sharp and well-designed cutting instruments. There is a space with no teeth whatsoever,

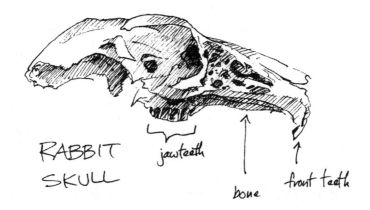

RABBIT SKULL   jawteeth   bone   front teeth

then a double row of strong molars embedded deeply in jaw-bone, nicely designed for eating just about anything the rabbit fancies—and this one fancies brambles. Each place wild rose leans over the ice there is that comical two-step, that bristle of cut canes, and I walk the creek as far as the road, inspecting each in turn.

Eventually I backtrack, noting my own slow, close-spaced prints, and step again where I had gone before. Or so I imagine. This time, the ice groans and billows until suddenly it gives beneath my boot and I am up to my ankle in ice water. The day is surprisingly warm after these weeks of below-zero tempera-tures—nearly up to the freezing mark feels suddenly balmy—and I continue my slow progress undeterred by soggy socks.

I still want to explore the hill path, to track the strange animal I had seen earlier, half sliding, half striding down the hill. It looked like a cat, but too big, too low-slung; it looked like a fox but too feline. I hope to find its trail to give me a hint—the round, flower-like tracks of cat, claws retracted, are distinctive. Digitigrade paw construction (meaning cats walk on their toes rather than with the flat-footed, plantigrade gait we share with the bears) helps lend roundness to their prints. Now, in winter, a heavier growth of hair between the toes and around the pads contributes to a softened, even more rounded effect. Front feet are larger than the hind feet; plantar pads are rela-tively large compared to the prints of the dog family.

In good tracking conditions, identification would be easy. But the snow is thinner on this northwest-facing hill; the afternoon sun, infinitesimally warmer, has melted it to a crust that fills only the spaces between the fallen leaves. Tracking is difficult, until I turn off the old trace road that goes uphill through the woods. There, down the length of a snow-covered fallen log, are the unmistakable prints of cat—very large, but very feline, and I wonder if the bobcat we heard years ago in these hills might still be about. This not the trail of the housecat I followed earlier.

As though I will learn more about my quarry from where it has been, I trace backward up its route until the tracks are lost again among the leaves. There is no sign of scat or urine markings—both, in the cat family, are strongly scented and used territorially. There is no indication of scratch marks on the trees. Like a genealogist just run out of leads, I stand looking about, perplexed. There is no further sign of cat, not in the woods, and not in the meadow beyond. I turn to go back downhill to cabin and warmth and a cup of hot mint tea, oddly satisfied with this encounter with mystery. The rabbit's tracks I could translate; the big cat's I could not; and one more than the other tugs at my curiosity, makes me smile into my tea. I like to begin the year with a question, not an answer; there's more mileage in it.

Maine Morning

"Good morning." My voice sounds unnaturally loud on the fog-muffled air. It is dark yet, or almost so. Here in Port Clyde, a small town on the rocky coast of Maine, morning comes early—but not this early. Being in a strange place among the stranger sounds of foghorns and gull voices has roused me from my bed before the sun.

And that comes early enough at such a northern latitude. Light pries at the windows by 4:30 and I am anxious to fill myself with every possible hour of these long days.

It is foggy, a gray blanket that muffles sound and imparts a kind of intimacy, a closeness to the scene. I can see barely fifteen feet, and each small lane fades into the background as though into a cloud.

"Good morning."

The old woman is working in her tiny yard in the near dark, rearranging the whitewashed stones that outline miniature flower beds. A cat rubs against her legs, sure of his welcome.

"Mornin'," she answers, startled by my presence. "You're about early."

"I like the fog," I answer, looking into the truncated distance, face lifted to the pervasive moisture. "It's beautiful."

"You like weathah, do ye? You don't meet many who like weathah," she says with a questioning twist to her voice, grinning at me. She's seen a lot of people here in this tiny town where the ferry leaves for Monhegan Island, but few at 4:30 in the morning in dense fog enjoying the weather.

It is a good time for a walk. Aside from the woman and her whitewashed stones and her big gray cat, no one else is about. The sound of my feet on the gravel roadside is the only sound beyond the wail of foghorns and the gentle waves investigating the spaces between the rocks.

In this protected cove there is no surf, only the patient rise and fall of the tides and the soft slap of water on rock. The quietude seems to underscore the silent fog that also comes in from the sea. The smell of fresh coffee from a tiny dockside cafe infiltrates the gray-white vapor like a drop of dye in a glass of water; now fishermen are up and about, ready to face the vagaries of that northern ocean—but not without coffee. The scent of it beckons to me as well, but the salt tang carried in the fog is more exotic. Coffee I can have at any time. This muffled gray morning with its cargo of strange smells and sounds is the stronger draw.

I like weather; always have. It's a way of experiencing life, of knowing I am here and fully sentient.

Suggested Reading:

Bair, Frank E., and James Ruffner, *The Weather Almanac*, Avon, New York, 1979.

Forrester, Franklin, *One Thousand One Questions Answered about the Weather*, Dover Publications, New York, 1982.

Kappel-Smith, Diana, *Wintering*, Little, Brown and Company, Boston, 1984.

Stokes, Donald, and Lillian, *A Guide to Animal Tracking and Behavior*, Little, Brown and Company, Boston, 1986.

Stokes, Donald W., *A Guide to Nature in Winter*, Little, Brown and Company, Boston, 1976.

· Four ·

Along the Central Flyway

THE SOUND IS HIGH, piercing, wild as a bobcat's cry: Hawk. It *must* be. There is a subtle difference from the hawk-like whistles the jays have perfected, the whistles that send me searching the sky, all senses alert, only to find the blue-gray trickster perched nearby, laughing at me and at the panic he has created among the other birds. There *is* something almost deliberate in that hawk sound, as though the jay did it just for the hell of it. But this time the sound is richer, stronger—authority rings in it.

I scan the featureless blue dome overhead, searching the negative spaces between newly bare limbs. The sound is closer, louder than before, cutting to the bone. The smaller birds of the forest—woodpeckers, chickadees, finches—rocket through the trees, scattering wildly, desperately, as though knowing they'd fill an old emptiness in the migrating hawk's belly. The grayish bird comes in low and fast, swooping just above my head, and pulls up abruptly, the sound of its wings braking hard against the air an audible *whoosh*.

The hawk screams again; hair rises on the back of my neck as the raptor suddenly appears, materializing out of the ether itself. The clear autumn sunlight, unsullied by the haziness of a humid midwestern summer, strikes the hawk's creamy underbelly and lights it like a beacon against the deep October sky, outlining broad wings and spread tail as though to cut a laser image from the sky. It's a red-tail, one of the more common hawks in my area.

This one has an odd double cry—*kee-eee, kee-uhkee*, syncopated and nearly overlapping—or so it seems until I find a second hawk riding the thermals, circling in a slow *pas de deux* with the first. They loop off in opposite directions, then come at one another, picking up speed, closer and closer on a convergent trajectory—and miss by a handspan, screaming in defiance or ecstasy, I can't know which.

Time and again the two light-phase red-tails circle, as if held on an invisible tether. Sunlight finds the undersides of their wings, rendering them opaque, then, as they reach the apogee of their orbit, shines through feathers suddenly translucent. Each primary feather is clearly delineated, outspread to catch the wind; each overlaps the next at the base, sketching a dark outline.

The hawks come together for a circuit or two, coming in low over the ridge, tangling their images with the trees, and I don't see how they avoid collision—with each other, with the close-spaced oaks on the hill. They are less than thirty yards away, slipping through the interstices of the angular branches as though the woods were home. They appear again unscathed just beyond reach of the tallest oak, then figure-eight away from one another, still low overhead.

I turn and turn to keep them in sight, trying to keep the image in my binoculars, frustrated by their speed and evasive tactics. Feathered bodies as powerful and graceful as young Nureyevs swoop above me, showing me their every aspect, and I wish I held a camera rather than my father's old field glasses.

One hawk breaks free of the dance and makes as if to stoop on some unseen prey, wings aerodynamically pinned back, talons extended. The sun catches those curved blades, and for a moment I imagine the searing pain of impact as the hawk plummets closer and closer. The hawk is close, so close I imagine I can see the scales on its feet, and I admit to a instant of unreasonable panic, stifling an impulse to shriek like a rabbit. But the big raptor pulls up and retracts its legs to normal soaring position, catching an updraft and resuming a lazy circling of the sun and the other hawk. I let out a long breath I hadn't known I held, the sound whistling through my teeth.

Both hawks come in close again, then spiral off over the far hill, come in overhead for one more look at whatever it was that attracted them here and held them, then cut the thread and catch the long arm of the next helix of air current down the ridge. They disappear—together, separate—over the east hill, and the silence is suddenly immense. The wind sounds different; vacant; ancient and inanimate.

It is the season of hawk migration. Great kettles of them— all kinds, all sizes, accipiters, falcons, buteos, kites—ride the thermals that spin down the ridges to the river bluffs. At Hawk Mountain, Pennsylvania, thousands of spectators line up to watch the big raptors wheel southward. Along the Great Lakes you may see any hawk that inhabits North America; at Cape May, New Jersey, a prime birding location, accipiters, falcons, and ospreys sail ahead of foul weather. Normally solitary hunters, at migration the raptors flock together to run before the advancing isotherm of winter.

Within minutes of the disappearance of the two red-tails, a broad-winged hawk and what looks to be a long-tailed northern harrier hitch a ride on the same invisible helix of air that passed unfelt over my head, and I continue to scan the sky the rest of the afternoon.

I don't go unrewarded—the urge to move out must be strong, its silent call irresistible. I count seven other hawks, anonymous shapes in the sky; identification from this distance is impossible, frustrated by distance and cryptic markings. Not surprisingly, either—Peterson's field guide to hawks lists more species than I knew existed, from the gray hawk of Arizona and Texas to the zone-tailed hawk of the American Southwest. Migration, even in this small sector of the country, is a raptor's melting pot of traveling companions.

A few hawks overwinter, ignoring the weather. Here in Mis-

souri we see red-tails all winter long, perched hunch-shoul-
dered and alert on telephone poles as evenly spaced as though
their territory were platted by township and fenceline. They
like the highway especially. These unnatural edge habitats are
popular with many small mammals and birds for their availability of food plants and for the nearby cover; where small prey
animals prosper, the hawks take up residence. In hard times,
they're not above scavenging. Roadkill—if it is fresh—may become the entree *du jour*.

    I am never able to get close enough to one of these big
hawks on my walks—ancestral memories of my kind popping
away at "chicken hawks" make the raptors jumpy, perhaps.
Their caution rivals that of the skittish black crows that take off

at my approach with a great clatter of wings and derisive laughter. The hawks, too, move off—though more discreetly and with a kind of unconcerned dignity—as soon as I infringe on their territory.

Though hawks are now protected by law, a few trigger-happy souls still can't resist target practice. If caught, a stiff fine will be levied against them. It is illegal, in fact, to have in your possession any part of a raptor; even the smallest feather is an infraction of the law, no matter how you came by it. My friend and veterinarian, Pete Rucker, says he must destroy all molted feathers even from those injured birds he legally rehabilitates.

When we think of migration, great lines of geese sketched against the sky come to mind, V shapes trailing off into the ether. But kettles of hawks stirring down the invisible thermals are a part of migration as well, and one I look for each year in autumn.

Living in the Flyway

Deep in the small hours of the night, the sound burrows into my dreams and calls me to wakefulness. The clamor, at first, is tenuous, only half heard. Is it really geese? Is it—as it usually is—only dogs, or wind, or my imagination? I lie in the darkness, listening—and then, inevitably, leap up and run out the door, standing on the cold sidewalk in my nightgown and looking up at the night sky. There; against the sounds of the small-town night—the cars on the nearby state highway, the buzz of sodium-vapor streetlights, the wind rattling in the bare branches—there is that magical racket. I was not mistaken. It is migration; the seasons tilt toward the future.

I live in a most fortuitous place, on the Central Flyway near the Missouri River; along with the Mississippi, which it meets at St. Louis, it is a great river of birds as well as water. Here time is still measured by wingbeats; twice each year the skies are traced with lines of geese. Interspersed with these big birds are many species of ducks, pelicans, herons, hawks, and smaller songbirds, though on a somewhat syncopated schedule that suits their inner itinerary. At night I walk out to hear the conversations of tiny migrants in the night sky, or watch the full moon for their fleeting silhouettes; small passerines migrate through the lengthening dark. Sandhill cranes, ancient shapes that seem to spring to life from a Chinese scroll, join the river of birds, their voices a harsh, chaotic cry that is nonetheless stirring. Large concentrations of them still find staging grounds in Nebraska each spring. Eagles follow the main migration in search of prey.

Worldwide, these invisible flyways sketch lines across the globe, connecting north to south. The main North American routes follow the coasts or cut through the center; a migration map of this country will show the Pacific, Central, Mississippi, and Atlantic flyways.

Here in Missouri there are four national wildlife refuges, with birds in astounding numbers. There are 300,000 geese—snows and blues and Canadas—give or take a few thousand, and up to 300 bald eagles in attendance at Squaw Creek, near Mound City, alone. Along with Clarence Cannon National Wildlife Refuge, north of St. Louis, Squaw Creek catches the first autumnal wave southward. Swan Lake, in north-central Missouri, is a stopover for 100,000 transients; immense Mingo, in the southeast, is Missouri's first port of call northward in the spring. Add to these the more than 460 other wildlife refuges in every state in the nation, and you will sense our human interaction with the ancient forces of instinct and need. Over 90 million acres go to make up these refuges; it sounds like a lot, and it is. But compared to the wetlands and feeding areas once available to wildlife (now lost to agriculture or cities), these acres are a tattered remnant.

Never was it more essential to try to meet the requirements of wildlife—and never was it more difficult. Before the coming of white settlers, the big rivers flowed free, forming broad oxbow lakes. Marshes fringed their borders in deep, fertile bands. Waterfowl by the millions found natural refuge here, and the welcoming landscape was far different from the shrunken wetlands of today. The rivers are no longer wild; in their natural state they provided habitat for hundreds of species of birds.

Now, they are drained for irrigation, dammed and ditched, straightened, channelized, and wing-dammed to a shadow of their historic selves—a boon to the cities in their floodplains, but a loss to dependent wildlife. It's not only the migrant water-fowl and resident nesters that are affected. Also on these lands set aside for refuge you may find muskrats and beavers, wild turkeys, deer, coyotes, foxes, turtles, frogs, and fish.

By the 1930s, the situation was recognized as critical; we were losing ground—literally, though President Theodore Roosevelt (perhaps our first "environmental president") had already set up a system of national refuges beginning with Florida's tiny Pelican Island in 1903. Today the 1934 Migratory Bird Hunting Stamp Act finances the acquisition and maintenance of refuges administered by the U.S. Fish and Wildlife Service, as a safety net designed to meet the needs of precipitously declining waterfowl.

Look at a map of the great flyways of North America and you'll see the immense ancestral routes of millions of migratory birds. One of those rivers of birds, the Central Flyway, flows directly through Squaw Creek National Wildlife Refuge. At the height of fall migration, 300,000 snows, blues, and Canada geese make a rest stop here, with thousands of ducks and the attendant bald eagles always watchful for a free lunch. When you are amongst them, it doesn't seem possible there could be a bird left anyplace else in the world.

The sound of their wings is a thunder, bearing the freight of bruised air that makes your ears pound with your own heartbeats. Their voices—near, far—are such a wildness that you forget you are civilized or even human. You are borne away by sound.

eagles on
muskrat mounds

geese like a
dark, floating raft

Birds rise in clouds to circle once, twice, and then land again, and you wonder what it was that sent them squawking into the air. Did an eagle fly too close, or was it just a daily jog to stay in shape while they lounge here before the ice of winter sends them arrowing south?

Squaw Creek has a mystique of its own, even without the migratory spectacle. Including a long, crescent oxbow of the then-wild Missouri River long ago abandoned in its bed, the spot was noted and remarked upon by the naturalists and explorers William Clark and Meriwether Lewis. I explore the refuge near the river and try to imagine what it looked like when the Lewis and Clark expedition passed on their way to the Northwest Passage.

The hills that bound the oxbow are odd, abrupt—convoluted and ridged in a way that subtly calls attention to themselves. And so they should. Legacy of the last glacier, these are loess monuments to the passage of geologic time. As the wall of ice retreated, clouds of powder-fine rock dust ground to flour by the glacier's weight blew out across the flattened plains and piled up here. Fifteen thousand years later they are softened in the spring with a different kind of cloud, the hot-pink mist of redbud flowers. Trails twine through the hills, inviting exploration.

The river that flows beside the refuge is itself a child of ice. There was no Missouri River before the glacier muscled its way

loess hills
and geese

Colors:
pale gold
clear, light blue
rich, red-gold hills
brown husks of weeds

clear to Kansas City, gouging the riverbed before it. In the long stream of time, the Missouri is only a nanosecond, an infant stream now tenuously constrained by the dams and locks and levees of the Corps of Engineers. She still gets her back up on occasion; in 1993, flooding rivaled the Great Flood of '51, when I was a child standing on the river bluffs watching the hungry brown water devour great hunks of city. The river still licks away at levees with a hunger that is older than time itself, and I remember that a floodplain is, in fact, riverbottom. It waits to reclaim its own. At Squaw Creek there is a feeling, always, of waiting.

According to Ronald Bell, the refuge manager here, the facility was carved from the remaining marshes in 1935, when the pools were deepened and expanded to ensure habitat even in dry years. At Squaw Creek, 2,500 to 2,600 acres of water are considered optimum; even after a dry summer there are still some 1,800 acres. It sounds huge; it is not. But it *does* offer hope for the future, as do all our refuges.

We are following the bald eagles, which in turn follow the migration of waterfowl from their nesting grounds in the northern tundra. If you imagine eagles visible only in Alaska or the coasts or the wild reaches of the West, think again. Missouri has the largest concentrations of bald eagles of any state in the contiguous United States except Oregon. Musician Barbara Duffy is a friend who lives at Missouri's Lake of the Ozarks (a man-made lake with a shoreline longer than the coast of California). On New Year's Eve she told me excitedly of a huge eagle landing beside her deck and devouring its fishy breakfast while she raced for her camera. I would have as soon imagined a condor at my finch feeder.

On a recent winter walk between two of the big marsh pools at Squaw Creek with our friends Grady and Terri Manus, we were delighted with the proximity of the eagles. The first time Harris and I visited the refuge some four or five years past, there were geese in the hundreds of thousands like a storm of birds against the red-brown hills, and eagles to be seen—but only in the distance. They looked like tiny specks in the bare branches, and my attempts at photography were frustrated by the lack of a telephoto lens.

This day each muskrat hut on the marsh sported a huge bald eagle, most of them fully mature and regal with the white head and neck that gives them their name. Some simply sat like living gargoyles, waiting for prey—or for renewed hunger; others actively fished or gleaned the marsh for dead and dying geese. Their wingspan, an incredible seventy-one to eighty-nine inches, gave them the aspect of sailplanes, but far too exotic to be anything so human. They were magnificent. One circled overhead on wings of such strength I could imagine the Psalm come to life; one *could* "rise up on wings like eagles" with such a span. The heavily feathered legs were clearly visible, and the legs were golden yellow, like the scimitar beak. Even the fierce hooded eyes were visible, glinting yellow as they scanned the water for prey; I was glad I was not it.

Here where the muskrat dens punctuate the open water, the geese were as active as the eagles, ignoring them like elands that knew somehow the lion in their midst had recently fed. A bit farther on, shallower water had frozen from shore to shore, and the birds had vacated it completely.

As we walked along the long spit of land into the winter wind, I noticed the variety of plants that grew there: American lotus, ground nuts, willows, sumac, reeds, and a brownish skin on the water that must have been dead duckweed. The ruddy bristle of staghorn sumac was laden with fruits still fresh and tart, lemony and acidic. At home the rains had stolen all the flavor already, and when I sucked on a hairy sumac seed beside my pond there was no taste at all.

The quiet was profound, except for the voices of the geese in the distance. Here where we walked, the ice stretched off in all directions; open water was invisible beyond the rise of land just ahead, but we knew it was there. The geese, rising and falling like drifting snow, had to be landing somewhere. We could hear their cries—but little else. A leaf, dead and December dry, skittered across the ice like a bird taking off, the whisper of sound magnified in the silence.

Coyote and fox tracks sashayed across the ice, looping off in great ellipses. A deep hole in the mud by the bank hinted at a beaver's bank den; nearby, white blazes on the twigs of a willow tree and the cut stumps confirmed the identification. Grady lowered himself onto the ice to get at a chewed twig for me, but when he found unmistakable evidence of the eagle's repast, I joined him in an instant. I couldn't have cared less if the ice only

thinly covered the mud at the marsh's edge; I mucked my way over to where he stood, snow goose skull in hand. Nearby, evidence of earlier feeds in the form of feathers and wing-tips confirmed the reason the eagles congregate here: food, and plenty of it. Drifts of down blew silently against the shore, tangled in the reeds as though someone's pillow had burst.

Back on dry land—as dry as it got this muddy winter day—Harris and Terri stood laughing at us, feet muddy to our ankles and hands full of the bloody remains of the eagles' dinner. "You're a real pair," Terri said. "You make quite a picture to this city girl."

Later, when we drove slowly around the perimeter, we saw a young eagle in a tree near the road. Edging the big truck off the gravel and out of the way of other refuge visitors, Grady pulled to a slow, silent stop. We gawked like a bunch of kids at a rock concert, amazed to be so close to this bird that has become a symbol for our country and all it should stand for. Grady opened the door and slid out, camera in hand; I followed suit, trying not to whoop with excitement. With only one shot left on my roll, I was lucky to get a silhouette. Grady had more film in his camera—and more patience than I could muster; he came home with two wonderful shots of the youngster. The telephoto helped; the color print looks as though you could stroke its curved beak and hand-feed it goose parts. And from the print I was able to identify the young white-belly as a yearling eagle, on his first jaunt southward for the winter.

When we finally returned to the car to complete our slow circuit of the refuge, we were treated with the sight of a magnificent buck whitetail, trying its best to blend into the woods. We were as silent as the day, just watching—tired but happy. Walks don't have to be solitary, not always. Sometimes it's nice to have friends who understand what interests you; we shared a great day at the refuge.

At Swan Lake, a mostly man-made wetland, turtles sun themselves on every log and splash warily into the water at my approach. Gadwalls and loons appear among the more common mallards and wood ducks. There is a sense of diversity, of plenty, that is lacking in our more civilized habitations. There is a sense of peace that goes deep as the bone.

Places like this were never more necessary than they are today; constant vigilance is required even to maintain the status quo. Despite President Bush's pledge of "no net loss of wetlands," early drafts of suggested guidelines to the designation of wetlands would have resulted in the loss of hundreds of thousands of acres nationwide; when scientists realized how great the loss would be, the administration decided a rewrite was in order. There are immense demands on landscape from the developmental and agricultural communities. As with any resource, there are conflicting agendas. But with a new emphasis on environment in high places, there's cause for hope.

The needs of wildlife are not necessarily more important than those of human beings (though I admit to a certain curmudgeonly inclination to honor prior claim). But when species are lost or endangered they act as indicators to our own situation. Wetlands are important in and of themselves. They not only encourage wildlife diversity, but help control flooding by storing runoff; most importantly, they are capable of naturally decontaminating polluted water.

Today, some municipalities are designing new water treatment plants that are, in fact, nothing more than giant man-made wetlands with the Everglades as a model. That sea of grass, as it has been called, naturally filters the water that flows through the state of Florida. Now in these man-made pools, I half expect to see a crocodile among the cattails.

Lowell Patterson, public works director of the city of Columbia, Missouri, confirms that the first phase of this progressive city's waste-water treatment plant will be in operation this spring; construction is almost complete. This phase will have a surface area of ninety acres, designed to process 16.5 million gallons of water a day.

It's not a primary water treatment plant, however; such a facility would require 7,000 acres of wetland to handle the waste of a city the size of Columbia, some 69,000 people. The primary water treatment plant will still discharge wastes within the recommended parts per million of solid pollutants. When the water that passes through the man-made marsh finally reaches the Missouri River, it will far exceed EPA standards—and will certainly be cleaner than the river itself.

Columbia's Public Works Department is operating in cooperation with the Missouri Department of Conservation, which has purchased an additional 2,700 acres, also to be converted to wetland use. Water from Columbia's marsh—or more accurately, three successive marshes—will feed into the Conservation Department's wetland, further purifying the water. But whereas the city's primary concern is cleaning the waste water of pollutants with only a secondary interest in wildlife, the MDC will directly benefit wildlife with their adjoining acreage. The two ends complement one another beautifully.

Ten years from now, phase two of Columbia's planned wetlands will be put into operation, more than doubling their available capacity.

"I know a river can refresh itself and that nature is capable of great healing. But how exactly is a man-made marsh constructed to clean waste water?" I asked Patterson.

"The same way the Everglades is, essentially," he answered. "Slow-moving water and thick marsh plants are an unbeatable combination. There's natural aeration—this is a shallow marsh, about a foot deep. That's aerobic action, oxidation. There's filtration through the biomass of the plants themselves. And there's sedimentation, when the cleaned solids fall to the bottom of the marsh. At thirty parts per million in the discharged water, that's a cleaner, clearer product than the Missouri River itself. At this time, the marsh is to be considered a polishing system for the entire setup, though; we'll still retain our sludge treatment plant."

Several smaller cities and communities are trying out the biomass/marsh system. In Taney County, Missouri, at least two such treatment facilities are being built. Near Fort Osage, the frontier outpost designed and built by the explorer William Clark where my friend Grady Manus is site administrator, runoff is also being diverted to wetland, and the land will begin to take on some of the aspects of Clark's day, as it did—in scope, at least—when the river reclaimed its ancient banks in 1993. If human enterprise had not been in the way of the river, the cycle of flood and cleansing would have been a positive event.

We discover, time and again, that nature knows what she wants to do; we can cooperate or get out of the way. We can take a lesson.

What that lesson may be is that we need to rethink our position when possible flooding is on the curriculum. In some communities, it is illegal to build in the floodplain; others charge a fee to cover disaster—because in nature, disaster can easily happen when the rains come.

Homes, farms, businesses, when put in the way of flood-plains, are at risk. Levees break or are over-topped. Even building on berms doesn't solve the problem. You can't build up the entire riverbottom, and living on an island is not an option.

Agricultural use is the safest, if farm homes and livestock are kept out of the way of floodwaters. Still, when hundreds of thousands of acres are lost, crops are washed away, and your land is covered with six feet of silt, "safe" is not a word a farmer wants to hear.

We need to learn to cooperate, to second-guess natural events and prepare ourselves to deal with them. We cannot prevent them; we can only survive.

A Walk Among Monarchs

Birds are not our only migrators, though they are certainly the most obvious due to their size, their numbers—and their vocalizations. Our most famous non-avian migrators are more silent and often overlooked—the monarch butterflies. Spring and fall they make their way up and down the continent, trailing beauty in their wake.

One fall day rich with the sort of loveliness that remains in a corner of your mind for decades, Harris and I walked beside Watkins Mill Lake and stopped to rest on a wooden bench. At first I simply absorbed the peace of the place, letting the sun warm my cheeks and the breeze kiss my hair. The wind was still

from the south. The pennywhistle voices of tufted titmice punctuated the stillness as they popped in and out of the cedars behind us, and a few fall leaves had started to blow across the meadow that tilted down to the lake's edge. At least that's what I thought I saw, from behind the half-closed lids of utter contentment. After a moment or two I realized the breeze was from one direction and the colorful shapes from another. I sat up and took notice: monarch butterflies. Ten—twenty—fifty—a hundred of them, drifting lazily southward.

According to J. Richard Heitzman, my expert in time of need when it comes to questions of lepidopterology, literally *millions* of migrating monarchs pass through this part of the country in a single season. Coauthor, with his wife Joan, of *Butterflies and Moths of Missouri*, Heitzman should know. This trove of information not only describes the moths and butterflies that decorate my corner of the country, but also tells how to find them, collect them, attract them, and understand them.

"The Kansas City area is very good habitat for migrating monarchs," Heitzman told me. "Western Missouri and eastern Kansas in particular are good for sighting these butterflies. They roost in trees in specific areas year after year. Near the dam at Warsaw there's an important gathering area where the butterflies congregate before their long flight.

"There are three areas nationwide where you're likely to see large migratory concentrations: the eastern migration and the western flight path—in California and Oregon—and our area of the Midwest."

It's amazing to think how many of these insects actually make it to wintering grounds in the mountains of Mexico— enough to turn the pine trees orange. Enough that the sound of their wings is an audible rush. The butterflies that make it to Mexico, of course, are not the same ones that return to our area in the spring. While in the warmer climes or on the migration route itself, butterflies lay their eggs and die along the way. This first batch of new spring butterflies never migrates at all, Heitz- man tells me, but simply eats and reproduces. It's a generation or two down the line when the urge to move southward—and the genetic knowledge of where to go when it does—enters the picture and sets them sailing across the meadows.

I asked about the toxins that monarchs are said to absorb from their host plant, the milkweed. Monarchs eat *only* milk- weed, their harlequin-striped larvae filling up on the sap that nourishes while it protects.

"Most do absorb toxins from milkweed," Heitzman told me, "but some in lesser degrees than others. It depends on what part of the plant the larva feeds from; concentrations of toxins are greater in some parts than in others. Still, it seems to be enough to protect them from most predators. It really isn't a poison in the sense that it *kills* the bird or mammal that eats a monarch, by the way. It's a heart toxin that will make the preda- tor so ill it disgorges the insect and won't try another.

"The larvae really seem to like it," he continued. "When a plant is damaged so the white sap oozes out, they've been known to leave wherever they were feeding and congregate at the injury to literally lap up the sticky stuff."

That the bitter juice is the draw is a fine example of ac- quired taste, as far as I am concerned; perhaps the butterflies really do know what is good for them and choose their diet accordingly. I've eaten milkweed myself, as a spring green or asparagus substitute, but properly prepared for human con- sumption. That means boiling *off* the bitter sap in several changes of water.

The sap makes it taste more medicinal than edible—as indeed it is, before it's processed. The *Peterson Field Guide to Eastern/Central Medicinal Plants* by Steven Foster and James A. Duke says the Indians used the root to make a tea for a laxative and diuretic, for kidney stones and dropsy. The juice was applied to warts, moles, and ringworm. Latex from the dried juice was sometimes chewed as a gum, but it's a dangerous practice; according to Foster and Duke, the toxins in milkweed contain cardioactive compounds—as Heitzman said, a heart toxin. This folk remedy for cancer also provided soft filling for pillows and mattress ticks from the silky seedheads.

Asclepias syriaca—milkweed—is oddly named, for this is a North American species; *Asclepias* comes from the Greek god of medicine, Asklepios. *Syriaca* means Syrian, which this plant definitely is not. The earliest inhabitants of this country had discovered the uses of this plant as a medicinal and foodstuff long before the first white settlers arrived. Omaha and Osage, Lakota, Pawnee, Crow, Cheyenne, and Ponca all used it in my area. According to *Edible Wild Plants of the Prairie* by Kelly Kindscher, the explorer John Fremont reported that he had found great quantities of milkweed growing along the Blue River in southeastern Nebraska in June 1842 and noted that "The Sioux Indians of the Upper Platte eat the young pods of this plant, boiling them with the meat of buffalo." I wonder if his bride, the indomitable Jessie Fremont, who often accompanied her husband on these expeditions (and later supported the family with her travel writing), added this useful plant to her repertoire by way of the Native Americans they met on their journeys. Perhaps *they* learned of its usefulness from the butterflies—and the insects have had plenty of time to develop a taste for it. Butterflies are thought to be over 23 million years old—older than dinosaurs, older than birds, and certainly older than us.

Dr. Orley Taylor, Jr., entomologist at Kansas University, noticed a marked decrease in monarch numbers this year when he was in Mexico to study Africanized bees. An unusually hard freeze in these high mountains was thought to have killed large numbers of the insects, and a tracking effort is under way to determine how great the losses actually were.

Butterflies are not banded as you would a bird, of course. Instead of a lightweight metal band around a leg, the insects are marked with a tiny, self-adhesive paper label folded over the leading edge of a wing. When I talked to Joan Heitzman to confirm how that was done, she laughed.

"I wondered about that, too, at first," she said. "At one time I had heard they actually stamped a wing, but I couldn't imagine how that would work. You'd have to rub the scales off completely in order for it to take.

"The paper labels work really well, though. They don't seem to interfere with flight at all," she said in answer to my query. "I could imagine butterflies flying around in a circle with the extra weight on one side, but they don't seem to notice it.

"We did learn a lot from the banding operations we've done. For instance, we thought that migrating butterflies would just be here overnight, to feed and then move on. But when we banded them we learned they often stay for several days in an area before leaving."

"I didn't notice a significant decrease in monarch numbers in our area this year," Richard Heitzman added. "It'll be spring, and the new hatch, before we can begin the count and know what to expect from the Mexico freeze."

It is not only the freeze that threatens monarch numbers in Mexico. Although their mountain habitat is protected by the government of that country, there has been illegal logging nearby. The big pine trees are just too tempting, and encroachment in this area would result in significant decreases in monarch butterfly numbers.

As always, habitat destruction is the main culprit in declining numbers of butterflies—as with other wildlife. Pesticides and herbicides kill still more, but many people are inviting butterflies into their backyards and gardens. Plantings of butterfly-specific food plants include some of the prettiest of cultivated plants.

"The flowering period of various trees, shrubs and herbaceous plants is often an indication of the presence of certain Lepidoptera," according to *Butterflies and Moths of Missouri*. "The habitat, emergence period and nectar preference of some species are known to coincide with the flowering period and habitat of certain plant species. This makes them odds-on favorites to be found visiting the flowers, providing the insect occurs in that region."

Look for monarchs, of course, near milkweed plants; you can add these to your garden from wildflower nurseries or from seed. Don't try to dig them in the wild and transplant them to your backyard; it is illegal in some areas and usually doesn't take, anyway. Cultivation is not difficult, however—these *are* weeds, remember, and by definition, hardy. They have also been in cultivation for a very long time; one of the earliest reported attempts at making a garden crop of these plants appears in the Gerarde-Johnson Herbal of 1633, which published in London.

Other butterflies love white sweet and red clover, heath asters, pale-purple coneflowers, clematis, hawthorn, lilac, honeysuckle, bergamot, the mints, marigolds, petunias, and even wild onion. (Check a good book on butterflies for a more complete listing; Heitzman lists seventy-eight wild and cultivated flowers, shrubs, vines, and trees that attract these insects.)

Why wait for your plants to flower to attract butterflies and nocturnal moths? The Heitzmans offer a recipe to attract them that sounds as though it would be delightful on ice cream. The mixture is called "sugar bait," but it's a great deal more than that: Take a can of beer, two pounds of sugar (preferably dark brown), two cups of molasses, and two pounds of well-ripened fruit. Peaches or soft bananas are fine. Stir well and allow to ferment in the sun for at least a day. Dab it on posts, rocks, or tree trunks and watch for the action. (Do be sure to store in a large enough container with a loose-fitting lid. Fermentation causes great expansion, as any home brewer will be glad to attest.) Once the mix has fermented sufficiently, keep it in a cool place. Reapply several times a week; results improve with aging, just as with a good wine, and the butterflies may need the boost during migration.

Monarchs get all the press when it comes to migrating butterflies; those incredible, insect-covered trees in Mexico get the credit for that. But painted ladies migrate in March, in especially large concentrations in Arizona and California. Cloudless sulphurs, little sulphurs, and several others of this clan are known to migrate, as are some of the fritillaries, buckeyes, and even red admirals, to a degree.

Patrice Dunn, administrator at the Martha Lafite Thompson Nature Sanctuary in nearby Liberty, Missouri, tells me of a wonderful sight that greeted her in their prairie habitat. It had been a good year for monarchs—their rich orangy wings were everywhere; she had become accustomed to seeing them, to looking for them.

This day a family came down the path—a young couple, a child, and a grandmother—visiting, apparently, from India. The child skipped down the path toward the sanctuary's main building, with the grandmother, dressed in a flowing orange silk sari, just behind her. A rising wind caught the monarch-colored fabric and lifted it like a wing, bright against the green and tan of late-summer prairie grasses. It was hardly a sight you'd expect, coming out of a midwestern tallgrass prairie; it was exotic as a monarch grown large as a dark-haired woman in butterfly-wing silk.

A Walk Among Aliens

When I arrive at the cabin there are only a few furtive dark shapes slipping through the bare trees, the beginnings of movement like the first slow, contemplative notes in a new symphony. Here and there a dark form drifts downward through the stripped branches, and another, and another, as though new leaves had appeared overnight only to fall again in an endless wintry autumn.

They are mostly common grackles, iridescent birds somewhat larger than a robin. A few larger specimens among them, somewhat off their normal territory, must be great-tailed grackles, which may attain eighteen inches long—plus. Both have odd, pale eyes that seem to stare back with a wary, enigmatic interest. Both are oil-slick handsome in shifting colors of purple and bronze, green and turquoise overlaying black; the birds glint like black opals in the sunlight.

An earlier migration of grackles had passed through in September comprising thousands of birds, and I had assumed they were all gone, ensconced in some warm latitude with others of their kind. Traveling companions of the redwings and other blackbirds or Icterids, here in northwestern Missouri the concentrations of migrating grackles are normally long past when the winter solstice is at hand, chasing the retreating light. But the birds' wintering grounds overlap summer territories throughout much of their range; it's a trick of weather as well as light that sends them migrating, and birds that summer farthest north must find our more southerly clime mild in comparison. The cabin feels almost hot when I step inside after walking outdoors in winter, though the thermometer reads a chilly fifty-five degrees; we are not so different from the birds.

We don't see as many Icterids in the Midwest as on the eastern seaboard. Here, the red-winged blackbird, brown-headed cowbird, rusty and brewer's blackbirds, and the sometimes unwelcome import, the European starling—plus, surprisingly, the meadowlarks and orioles, also Icterids—are the most common family members. Elsewhere, fourteen nesting species plus four accidentals swell the populace. Eighty-eight species worldwide make our life list look puny.

As I enter the cabin to begin my work, I spot still more grackles across the creek, drifting through the trees like heavy, black smoke. The first ones were not stragglers, then, but part of a larger band—visitors from Canada, perhaps.

I try to concentrate at my desk, but I can't help but attend to the sound of these garrulous, intelligent birds, swelling and rising just beyond the edge of my attention like the sound of continuous surf. Twice I step to the door to listen, and each time a cloud of them rises with a rush, disturbed by the sound

of the door opening—or by some more mysterious and instinctive force. A dense cadre of birds drives itself through the woods, feathered missiles that manage not to collide with a single branch. Moments later, a matching wave retraces its course, surging back across the creek and into the trees. At the crest of the hill beyond, visible now in the barren woods, a squall of dark birds rises with a muffled roar; the birds scatter themselves down the slope, falling random as shrapnel, feeding again and moving on.

At first I thought them gone, an army passing in review by my small cabin, but the bivouac is of a more lasting nature. The tenuous quiet is soon broken by the sound of shelling on the cabin's metal roof. The grackles have returned, flying low through the walnut grove, streams of birds breaking and parting around the cabin like water around a stone. I feel their presence as palpable as current in a deceptively smooth river. They have found the year's heavy crop of acorns in the woods, still visible through the thin snow or clinging here and there to a limb. Many of their heavy bills are loaded with nuts that look much too large to swallow, but these powerful tools are strong enough to get at an acorn's meat with apparent ease. When a nut slips from a bird's grasp it shells the cabin with a gunfire rattle instead. Their actions mesmerize me by the door; I want to catch them at it.

More and more birds join the fray. The clouds of dark birds are like an inland hurricane, too exciting and too foreign to ignore. Who can work when such a phenomenon impinges on the ordinary, shouldering it aside as if it were too weak to resist? As indeed it is. Duty—responsibility—inertia; they seem intertwined and entirely superfluous when there is something like this wild, pulsing migration to see. The sounds in the woods and the rush of wings excite me. It's not an invitation; it is imperative. Leaving coat and hat behind, I step out into the woods to follow.

An iridescent wave of birds rushes back up the hill away from me, following the tractor road and spilling over into the woods that crowd it; I push my way through the tangle of buckbrush after them, feeling only slightly foolish. Overhead, a few birds watch me with unconcern, as though I mattered no more to them than a stone in the path, but others rise at my approach with a thunderous roar of wings—there are thousands more than I had originally assumed, filling the trees and the underbrush with their clattering voices, somewhere between song and screech.

They fly only a few feet and land again, waiting for me to catch up in a strange version of interspecies tag; war games in the woods, catch-me-if-you-can. The incurious watchers overhead express their opinion without moving, their voices individual in the overall cacophony, but as I come on up the path the flock rises again and again, leapfrogging through the trees just ahead. The sound is everywhere, a rushing roar like a waterfall; it rises as I approach, and I don't know if mere proximity or panic among the birds ups the volume. My blood pounds in my ears—or is it just the sound of their wings? I can't hear my own shouts; the sound of battered air and bird voice hurts my ears; something in me wishes it louder still.

I've long since left the path; the birds forge their own invisible route through the trees, and I follow, frustrated and earthbound, never coming closer than twenty feet to the main band—and never disturbing the implacable watchers above me, commenting desultorily on my strange actions. I follow the waves of grackles through the woods, now paralleling the creek rather than angling away, slipping and stumbling for footing in the thin, icy covering, trying to keep up with the waves of birds without ever looking down—as though they would disappear if I looked away and I'd find myself bereft and foolish among the trees.

The clouds of birds remind me of tales of the great flocks of passenger pigeons that eclipsed the sun; I would like to have seen that spectacle before the sky emptied. I imagine the thunder of the hooves of bison shoulder to shoulder, mile after mile across the flats. It is as though numbers alone have power over our imagination—and perhaps they do.

These grackles are common as dirt—as were passenger pigeons—but their swollen numbers are decidedly not typical. These are not the two or three adults that frequent my summer creek; these are legion, as though the normal numbers that inhabit a Missouri woodland had been mathematically increased to the tenth power; to the hundredth; to the thousandth. But finally I can no longer ignore the pervasive chill. A flannel shirt isn't sufficient against the December day, and my feet in their soaked sneakers begin to feel the snow; I might as well be barefoot. Reluctantly, I give it up and return to the cabin by the upper path, having circumnavigated a large portion of the woods in search of belonging. If I learned anything from the experience it is this: It's easy enough to forget our veneer of civilization when faced with wildness that comes in migratory waves. I surrendered work and comfort and identity willingly just to enlist, however briefly, in the force of migration.

Suggested Reading:

Carter, David, *Butterflies and Moths*, Dorling Kindersley, Limited, London and New York, 1992.

Clark, William S., and Brian K. Wheeler, *Peterson Field Guides: Hawks*, Houghton Mifflin, Boston, 1987.

Cutright, Paul Russell, *Lewis and Clark, Pioneering Naturalists*, University of Nebraska Press, Lincoln and London, 1989.

Foster, Steven, and James A. Duke, *Peterson Field Guide to Eastern/Central Medicinal Plants,* Houghton Mifflin, Boston, 1990.

Heitzman, J. Richard, and Joan Heitzman, *Butterflies and Moths of Missouri*, Missouri Department of Conservation, Jefferson City, 1987.

• **Five** •

Among the Trees

The Urban Forest

Bethany Falls Trail begins without fanfare, a darker green opening in green summer woods. Like many another forest path, this one looks inviting, cool—and uneventful. The wide wood-chip path as it is maintained by the state of Missouri is one way only, so you don't meet yourself coming and going; there is a feeling of solitude that deepens as you penetrate the green glow of the woods. Birdsong and the whisper of leaves are braided among the fading sound of voices left behind at the trailhead and picnic area.

Only yards down the path, history reaches out its frail human fingers to touch the walker. Hidden among the trees are the mossy remains of foundation stones; someone found a home here in a tiny cabin no larger than ten by ten feet. It must have been a lonely existence tucked into these steep hills, screened by the massive trees—but if it was so lonely, why do I wish I were there, looking from the small windows in square-hewn log walls? Why is the image so attractive? It would have been a hard life, but a walk in beauty as the Navajo say—and beauty does much to salve the abrasions of loneliness.

A bit farther on, the circular eye of a stone-lined well blinks up at the sky and I bend low to see the water held deep in the earth. The foundation stones of a larger cabin, nearly hidden by thick summer underbrush, appear just up the trail; there was company here, after all, the human need for community written in ivy-covered rocks.

A wooden-decked overlook hangs over a small creek far below; I can barely hear the water's voice beyond the screen of trees. The deck, an anomaly bounded by railings and reached by a catwalk over the forest floor, is not what you expect to find on a rugged path barely three feet wide, but it's a welcome surprise nonetheless. It offers another aspect, a vantage point over steep, wooded hills I could not have achieved by myself—without climbing an overhanging tree, that is. There is a sudden island of space in the forest invisible from the closely fringed trail.

Burr Oak Woods is beautiful, but except for the unexpected, intimate panorama from the overlook, not unlike many hundreds of other walks I've taken in Missouri woods—until I come upon the trail's namesake. The massive outcroppings of Bethany Falls limestone are the legacy of an inland sea some 300 million years gone. Here, these form huge stony bluffs, freestanding as a herd of elephants on the side of the hill. The mammoth stones are taller than I am; the ground drops off beside them so there is a deepened sense of isolation. Everything has changed; it is common woodlands no longer. Here the trail leaves reality and enters . . . magic.

The limestone monoliths take woods and weather by the scruff of the neck and change them to suit themselves. The growing heat of a midwestern summer day is suddenly cooler by degrees. Quiet is thrown across the air like a down comforter. As I step into the fissure between rocks as big as prehistoric pachyderms, I am reminded of Loren Eisley's descent into a sandstone crevice in *The Immense Journey*, a journey—like this one—backward into the unimaginable past. Instead of Eisley's featureless and innocent prairie, I enter through dense and varied woods. Instead of the soft, tawny sandstone, I reach out to touch the cool gray limestone that underlies much of my

area. But the sense of entering a reality far different from the one I've just left is the same.

Even the vegetation changes. The stone's propensity to act as a sink for the cooler air of night makes it a fine habitat for soft, acid-green mosses in as many varieties as I've seen anywhere. It is a miniature patchwork of fine, green shapes. Common beard moss, cushion moss, and twisted moss grow here, cushioning the rock—and the sounds that find their way between them. Ferns punctuate the velvet covering as though planted for a centerpiece. Lichen patiently devours the stone, returning it to earth. These ancient plants—mosses, ferns, lichen—reinforce the feeling of the prehistoric, and although I know better—Bethany Falls limestone is notoriously devoid of fossils—I can't help but look for the remains of something old beyond the edges of our time.

But instead of the deep shadows of prehistory, there are the more recent shadows of the historical cougar, the red wolf, and the black bear once populous in these woods. Cougars—a.k.a. mountain lions, pumas, or "painters," as they were called in the backwoods—are thought to have been extirpated from their ancestral ranges here in the Midwest. Extirpated is an odd word; it means the big felines have been driven from the area. Cougars are not extinct in the wild, not yet. It is possible, even, to see an individual animal in the deep primal privacy of the woods— remotely possible. Breeding populations, however, are thought to be completely absent.

Nonetheless, there is an occasional tale of sightings throughout the state, an occasional scream in the night. Rosalyn Johnson, wildlife ecologist with the Department of Conservation, tells me there's been no hard evidence of their presence— no tracks, no roadkills—but certainly plenty of reports. People describe the size and length and the way the big cat looks—but the cougar itself is as elusive as Bigfoot (which also is "sighted" in the Missouri hills on occasion—perhaps after an ingestion of a bit too much "white lightnin'").

"There are several wild animals parks in the area," Johnson tells me. "The reported cougar sightings could be escapees; maybe someone's pet has gotten loose. Or, it could be a remnant of the state's original population. We just don't know."

The red wolf—also extirpated from the state—is a candidate for reintroduction in its ancestral range, but as in Yellowstone, human resistance is formidable. When the question is "Who's afraid of the big bad wolf?" the answer is, we are. And in spite of the fact that populations of white-tailed deer have exploded so as to become pests in many areas, we'd still rather live with them than with the natural system of checks and balances that is prey and predator.

Doug Hamilton, a wildlife research biologist with the Department of Conservation, tells me reintroduction is not likely, not here, at any rate. Habitat conditions are too degraded. In spite of acres of timber in the more rugged parts of the state, there are still too many people, too many highways and roads.

"Red wolves require a larger landscape than we're able to provide," Hamilton says. "It's still a controversial subject; they'd come into too frequent contact with people, and not everybody is enlightened about wolves. The biggest factor in a successful reintroduction, though, is the presence of coyotes. That's part of what did away with the wolves in the first place—interbreeding."

Gray wolves once existed in the northern two-thirds of the state; as near as we can tell, they were all gone by the late 1800s.

Red wolves were common in the more rugged Ozark areas, but they were gone by the '30s or '40s. Although there are captive breeding programs for these beautiful animals in North Carolina and other southeastern areas, it's not probable that such a program would work in the Midwest.

"Even if we tried to release them into the wild, red wolves would soon crossbreed with coyotes and their genes would be swamped," Hamilton said. "Originally there weren't such widespread populations of coyotes; now they're everywhere."

Black bears, once common throughout much of the Midwest, seem to be making their own comeback, thank you, with no intervention from humans at all. Tracks of bear *have* been found. Black bears are smaller and less aggressive than grizzlies, and reclusive—not the usual stuff of bear-mauling stories. These bears are less territorial than grizzlies, as well—and less likely to attack a human even when provoked (although it has happened).

Our current bears may be what are left of the original population—or they may be a remnant of a captive breeding program undertaken in Arkansas.

Black bears had all but disappeared by the early 1900s. They had been absent in the whole area for thirty or forty years, when Arkansas brought in 254 animals from Minnesota and Manitoba, Canada, and released them in three locations.

"The program lasted twelve years and was given up as an expensive failure," Hamilton said. "They thought the bears had all been shot or had died out naturally. But after five or six years they realized they were getting new bear sightings and that they had a breeding population somewhere. Some of the bears that were shot were still wearing the ear tags the project used in the latter years; some weren't.

"Now we think the bears we have here in Missouri are either descendants of those original animals or new ones recently come up from Arkansas. We have at least a few breeding females in the Current River watershed and near Lake Taneycomo."

"How do you think these bears will fare?"

"The prospect is excellent," Hamilton replied. "They're capable of coexisting with humans, unlike the red wolves. They're very different from grizzlies, shy, retiring—not nearly the problem to hikers. We *do* need a public that's tolerant of bears, though. The Department is prepared to deal with nuisance animals."

In the Great Smokies black bears are making a record comeback; they've become a tourist attraction. I'd be surprised to see one near a Burr Oak trail—it's too far north—but not sorry.

"We get all kinds of reported sightings," Hamilton said. "Panthers, *black* panthers, hyenas, wolverines—even Bigfoot himself."

"But no unicorn sightings, I guess," I said, laughing.

"Not yet. But I wouldn't be surprised if somebody called one in."

It's sobering to think how much we've lost; how much we're in danger of losing. There is already so much I will never see. Clouds of passenger pigeons no longer hide the sun, and the realization casts a cloud on my mind instead. Dodo birds have become a joke rather than a living, breathing entity. A new forty-two-page booklet just revised by the Missouri Department of Conservation in 1992 updates listings of rare and endangered species. Among those counted as rare are the black bear, swamp rabbit, plains harvest mouse, pocket mouse, eastern small-footed bat, and long-tailed weasel. Among the endangered are the black-tailed jackrabbit, plains spotted skunk, and the gray and Indiana bat. Birds, reptiles, amphibians, mussels, crayfish, insects—the list goes on and on, and absolutely stops me in my tracks.

Pockets of urban woods like Burr Oak are too small to support breeding populations of most of these creatures; they are too close to burgeoning human populations for more than accidental sightings. But large expanses of land like that just bought by the Nature Conservancy in southern Missouri, which includes the wild and lovely Greer Spring, are just the ticket. Mark Twain National Forest, although subject to logging, is also prime habitat. The debate goes on whether to allow clear-cutting or to require more selective logging practices that would reduce erosion and preserve large tracts of habitat.

Still, the smaller parcels of woods are precious and well worth preserving. In my part of the country, both public and private nature sanctuaries keep safe small tracts for wildlife—and for humans. We need them as much as they.

Today the trail is labyrinthine, weaving between and among the huge stone monoliths. There is something to discover at every turn—wild columbine growing from a minuscule crack in the rock; a water-dug tunnel through the bluff's face that looks the perfect den for some small creature. The trail goes on and on, twisting and turning until you couldn't begin to know which way you went without a compass—or without the implied promise of a wood-chipped path. It's a most satisfying confusion, couched as it is in the assurance that someone surely maintains that trail and that it must lead *some*where.

But like everything touched by the human, the trail is not without its tragedy. A few years ago a man was murdered among these rocks; his body was found by a frightened hiker, and for some time afterward the area was less used. What if the attacker returned?

In the end, it turned out to be an isolated incident, a crime with a motive and not a random killing. My friend Judy, who often walked here winter and summer, says that her family was concerned for her, for a time—and that they insisted she at least investigate Mace. For a time she walked accompanied by a grown daughter. But the peace of the place reasserted itself and the memory of murder receded into the past.

There are other trails at Burr Oak, including a handicap-accessible trail that is an easy stroll through spring. The picnic areas attract local families and schoolchildren. A modern interpretive center provides a preview of the surrounding ecosystem in graphic, easy-to-understand terms. A large three-dimensional map allows the casual visitor to see just what to expect, in miniature (though like a painting or a photograph—like these words—it is no *real* preparation for being there, and my best advice is to find the door and step outside).

On a table near the map are wooden balls of many sizes. They are carved from various woods, but as I heft them I find they are all the same weight because of the different densities of the woods. Dioramas show the wildlife and plants that may be seen along the trails, and an expanse of glass opens onto some of the most active bird feeders I've ever seen. (The squirrels enjoy them, too, and gather below the platforms to glean their share of seeds.) A fourteen-foot-long aquarium mesmerizes visitors as indigenous Missouri fish swim slowly by—including the prehistoric-looking gar. A huge snapping turtle paddles lazily to the surface; soft-shelled turtles watch it warily.

But the real draw is the forest, so accessible to the growing town of Blue Springs and only a few minutes from downtown Kansas City. Directly behind the nature center, the asphalt-paved trail makes exploration available to anyone; it is a beautiful place to wander if you have only a short time or limited energy. But for those with the desire and the ability to explore—and with perhaps a need to get a closer sense of what these woods are like to their original inhabitants—the less civilized trails are the ticket.

Urban forests are invaluable learning tools; they're also islands of peace and sanity in cities that show no signs of slowing their rapid outward growth. On the Bethany Falls Trail you are surprised, as you near the end of the forest section, to hear the traffic on nearby Missouri 7 Highway—how can civilization be so near when you'd forgotten its very existence, immersed in prehistory among the stones?

There is a great variety of plant life in these woods. Bittersweet climbs the trees as though for a better look—it is life-giving light the vine is looking for. Close to the ground, eastern wahoo or spindleberry opens hot-pink drupes like gaily painted, triangular boxes. A relative of bittersweet, this plant is often overlooked for its showier cousin.

The rich soil of the forest floor is hospitable to a variety of plants and wildflowers. Spring to fall, you may find tiny wild violets, bloodroot, mayapple, sweet William, starry campion, bellwort, cranesbill, tall bellflower, or aster. Mushrooms and other fungi from morels and chanterelles to woody bracket fungi appear as the season dictates or cling to their chosen trees year after year, as though put there by a carpenter influenced by art nouveau. Once, in the winter woods near Watkins Mill, I found the vegetative remnants of puttyroot, a wild orchid not often found in these parts.

The diversity of tree species you discover on your rambles depends a great deal on where you live. The Ozarks are largely clothed with oak-hickory forests, with a variety of smaller trees like redbud, dogwood, sassafras, and serviceberry claiming space in the understory. In the eastern forests, you will find the typical New England mix of sugar maple, yellow birch, yellow poplar, sweetgum, and the basswoods that make this area a must-see destination in the fall. In Canada, Alaska, and parts of the Great Lakes area as well as in cool Appalachian elevations as far south as Georgia, boreal forests of spruce, jack pine, and fir mix in some areas with quaking aspen, paper birch, and balsam poplar. In the mountains, evergreen-aspen forests predominate. Rounded patches of aspen that change in autumn in syncopated sequence are called clones; they grow outward from a single tree.

Near a water source, the forest community may alter to reflect habitat change. Cottonwoods, sycamores, willows, and other water-loving trees take their place beside the more drought-tolerant species. When I walk to the old meadow on my place—the highest elevation at 950 feet above sea level—I look back down into the woods and see the line of ghostly white sycamores that mark the path of the creek that empties into the Missouri River, ten miles away. If I were in a light plane, I could find the creekbed all the way to the river.

In a natural mixed forest community the variety of tree species and small understory trees sharpens my powers of ob-servation; learning their names and habitats provokes a forester's concentrated interest. Scientifically, trees are divided into gymnosperms, those that produce fruits without flowering first, and angiosperms, those that flower before fruiting. Pines, which are gymnosperms, may bear fruits hidden in protective scales; watch a squirrel as it carefully dismantles a pine cone to get at its rich, oily repast. Yews, cedars, cypresses, and the non-native ginkgoes (non-native in historic times, at any rate—the fossil record proves it was once common) are all gymnosperms that have developed individual ways of protecting their seeds. Apple, nut, and cherry trees are angiosperms that flower in a variety of ways; in midwestern woods the leguminous honey locust scents the air with waxy hanging flowers that resemble wisteria. They are in fact first cousins.

In spring and much of summer, many trees send out small packets of hope for the future in the form of seed snow, a profligate production intended to ensure a good supply of new trees. Some years there is almost a blizzard of varied seeds and samaras, and when the wind blows they pile in yellow-brown drifts. If all of these sprouted to become young saplings, there would not be enough light and nutrients available to support them to maturity. But like the thousands of seeds put out by a single cattail, most are destined to another fate. Some simply die where they pile up in thick, mulching drifts; there's not enough available moisture to sustain them, nor room to grow if there were. Most end up as food for birds from turkeys to grouse, as well as for a variety of mammals. Deer and squirrels find these succulent seeds a welcome addition to their diets, as do other small gnawing creatures. And a few sprout to become the understory of a new wood, new trees in the making.

If we notice *only* these forest giants when walking in the woods, we truly are "not seeing the forest for the trees." Fire-red cardinals seem especially abundant in winter, but perhaps it's their coloring against the pale landscape creating an illusion. Yellow-shafted flickers streak through the trees like arrows made of sunlight. Bluebirds nest in growing numbers at the forest's edge—or so it seems. Considered threatened as pushier birds take over nesting sites, these birds appear to be making a comeback where I live. A concerted effort to educate the public about making proper nest boxes available where woods meet open areas and maintaining them to meet the needs of bluebirds seems to have helped.

More subtle in coloration, the chickadees, titmice, brown creepers, and nuthatches—as well as many other small passerines—are also in residence. Owls and whippoorwills ply the night, and hawks circle overhead, never seeming to stoop among the trees for prey.

The graceful shapes of turkey vultures on black dihedral wings sail lazily overhead; they roost at night in dense stands of trees. I find their huge black primary feathers on the ground and note the white splashes of excrement on their chosen trees; these big birds provide their own insect repellent by spraying their lower extremities with their own dung.

Once my godchildren called me excitedly from their home near the Fishing River abutting Isley Park Woods, the Missouri Natural Area in my town.

"There's a buzzard down by the river; I think it's hurt! Can you come?"

I grabbed my camera and raced for the park. In the fringe of woods beside the river, a young turkey vulture (or buzzard, as it is commonly known), its head still black and almost unwrinkled instead of the adult bird's hideous red, burned-looking visage, glared back at me. It did appear to be hurt, although I could see no blood nor discern a break in a foot or a wing. It lumbered awkwardly away from me, silent and sepulchral. I could get no closer to find out why it walked rather than flew, so after a few quick snapshots I hurried up the hill to the children's home and turned the problem over to Pete Rucker, my veterinarian. As a wildlife rehabilitator, Pete could fix the creature up if anyone could.

It's not always the normal denizens of the forest I see here. Once, a prehistoric *schronk!* startled me with its harsh assault on my ears; a great blue heron had landed in a tree just overhead, and protested my presence in the forest. Another time a

The Little Green Heron can extend its neck or retract it back into loose skin and feathers so it looks as though it has a short neck like a Night Heron.

little green heron also voiced its complaint deep in the woods. It had found a tiny creek and fished its hidden waters in private. I was not welcome in my own territory.

The little green heron, by the way, is named quirkily enough. It is not very green at all, but more of a colonial America black-green and brown; when you see it you may wonder why the name, as I did. One source said that the "little green" part comes, indeed, from the fact that there is so little green in its plumage. Someone had to stretch a long way for that description.

Tree bark provides the perfect hiding place for a variety of insects. Catocala moths have so perfected their camouflage that you'll hardly see them until they move, flashing colorful underwings. Elegant luna moths move like duchesses dressed in pale green silk; their larvae feed on the locust trees that abound in these woods. Bark beetles carve ornate tunnels beneath the corky upper layer; their distinctive designs tell you which kind of beetle excavated these mazes.

Deep in the old-growth forest on the east hill, I found an oak seven feet in diameter. It towered above me, reaching twisted arms as though to snag the scudding clouds. At its base was a fantastic gall, big as two bushel baskets, with a cave-like opening filled with acorns. Delighted with my find, I knelt for a better look.

The red oak clung to the edge of one of the many gullies that scribe the north hill; this one is salted with glacial erratics, visitors from another age shoved here some 15,000 years ago—raw newcomers beside the limestone rocks I'm used to. These pink quartzite anomalies appeal to my imagination; I return their visit, touching their smooth coolness. A subtle shine, facets of natural glass embedded in the rock, sparkle like a dusting of new snow.

There is death as well as life in the woods. I had headed up the little gully toward the biggest of these rocks when suddenly I became aware of the red-brown fur of a squirrel's tail on the ground and the avid buzz of flies. On closer inspection I found not just a tail but an entire dead squirrel, and I bent toward it with a naturalist's interest. What had killed it? Why was it here? How was it that none of the other scavengers had found the squirrel—why was it the sole province of the flies?

There was an odd, fungus-like growth sprouting from the eye that stared sightless up at me, like the sulphur-colored growth that sometimes grows on forest deadwood. I took a stick and tried to scrape it away.

And the squirrel moved. There was a faint, weak movement of a forepaw. Suddenly the world changed focus with a lurch and my stomach with it; I was no longer the detached observer. Something had to be done. I couldn't leave the animal like this.

I felt ill. My heart began a heavy, erratic thumping as though I had run a long way. I picked up the heaviest stone I could find and dropped it toward the squirrel's head—but I couldn't watch the moment of impact. Please God, let me kill it, let me put it beyond pain. I looked again and there was still that faint, almost imperceptible movement.

Damn! It wasn't dead. I lifted the stone and let it fall again, and again once more. I felt like an animal in a trap, appalled at the situation I found myself in.

But finally the job was done and I could look again as an observer, although a sickened one. I felt as though I had witnessed a terrible accident; as though I had been in one. The question of what had injured the squirrel remained. My land bristles with "No hunting" signs, and I hoped—hard—not to find evidence of trespass.

There was none. I turned the animal over to discover that it had broken its leg. It was a bad break of the right rear femur, the big bone of the upper thigh. The flesh around the ivory bone was exposed, discolored. The animal evidently had licked the injury until the fur was gone and the flesh exposed; it looked infected, but there was no sign of bullets of any kind. Perhaps it had missed its footing, unable to see clearly with that eye, and fell from the tree; perhaps it was hit crossing the road, only thirty feet away.

I still didn't know what had happened to the eye; didn't want to. The afternoon was shot through with pain; only the vigorous exercise of the rest of my walk and the profound, incandescent beauty of autumn woods could put enough space between me and the dumb agony of the squirrel.

Most of the woods in my part of the country are oak and hickory forests, with an understory of smaller trees like redbud, hawthorn, and pawpaw. Typically dense and opaque with this mix, the woods are deep and cool on a summer day. Deer move cloaked in anonymity through this screen of leaves; a fox drowses invisibly at the base of a tree. Near my cabin the forest is so thick that when I walk in through the woods to the north I can't see the cabin's roof until I make the final turn. And that's in winter, when the leaves are gone. In summer I don't even try.

Old forest giants are interspersed with mature trees and young saplings—where they have managed to get a foothold. It's light that's in short supply; in order to thrive—in order to survive at all—these strappy youngsters have to get enough of it. They make up for the competition in a variety of ways. Often

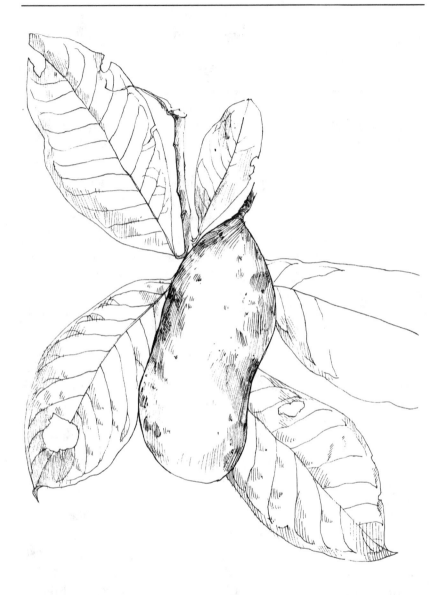

waiting to branch until their skinny adolescent trunks wave twenty feet in the air, they reach for the light with a single-minded grasp of survival techniques. Many young trees have disproportionately large leaves—the better to grab for light and the exchange of sugars, water, oxygen, and carbon dioxide that makes life possible on the vegetative level.

hairy

PawPaw
flowers

←—— Young,
green w/
mahogany
veins

Mahogany - colored

—Center is
green and
textured

Pawpaws wave huge moccasin-shaped leaves in late spring and summer. In spring *Asimina triloba*'s odd brownish flowers look carved, glossy and angular; these flowers develop into sweet, buttery pawpaw fruits. Lewis and Clark's journals mention making a special stop not far from where I write "to let the men gather Pappaws or the custard apple of which this country abounds, and the men are very fond of." The spelling and grammar of these early explorers could use some improvement, but their taste in wild fruits is excellent. I never beat the raccoons and squirrels to those in our woods; they are Johnny-on-the-spot at the moment of ripeness.

In a climax forest, there's typically a mix of ages and sizes of trees. Here and there a limb will die, its pithy wood providing fine and easily excavated nesting sites for woodpeckers and subsequent tenants like chickadees and bluebirds. Eventually, the dead limb or the whole tree may succumb, crashing to the forest floor to offer the raw building materials for carpenter ants and powder-post beetles and habitat for the fine white tatting of mycelia. Shelf fungus grows from the side of the damp log; rabbits find shelter in a hollow center. On a winter walk through wood such as these, I thunked absently on a fallen log with my long stick, only to be startled when a cottontail rabbit exploded from the open end like a cannonball. Bending to inspect the hollow, I discovered a snug chamber that could provide cover for any number of rabbits, skunks, raccoons, or even foxes or coyotes. Tracks in the snow nearby confirmed the supposition. With its crumbling lining of soft, pithy wood, it looked quite comfortable. Given time enough, the log will rot, becoming new soil and offering nourishment to the seeds that fall there. Old forest becomes new.

In the woods where I walk today, the scenario is a bit different. Once open territory except for a few large trees, this land was abandoned and allowed to grow up in brush years ago. There must have been cattle here at one time; here and there old bones gleam against the dark forest duff, oddly out of place in this unused corner. Barbed wire fences snake through the woods, posts sagging, wire slowly turning dark brown and brittle as rust claims dominion over steel. This young forest— kept open for years by livestock or by mowing, then suddenly

abandoned to the inevitable by a new owner—has grown up virtually all at once, and most trees are approximately the same height, the same girth. Their canopy is compact as rain forest. Underneath its dense shade, the normal understory plants have given up the attempt; almost no light reaches the ground. There is only a thick bedding of leaves underfoot, and an occasional mushroom.

Once in the forest, I can see for a long distance through green-tinted light. It is as though the transparent canopy were a dense congregation of emerald kites on dark, skinny strings—and so it is. The leaves—far from the ground in this crowded young forest—are held up at the ends of myriad thin, wiry trunks. The woods are so open I swear I could see a tick for a quarter of a mile—but of course I could not. These tiny parasites are furtive, hanging on the brush, lying in wait in the trees. They're patient. They can go a long time without a meal, as long as they get that fix of blood at the end of their wait.

I've gotten used to them. When I was a child, finding a tick attached to my pale skin was an occasion for hysteria; when I was older, disgust. Now I remove them like a pro and throw them on the fire or down the toilet with hardly a shudder. They're an occupational hazard like any other, and one the OSHA can do nothing about.

The little seed ticks are the worst, though not for sheer revolting size like a fully engorged adult tick. The problem is that these tiny creatures are easy to overlook, particularly if you're freckled or tend to moles. If you're the sensitive type, you may feel the larger wood or dog ticks as they move on your skin and remove them before they complete their agenda; if one has already bored into your skin, they're easily grasped and removed. Not so the seed ticks. These are much harder to find, much harder to remove, but anyone who spends time in the woods knows the drill. Drop your pants, shinny out of your clothes at day's end, and have a friend or spouse look you over. Lacking a helper, a mirror and a good light source are necessities. Keep the tweezers handy; some of the smaller ticks are impossible to grasp without them. A drop of disinfectant or

Eastern
Wood Tick

antibiotic lotion will usually do the trick, though I admit I am sensitive to tick toxins—a bite can itch for weeks and make a hot red welt.

Last summer I walked through the woods uncharacteristically clad in a denim skirt; jeans are my usual uniform. This time I looked down to find my ankles and calves covered with an army of tiny, moving dots. Seed ticks marched up my legs and all I could think was "Get them *off!*"

I raced inside to get a filleting knife—they were far too small to pick off, and there were far too many of them. Sitting on the deck, I shaved them off, wielding the knife like a straight razor.

It took quite a while to get them all; not being able to see the backs of my knees was a distinct disadvantage. And next time I walked in the summer woods I remembered the DEET.

Seed ticks may be a misnomer; the name is used to cover a range of situations that all mean some form of especially small arachnids. Some of these tiny ticks are adults; others are the nymphal form of large ticks. (*Ixodes dammini* is the culprit that caused the original outbreak of Lyme disease in Lyme, Connecticut; we don't even have that tick in Missouri. But a tick vector in my state *is* carrying Lyme or something just like it. *Ixodes scapularis* is widely found here—and in fact the January 1993 issue of the *Medical Entomologist* redefines *dammini* to include *scapularis*, effectively putting a stop to the debate.) Get out your magnifying glass; if the offender has six legs it's an immature nymph. If eight, it's an adult.

I had always assumed the nymphal form carried no diseases, but I was wrong—or at least I jumped to that conclusion. We simply don't know if they do or not. The key is to remove *any* tick, as quickly as possible after exposure.

We in Missouri don't have the problem that those on the East Coast seem to—not yet, anyway—but we're certainly aware of the danger. For a time after the news of Lyme disease hit the media, a bottle of our usual insect repellent couldn't be bought at any price; the factory was selling by the case to linemen, lumberjacks, and others who make their living outdoors.

When I first checked with the Kansas City Health Department several years ago about the threat of Lyme disease, Missouri had not yet had a problem. The Center for Disease Control in Atlanta had stopped testing for Lyme, as had the state of Missouri—the tests are considered extremely inconclusive. (However, the state will forward tests from referring physicians to the CDC, according to Michael Fobbs, health program representative of the Bureau of Communicable Disease Control in my state.)

The first time I checked with Dale Giedinghagen, public health specialist with the Kansas City Health Department, he confirmed that the disease had probably not made its way this far west. At that time there were only four confirmed cases in the state, and those were people who had visited back east and could have brought the illness with them to incubate and develop. Now, by the fall of 1992 there had been 675 cases reported since 1988.

It's still up for grabs as to what's causing the disease in my state. No ticks have been found in Missouri with the actual Lyme spirochetes in their system, and some experts are calling our particular manifestation of the disabling malady "Lyme-*like*" rather than the actual disease. (Other expects assert that it is indeed Lyme.) There are many more people who see their doctors each year who fear that they've contracted Lyme and there are more cases diagnosed as Lyme than actually are confirmed by the Center for Disease Control. And it is still more likely that you could pick up one of the tick's previously known diseases—Rocky Mountain spotted fever (or Rocky Mountain "spotless" fever, as Giedinghagen says it should be called; many cases occur without the characteristic rash), tularemia or rabbit fever, or ehrlichiosis, an arthritic malady similar to Lyme.

"All the tick-borne illnesses seem to be picking up," says Giedinghagen. "There are more people, and more people out in the country spring through fall."

The precautions against any tick-borne disease are formidable: Stay out of the woods or brushy areas (an impossibility for some of us); wear light colors, tight socks, long pants tied or bound at the ankle, and long sleeves (in my state's 100-degree-plus summer with 90 percent humidity this is not possible either); and douse well with repellent.

That was the preventative of choice until recently, when some products were voluntarily recalled for undesirable side effects. Oddly, it wasn't the deet (N-N diethyl-meta-toluamide) that was the culprit, though that stuff can melt the plastic lenses of your eyeglasses and render your steering wheel a sticky mess; it was one of the related isomers. My husband, a dedicated user, can rest easy; the recalled products are back, minus the offending member.

I'm somewhat unimpressed by their effectiveness, in my case. I took a walk through the summer woods the other day, knowing full well I would pass through prime tick country (ticks are most numerous where the woods meet the grasslands), and for a change decided to dose up. When I got home later that night I found six ticks, four already embedded up to their necks.

If you do find a tick on you, by the way, first check to see if it has become embedded. If it has, be careful how you remove it. Grasp it gently with tweezers and pull it loose (some say "unscrew" it with a counterclockwise movement). The point is, of course, not to kill it or tear its body loose from its head; if that happens it may regurgitate, causing it to release spirochetes into your bloodstream.

But as Giedinghagen said, if a tick doesn't get on you, it

can't bite you; if it gets on you but doesn't bite, it can't infect you; if it bites but you find it before it's engorged, it's probably safe given the low percentage of ticks carrying the Lyme spirochete. Even then the chances are fairly good you won't become diseased—just disgusted. Still, it depends on how long the tick has been on you; a seventy-two-hour window used to be considered the norm, but the sooner you remove it the better.

"My best advice to prevent Lyme is to check carefully when you come home," says Giedinghagen. "Change clothes, take a bath, and remove any ticks promptly."

For those particularly concerned about ticks, you can purchase a Lyme-tick kit, a $25 outfit consisting of specialized tweezers that unscrew the little devil, a magnifying glass, a "tick receptacle" to put the critter in for later identification by an expert, and a booklet on Lyme disease.

It's as good a defense as any. In the East some people are keeping their children, their pets, and themselves indoors, and advocating poisoning everything that moves, including the deer that play host to the offending tick—never mind that birds and rabbits, raccoons, horses, and your family dog can carry them as well. The best defense is still simple vigilance, a good bath at day's end, and a mirror. I don't make light of the consequences; my sympathy goes to those who suffer from the malady and its arthritic pain; the latest information suggests it may be incurable, once it has progressed too far. It's not the kind of pain you'd wish on your worst enemy.

If a tick _does_ bite, watch for fever, nausea, headaches, aching joints, and—Giedinghagen says—_sometimes_ a rash around the area of the bite. There is not usually an immediate reaction; an itchy welt like mine may just be the normal allergic reaction. Watch a few days—or even weeks—later, and be sure to tell your doctor of exposure to tick bite. The symptoms listed above, plus fatigue, and that characteristic bull's-eye skin rash (erythema migrans) may develop after exposure. Severe arthritis may develop in secondary stages, as well as weakness, tremors, and/or facial paralysis. In the third stage it is possible to develop chronic meningitis, severe arthritis, and in extreme cases, cardiac problems. Death is a distant possibility, but a possibility nonetheless.

Bob Buzard, my family doctor and a good friend, says he has only treated two cases of Lyme in his career: one while he was still practicing in Arizona, the other here in Missouri. And the word to remember here is *treated*. If diagnosed correctly— and early—Lyme disease can be treated successfully with a course of antibiotics, from fourteen days to thirty days or more, if the disease is well established. Some doctors prefer intravenous antibiotics, and some say it's best to keep giving them until all symptoms have disappeared. Catching the illness before it becomes too advanced is the key to most successful treatment. If you suspect Lyme, check it out.

Buzard agrees that the blood tests for Lyme aren't all that accurate. "There is a relatively high incidence of false negative and false positive results; blood tests aren't enough. You need good clinical diagnosis as well. But caught in time, sure, Lyme is treatable."

I check for ticks and remain alert for problems; staying indoors is not an option. Those transparent green woods are calling, and walks there are full of mystery and discovery.

There is a certain place between the Missouri River and the edge of town that maintains a steady out-of-sync-ness with the prevailing temperature year-round. It has a deeper chill in winter, a definite cooling in summer, noticeable by degrees from the farmlands that bake in the relentless sun. It is cooler, even, than the surrounding forests. To walk there is to be refreshed, and to wonder if those ancient trees possess a power we do not understand. It is a deeper cool than in the common woods, a cool that never fails to catch my attention no matter how distracted I may be.

Druids worshipped trees such as these, trees that have a strength and a secret; I don't wonder why. Even my skeptic's mind enjoys a momentary chill as I walk here, five degrees cooler than I was a moment ago, five degrees cooler than I will be just down the road.

There may be a cold-water spring just underground; there may be a limestone sink that so affects the local temperature. I don't know. What I do know is that the variance is real, and constant. My thermometer mirrors the change.

Local historian Harry Soltysiak tells of a crime committed in these woods. A pair of sisters who lived alone together did not trust the small-town banks to store their family fortunes. Someone—an outlander, according to legend—heard the tale of their storied riches and determined to take it from them. They were beaten senseless and left near death. Each time I walk through the deeper cool of the Howdershell Woods, I think of the two sisters; it beats Jason stories six ways to Sunday, and the chill I feel may be caused, on occasion, as much by speculation as by temperature.

Trees capture something atavistic in our imaginations—or our gene memory. They have meant too much for too long for our kind; they have meant survival. They provide homes and food, heat for cooking and comfort, shade in the summer. We make our beds and chairs from them, and fashion wooden bowls and spoons. Native Americans taught us to use acorns for flour; the oak's tannic acid is used in tanning leather. Many native trees have edible or medicinal properties, from the "tea" made from pine needles to the throat-soothing bark of the slippery elm or the purported "spring tonic" of sassafras, once so popular with our forebears. Myriad familiar and arcane uses abound in folklore and in the medical manuals. In the Pacific Northwest, a yew tree is found to contain substances of use in treating cancer. The pawpaw provides both food in the form of buttery-sweet "custard apples" and clothing or cordage; Native Americans once used the strong fibers of the bark to make necessities from strings for their hunting bows to finely woven baskets. Kentucky coffee tree provided our pioneer forebears with a substitute for coffee, as the name suggests. And the nuts, from pine nuts to acorns, have kept our bellies from meeting our backbones more than once in our history.

Walnut is a dense, fine-grained wood, satiny, the color of a sable mare in shadow. Since colonial times people have delighted in the uses of this hardwood. In southern Missouri where it is plentiful, walnut finds its way into handsome salad bowls, hand-carved gunstocks, and sculpture. We bought firewood last winter, and were both pleased and dismayed to find that it was walnut. This wood burns hot, and long, with a delicious scent on the winter air—but what a waste. I hate to throw such beauty on my blaze, but I'm too practical to refuse it. If I don't use it the carpenter ants will.

In summer the trees pelt us with the immature fruits as though to drive us out, raining down hard little knots that will be black walnuts. We watch where we walk to avoid the worst of the shelling and monitor the wind direction carefully. These nuts have deadly aim, and as they mature they may be two inches across; when they strike you know you've been hit. We take our revenge in the kitchen; the nutmeats add richness to baked goods.

Walnuts are encased in acid-green husks that turn slowly to a deep brown if allowed to ripen fully; if you touch them your hands will take on the same sable hue as the wood. My friend Terri collects them to dye the eighteenth-century clothing she makes; I watch her stir her steaming cauldron as though preparing a feast for a hundred. Instead, my husband's breeches come forth, drying in the sun to a rich, warm brown.

Suggested Reading:

Hancock, James, and James Kushlan, *The Herons Handbook*, Harper & Row, New York, 1984.

Little, Elbert L., *The Audubon Society Field Guide to North American Trees*, Alfred A. Knopf, New York, 1980.

Phillips, Roger, *Trees of North America and Europe*, Random House, New York, 1978.

Sutton, Ann, and Myron Sutton, *The Audubon Society Nature Guides Series, Eastern Forests*, Alfred A. Knopf, New York, 1985.

Thomas, Lisa Potter, and James R. Jackson, Ph.D., *Walk Softly upon the Earth: A Pictorial Field Guide to Missouri Mosses, Liverworts and Lichens*, Missouri Department of Conservation, Jefferson City, 1985.

Six

Prairie, Past Perfect

THE TALLGRASS PRAIRIE in winter is a place of great subtlety. The colors are richly subdued. Against the blue-shadowed snow of a January afternoon, the tans and wheats and russets are tawny as the coat of some great, rough mammal. The tallgrass is not so claustrophobic now; the winter's snow and ice have joined forces to lay the tall stems over in many places, especially where the wind leans on the grasses near the summit of the hill. It is an impossibly complex game of pick-up-sticks, made with the tangled stems of tallgrass.

There is no path here to lead me on a civilized walk, just amoebic patches of melting snow and the luxuriant fringe of grasses. I lift my feet high to get from one bent-over open patch to the next, and it shifts underfoot as though I stepped on the back of some shaggy beast.

These clumps of tallgrass are untouched; no one has walked here, no one but the coyotes that blend with the color of winter grasses in their gray-tan coats. The thick, folded hummocks are springy; they give only slightly with each step. For a moment I imagine the dense mat will hold me up, but again and again I fall through to *terra firma*. The grass crunches and crackles underfoot, disproportionately loud in the blue and gold silence. A few hundred yards away a bird takes note of my

presence and scolds repeatedly. It is far too distant to make out
more than a dark shape against the pale grass, and the single
note is ambivalence itself. To my untrained ear, it could be one
of a hundred birds, but here in this small prairie, Harris's sparrow abounds. This larger-than-average sparrow was first described by Audubon as he traveled near here in 1843. He named
it after his friend, Edward Harris, but I like the connection to
my husband's Christian name. "I saw your bird again today,
playing hide and seek in the tallgrass."

This late February day, the prairie is a graph of wind direction written in the sweeping, elegant calligraphy of stems.
Every blade, every leaf is bent away from the northwest, from
whence comes winter. When I look in the direction of the rising
sun it seems to me as though the wind is right-handed; when I
sketch, everything sweeps away from left to right—by instinct
or by habit. But looking toward the sun that hurries off to the
west I see that the wind might as well be a southpaw.

I thought no one had been here before me in this trackless
expanse—no one but the coyotes and foxes and a thousand tiny
rodents. But as I take a different direction, I discover a rough
path and look down to find the spreading footprints of a booted
man melting into the snow. It's impossible to tell how big he
might have been; the tracks lie to my face about a veritable
Sasquatch in gumboots. It has been several days since he passed,
several days of intermittent sun and warming temperatures. As
they have thawed, the tracks have spread in breadth and length
as well as depth.

I've bent down to inspect the trace and to make notes, and I
look up to find the world transformed by this new perspective. I
am a meadow vole here among the towering stems that come
together like an artist's perspective drawing in the intimate distance overhead.

Just over the crown of the hill the wind has been kind, the
strength contained in the stems more assertive. The grass stands
taller and thicker here, the hummocks of bent interwoven
grasses fewer. Even so I find one to sit upon, protected by upright stems all around. It is comfortably dry, soft, and warm

though surrounded by snow, a natural insulation that reminds me that our forebears once used the grasses for insulation in the walls of their homes and stuffed into their shoes.

Here, the wind whispers rather than shouts. The stringed instrument of prairie grass stems is like a wind-harp, played so softly I can barely hear. Now that my vantage point is a low-profile one, the birds I had imagined to be so few in number have begun to accept me and resume their feeding. The pickings are slim. I wonder how the long days and nights of remaining winter will treat these creatures, for where I expected to see myriads of seeds I find that most heads retain only a few. I wonder if they have dropped off in the weight of wind and snows of this winter, to reseed themselves in the spring, or if the birds have fed so greedily. There must have been millions upon millions of seeds here at the end of a bounteous midwestern summer. Now, within my sight, only a handful remain.

There is a delightful sense of concealment down here
among the stems. Where I had expected to feel claustrophobic,
instead I am reminded of childhood's hiding places, this one
done up in Scandinavian colors of wheat, pale blue, and white.
The sun is warm in this protected place, and the birds anticipate
the season to sing snatches of spring song mixed in with winter
calls, a medley of favorite hits. Alone among the stems, face
lifted to the sun, ears full of birdsong, I realize I am more con-
tent than I've been in a long time; it's like coming home. I do
not want to leave. I can't imagine what people mean when they
say winter is colorless and dead; the whole world is like some
big gorgeous sun-struck daisy, all white and gold and subtle blue
shadows.

Later, as the winter turns to early spring, the possibility of
claustrophobia all but disappears as late snows and heavy rains
continue to beat the stems to the ground. I am waiting for a call
to help with a burn this spring, to watch and contain the blaze
when a portion of the small prairie at the Martha Lafite Thompson Nature Sanctuary in nearby Liberty gets its annual grooming
by fire. But it may be a long wait; a wetter than normal winter
followed by a gloomy early spring has kept the grasses waterlogged and impossible to burn. I am both chagrined and re-
lieved; a prairie burn gives new meaning to "fighting fire with
fire," and lighting backfires is only one of the better ways of
controlling the beast.

The wind moans across the wide bands of prairie, a wraith
with a thousand voices that tell of the past, the bison, and the
pronghorn—and the woolly mammoth. There is nothing to
stand in its way; the western midlands are relatively flat, with
only an imperceptible overall grade from the western border of
the Appalachians, where the land is just above sea level, to the
foot of the Rockies. Here, the long erosion of the mountains has
deposited rock dust enough to raise the level of the land on the
lee side inch by inch, and although you'd never know it by
looking, you are standing mile-high with nothing to tell by but
the popping in your ears.

This broad incline is mum; it tells you nothing of its secrets, nothing of how the great stable cratons—Precambrian portions of the earth's crust that underlie the Midwest and the plains—came to be, or even that they're down there at all. Unlike the constantly shifting tectonic plates of both coasts—or the fault lines a few hundred miles away near New Madrid, Missouri, that make their presence known, moving measurably daily—the cratons are still, the grasslands calm, silent with their secrets; silent as stone. "What do I believe in?" asked Ed Abbey. "I believe in sun. In rock. In the dogma of the sun and the doctrine of the rock." Here in the ungentled glare of the sun, feet planted firmly on the rock that juts from the prairie, so do I.

There is sun, and rock; there is time. And there is mystery. The slow inclines and declines give away nothing about the inland sea that covered this landscape and mirrored the swells of wind on grass, nothing—unless you read the rocks in Kansas chalk beds, rich with fossils; unless you know the story behind the strange wind-and-weather-sculpted monoliths near Nebraska's Fort Robinson that mark the line of a prehistoric sea. I find

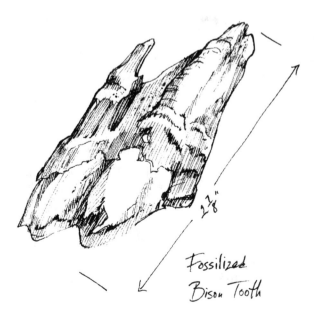

Fossilized
Bison Tooth

the fantastic shapes of ancient sea creatures and prehistoric fish, crystallized, turned to lifeless stone that nonetheless mimics today's clams and corals, snails and land-dwelling arthropods. The swells of wind on grass are a golden sea, mirroring the past. Elsewhere in these grassy plains are the remains of mammoths and mastodons, dinosaurs—and their eggs, with the tiny nestlings still in them, turned to stone as they hatched. It is an ancient land.

Speeding along by car or crossing the broad, lonely prairie of 150 years past in a creaking Conestoga, the casual observer sees only surface. One with an agenda to move, to progress, may discern nothing about the time when, some 70 million years ago, grasses evolved to give the prairie its own true face. What the early travelers saw in the last century—what I see now, in small pockets of remnant or restored prairie—seems timeless, unchanged and unchanging. But change, though subtle, is constant as the wearing of the rock.

This long timeline, sketched in broad, simplified lines, is easily overlooked in the open wind. The wind is monolithic in and of itself, reaching from horizon to horizon in abstract strokes too large to be seen from ground level. Mare's tail clouds played out into delicate veils mirror the energy of wind; what I see in the sky I feel here among the stems.

I love the prairie. It feels clean—and cleansing; uncomplicated—and wonderfully complex. Walking to the top of a long rise that bisects the blue prairie sky, I feel as though my small concerns have been swept away, a blown leaf chasing ahead of the prevailing wind.

My reaction is not the historic one, nor the one most travelers admit to as they fly over expanses that appear featureless from the air. As one drives through mile after mile of gently undulating grassland it seems the only punctuation is an occasional lonely farmstead. Many are abandoned. The prairie is, and was, most often seen as a necessary evil, something to be gotten through—quickly—on the way to something else.

The grasslands have created a tough breed of survivors. The

people who call the Great Plains home are the remnants of pioneer stock. In order to have survived here at all—by 1895, more wagon trains were headed back east than were going west—they had to be stubborn, stoic, and strong. They still are. All this emptiness, all this windswept, noisy silence, is a shock to the system, if one is used to a busier landscape.

The French were among the first Europeans to break free of the thick woods that stretched from the East Coast to the Mississippi, and they were both amazed and delighted. Traveling down the Illinois and Mississippi rivers in 1673, Louis Joliet wrote: "At first when we were told of these treeless lands, I imagined that it was a country ravaged by fire, where the soil was so poor that it could produce nothing. But we have certainly observed the contrary; and no better soil can be found, either for corn, or for vines, or for any other fruit whatever. . . . There are prairies there, six, ten and twenty leagues in length and three in width. . . . Sometimes we saw grass very short, and, at other times, five or six feet high. . . . A settler would not there spend ten years in cutting down and burning the trees; on the very day of his arrival, he could put his plough into the ground."

Prophetic words. That is exactly what happened, to this biosystem's great detriment. The dust bowl and continued erosion of subsequent years coupled with the destruction of millions of acres of native grasslands are an indelible legacy of change.

"Prairie"—a French word derived from the Latin *pratum*, or meadow, given to this landscape by the early explorers—is too simple to capture the truth of our varied grasslands. There are, in fact, tallgrass, mid- or mixed-grass, and shortgrass prairies. There is wet prairie and dry prairie. There are old fields as well as the true meadows the early French explorers remembered. There are desert grasslands, intermountain grasslands, and the vertical grassy slopes of California. I've walked many of them and find them seductive as the expanse of ocean. I look across a sweep of landscape so broad I can almost see the curve of the earth and find that, although I am a child of Missouri woodlands, the prairie calls my name with a sound indistinguishable from the wind.

The first band of grasslands as you come out of the eastern forests is tallgrass prairie, with twelve-foot-high big bluestem and Indian grass interspersed with cordgrass, switchgrass, and other shorter grasses. In the spring, before these towering grasses have attained their full growth, the prairie blooms with a rich tapestry of wildflowers, less ambitious, cool-season grasses like Junegrass and dropseed also claim their moment in the sun. Farthest from the rain shadow of the Rocky Mountains, the tallgrass prairie receives the most precipitation, a major influence in its lusty growth.

Presettlement tallgrass extended a long, pointing finger of itself far into Indiana as though to beckon travelers, but on its western border it cut in an almost straight line along the ninety-eighth meridian, a few miles across the border into present-day Kansas from its eastern neighbor, Missouri. On one side was tallgrass; hard by was mixed-grass prairie. This line might dance back and forth with the fluctuations in seasonal rainfall, retreating in drought, advancing in wet years, but the ninety-eighth marked the general boundaries. East of that meridian, the drying wind is not as intense, nor does the rain shadow of the mountains reach so far across the plain to dwarf the grasses that could survive there. West of the ninety-eighth, mixed grasses

Koeleria
cristata —
Junegrass

were shorter, perhaps only eighteen to thirty-six inches as compared to the ten to twelve feet of tallgrass.

There are those who say this mixed-grass band marks the beginnings of true prairies, the demarcation where trees still grow, from the plains, where they do not. It was this landscape that was known as the Great American Desert, first called so by Major Stephen H. Long in an 1820 report to the United States Congress. Unlike the tallgrass prairie, which exists mostly in memory and in protected parcels, there are still large tracts of mixed-grass prairie across Kansas, Nebraska, central Oklahoma, parts of Texas, and most of the Dakotas, where little bluestem abounds.

Because of the numbers of glacial "potholes" in this area, particularly in the Dakotas—potholes resulting in many natural ponds and lakes—this area is important to millions of migrating and nesting birds. Prairie chickens boom across the grasslands, as they have begun to do again in isolated pockets in my part of the country, as well. Here, too, are the ancestral grounds of great herds of bison, pronghorn, jackrabbits, and swift foxes. Though now you see bison only in protected areas and vastly reduced numbers, still they are impressive in their rough woolen coats and great size.

They are curiously docile creatures for the most part—at least that describes the small herds we have domesticated and fenced in. One day while I sketched a handful of them in a restored prairie, several came close as though to see what I was doing. At first when I spoke to them they started, snorting and moving away, but as I went on with my work they returned. I touched their damp noses through the fence and rubbed their woolly heads and inhaled the good, wild smell of them, continuing to draw until they lay down a few feet away and fell asleep.

They are not always so sanguine. A friend tells me the big ungulates apparently don't care for horses. While attending a reenactment of a mountain man rendezvous, he witnessed the goring of a horse by a free-ranging bison. I prefer the protection of the fence as I sketch—several tons of irritable bison packs a wallop.

American bison, erroneously called buffalo, were once common all the way to the Appalachians. They were indigenous to much of the grasslands, though nearly wiped out for their hides, tongues, and livers—and as an attempt to demoralize and disenfranchise the Native American peoples who depended on them for their livelihood. When the railroad came to the American West, buffalo hunters and early-day tourists shot from moving trains with no intention of butchering or eating their trophy at all but only to kill and keep on killing.

Bison still ran through the streets of Liberty, Missouri, as late as the 1850s according to old newspaper accounts, but that far east into the tallgrass—and into the more populous areas—they were already becoming scarce. Today they are found east of the Great Plains only in wildlife preserves.

Still farther west and deep into the rain shadow, shortgrass prairie laid claim to the land, here known as the Great Plains or High Plains. Close to the Rockies, this broad expanse—the size of western Europe—is the more arid of the grasslands. Because of the harsh conditions, it is possible to travel for miles in this last decade of the twentieth century without seeing a sign of human habitation. If you want solitude, this is the place to find it.

Some botanists (and some lovable curmudgeons) have referred to shortgrass as simply overgrazed mixed-grass prairie, but it is more than that. Here the plants suck up all available moisture in the soil before the end of the growing season. The earth is rock hard, down to the subsoil. Buffalo grass and blue grama are the most common. Hardy buffalo grass colonizes large areas with above-ground runners or *stolons* that can grow an astounding inch or two a day; they were capable of recolonizing an overgrazed area—or a buffalo wallow—in a very short time.

But for all its harsh mien, this high-plains grassland nonetheless provides habitat in plenty for the ubiquitous prairie dogs, badgers, pronghorns, deer, elk, eagles, foxes, rabbits, skunks, hawks, eagles, and more.

Historically, these divisions between tallgrass, midgrass, and shortgrass were as easily seen as though marked by road signs and lit up in neon. Were it not for the richness of the soil and the settler's plow, all this would still be true. But today, where farms and ranches abound and crops may supplant native plants, the lines are blurred. Instead, the prairie landscape—especially in tallgrass territory—exists as hints and shadows of itself, small corners of native prairie and bits of restored grassland that prove the soil and climate, at least, are still hospitable. In the Great Plains, huge circles of irrigated green are visible from outer space, and astronauts orient themselves by the sight. Left alone, prairie would reclaim its former boundaries, erasing all signs of our intervention. Or perhaps not.

Those green circles of cropland have robbed the Great Plains of most of its ancestral water supplies stored for millennia in the Ogallala Aquifer. Not the underground ocean many of us picture, the aquifer is instead a water-saturated layer of rock. One-sixth water, five-sixths gravel, this is rainwater that fell during the Stone Age. As with all our other natural resources, we in the twentieth century seem bent on using up our future's reserves. Where 250 wells pumped the reserves of ancient water in 1950 Kansas, today there are more than 3,000. The aquifer ran nearly sixty feet deep; now, in some places, it is reduced to less than six feet. We're running out. Forty years' hard use has pushed the Great Plains to the brink, and whether it will be able to support anything like its former ecosystem is up for grabs.

Probably, it will, most of it—the prehistoric prairie itself was well adapted to surviving on very little water. If instead you cast your lot with croplands and towns, green lawns and trees, it's doubtful. There's been a forty-year run on the bank and reserves are about to run out. The area will soon be bankrupt unless we look to the future. There is no natural F.D.I.C. to protect investors in this landscape.

Looking out over the waving grasses and bright wildflowers, this still appears far from the barren vista the first Europeans supposed, from the rumors that reached their ears. Compared to the dense eastern forests that once blanketed the land, this sudden openness was unnerving; it was understandable if the early settlers wondered how the soil could sustain crops if it could produce only a thin connect-the-dots of trees along a watershed.

Appearances, then as now, can be deceiving, and first impressions and hearsay are not to be trusted; the French explorers discovered that. Barren was hardly the description for these grasslands, underlain with deep, rich soils, slightly alkaline in makeup and extremely fertile. Soft, rich mollisols beneath that mat of roots that may reach fifteen feet deep are among the richest in the world. Where they have remained relatively undisturbed (often, oddly enough, in suburbs and backyards where no plowing has occurred for a hundred years), you can dig down three feet and more without ever finding subsoil. Now we know this area as the breadbasket of the nation, the Corn Belt; we still manage to feed the world on this soil we deplete more with each passing season.

The destruction began when the first plow ripped through the mat of roots that held the soil in place; with each successive season under the plow, more is lost; with each application of chemicals, the earth is depleted, its matrix more subject to erosion, its soul less able to sustain life. This area of America, the last to be settled, may also be the first to be abandoned, as the empty farmhouses and ghost towns across the region attest.

The astronomer Carl Sagan recently visited Kansas City to speak to the National Science Teachers Association, and commented, "When you look closely, you find so many things going wrong in the environment. You are forced to reassess the hypothesis of intelligent life on earth."

Sagan was speaking hyperbolically, but there is a disturbing edge of truth in his words. From the disappearing rain forests to the hole in the ozone layer to the depletion of the ancestral prairies, we have caused our own problems. The solutions are slow and excruciatingly complex. They will require sacrifice, an unpopular word with most of us in this last decade of the twentieth century. As someone I knew once said, "We did it to ourselves—but that doesn't make it hurt any less."

An old farmer once told me, "We don't even need dirt anymore, except to hold the plants up—we do everything with chemicals." At the rate erosion is claiming the earth, we won't even have that to hold the roots in place. Tons of topsoil are lost to each rain, and creeks run muddy with its lifeblood. The dust bowl of the 1930s was the direct result of our unthinking destruction of ancient prairie; as the Ogallala disappears we may again see more dust than crops.

The prairie is worth saving—or at least a part of it, a remnant. The effort is not without its challenges—nor its dissenters; until recently, not much of anybody saw the sense of saving these desolate grasslands. They *did* see the sense of putting more and more land into cultivation; that went without saying. More land and bigger machines equaled more crops—and more substantial profits. The balance of trade in international circles turns, at times, on a stem of prairie grass, and wheat and corn futures are traded by pin-striped suits who never crumbled a handful of soil to test its tilth. Commodities become abstract; the concrete is forgotten, lost in the cacophony of the trade floor.

But here and there, people are beginning to sense what was almost lost. They are joining together to protect remnants of presettlement prairie—in Oklahoma and Kansas, in Indiana, and bits of grassland in Missouri. Some biologists and ecologists who study this area believe we are heading toward returning the landscape to the bison, willingly or not.

Like the rain forests of South America, the grasslands have much to teach us. Recently, purple coneflower—long a medicinal used by Native Americans as a painkiller and cough medicine among other things—was confirmed as an important source of pharmaceuticals. It is believed to boost the immune system, and is used to fight everything from the common cold to infections. *Echinacea angustifolia* has been widely studied in Germany, as has *E. purpurea*, where, as ethnobotanist Kelly Kindscher points out, "there is a greater scientific interest in medicinal plants because more liberal laws govern their commercial availability and use." Scientific literature boasts more than 300 papers on these plants and their chemical makeup, pharmacology, and practical applications. White clover, buffalo gourd, evening primrose, prairie willow, compass plant; all these and more were used as medicinals, and many have been found to have value today. Still others are under study for their possible clinical applications. Who knows what is yet to be discovered?

Near Manhattan, Kansas, the Konza Prairie Research Project has provided material since 1978 for literally innumerable research studies on insects, small mammals, weather, wildflowers, watershed, and grasses. The Konza crawls with scientists—or it would if it were not so big. Containing 8,616 acres owned by the Nature Conservancy and leased to Kansas State University for research, the Konza (named for the Kansa or Kansas peoples who once lived here) provides plenty of space for study. Once part of the 10,000-acre Dewey Ranch owned by the C. P. Dewey family between 1872 and 1926, the Konza Prairie Research Project was bought by the Conservancy in 1977.

When spared the extremes of human intervention, prairies are a relatively stable ecosystem that maintain a characteristic mix of species and continued productivity over long periods of time. Protected from natural events like fire or grazing, however, both the mix and the productivity decline sharply. Scientists on the Konza study what that means and how it works by setting a burn schedule to study the long-term effects of fire on the soil's

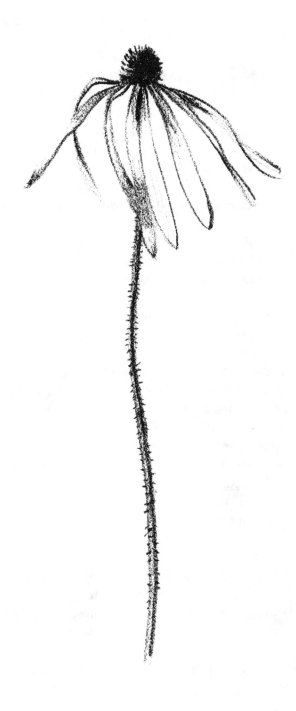

chemical, physical, and biological makeup. Grazing patterns and effects are studied. Mowing—a decidedly non-traditional prairie management tool—is also under study to see how using these grasslands for hay can help maintain them.

A list of prairie studies under way here includes comparisons of these mowed or burned areas, productivity of grazed and ungrazed plots, nutrient cycling, population dynamics of the animals that appear here and wildlife populations, and studies of watersheds, including the composition of prairie streams and water quality regulation. Perhaps we will be able to use what we learn here to save the prairie—not only for itself, but also for human use as we develop a more efficient operation of our agricultural system.

There is room for amateur prairie buffs on the Konza as a self-guided nature trail is maintained by the Conservancy. The trail guide available on-site leads you through three separate walks; you choose according to your energy level. The 2.8-mile-long nature trail closest to the parking area can be supplemented with King's Creek loop, which makes a 4.7-mile walk, or the Godwin Hill loop, which extends the trail to 6.1 miles. Smoking is prohibited for obvious reasons. Fires on the Konza, with its tremendous fuel load, are best set under controlled conditions, and for your own safety it's asked that you leave the cigarettes in the car.

On the nature trail you will see typical prairie grasses and wildflowers in addition to chinquapin and bur oak trees, cottonwoods, and willows near the watershed. Farther down the trail, you'll find rocky outcrops and shrubs that offer habitat to collared lizards, wood rats, and various prairie bird species including Bell's vireo.

In the Flint Hills of Kansas, ridges of chert, limestone, and shale protrude through the mantle of grasses like broken bones. The softening grasses blow in great, slow waves; the prairie blooms spring and summer with wildflowers. South of the Kaw River, wind and water have carved the landscape into long escarpments that look out over the Osage Plains. Because of its rocky character, much of this land has escaped cultivation and instead has been used to pasture cattle. It retains much of its original appearance, and for that reason efforts are under way to create a national tallgrass park, efforts that have been start-and-stop from the beginning. At this writing, Senator Nancy Kassebaum has suggested that the land be purchased privately rather than federally; neighbors fear the traffic and vandalism possible in a national park as well as federal regulations of lands bordering their property. What will happen to this large tract of relatively undisturbed prairie in the Flint Hills is anyone's guess, and meanwhile the smaller tracts of grassland become front lines of an effort to save the tallgrass.

It is not easy. Grasslands don't have the cachet of a Wild and Scenic Rivers designation, the national allegiance of a Yosemite or a Yellowstone. Often we don't even know what we're looking at, or care; consequently, less than 1 percent of our ancestral grasslands remain. A small plot of presettlement prairie, never touched by a plow, was recently turned under by its owner. Those who had known and loved it for what it represented reacted instantly, banding together to try to buy the plot. If it could be turned back over within twenty-four to thirty-six hours, the grasses would recover and the prairie would be as it was in less than a year. It was too late. The farmer had sold the land to someone else, and it remained as it had become—another plowed field, changed forever. Like a virgin once spoiled, there was no way to regain innocence.

Not all prairies are the typical broad expanse of undulating flatlands and rich soil. Historically, tallgrass prairies topped many Ozark hills. Here the soil is thin and rocky, and not conducive to the deep taproots of trees. Referred to by the original settlers as "balds," most remain in name only. Travelers to the Branson area may remember Dewey Bald, if not from the Harold Bell Wright book *The Shepherd of the Hills*, then from the road signs between Silver Dollar City and the strip in downtown Branson. To stand on top of one of these open, grassy domes is to see blue hills retreating forever into the distance. Today, "forever" is uncomfortably crowded with humanity.

The naturalist Henry Rowe Schoolcraft found a far different sight when he explored the Missouri and Arkansas territories in 1818. Few white people had ventured into this wilderness, and he and Levi Pettibone, a traveling companion, set out to discover likely spots for settlement. That they were successful is all too evident today.

Following the clear, cold, spring-fed rivers of the region and trails made by Native Americans, Schoolcraft made a great loop through wooded mountains, open grasslands, "extensive prairies, and a pretty fertile black soil" near the rivers—and topping the bony Ozark mountains, balds. Wildlife was unused to human presence and curiously unafraid. Elk, bears, and eagles were common. The sights Schoolcraft saw were remarkable; most are altered forever, and journals like these are our only record of the landscape that was.

"The country passed over yesterday after leaving the valley of the White River," he wrote, "presented a character of unvaried sterility, consisting of a succession of limestone ridges, skirted with a feeble growth of oaks, with no depth of soil, often bare rocks upon the surface, and covered with coarse wild grass; and sometimes we crossed patches of ground of considerable extent without trees or brush of any kind. . . . Frequently these prairies occupied the tops of conical hills, or extended ridges, while the intervening valleys were covered with oaks, giving the face of the country a very novel aspect, and resembling, when viewed in perspective, enormous sandhills promiscuously piled up by the winds."

Schoolcraft and Pettibone pitched camp that night at the foot of one of these conical landforms "called Bald Hill, and known among hunters who travel in this quarter as a landmark." Aside from a few tiny settlements where a family or two had banded together for community and protection, the explorers encountered few humans. What people they found in the backwoods impressed Schoolcraft only with their difference from the more educated and refined easterners he knew.

They were people "who could only talke of bears, hunting

and the like. The rude pursuits, and the coarse enjoyments of the hunter state, were all they knew.''

The company of explorers was fortunate to have found these backwoodsmen. In spite of their "disgusting, terrific, rude and outre" mien, the people supplied them with enough food to replace that lost crossing the North Fork River. Without their expertise in surviving the wilderness with enough to spare, Schoolcraft and Pettibone might have perished before completing their task.

This area was true wilderness in Schoolcraft's day; as he noted when he began his journey on November 5, 1818, "I begin my tour where other travelers have ended theirs, on the confines of the wilderness, and at the last village of white inhabitants between the Mississippi River and the Pacific Ocean."

Still today, these hilltop balds are habitat to some of the area's rarest wildflowers and plants, remnant populations found nowhere else.

Undisturbed, grasslands are a highly successful ecosystem, claiming over one quarter of the earth's surface, from the Russian steppes to the pampas of South America. And grasses do dominate these ecosystems in measurements of biomass. In the tallgrass prairie, four species of grasses dominate: big bluestem, little bluestem, Indian grass, and switchgrass. Sideoats grama and prairie cordgrass appear where conditions are hospitable. Still, these places are wonderfully diverse. Over 500 species of wildflowers are found here.

Meager in number and few in species as compared to the eastern forests, trees do appear here—in the prairies if not in plains where, according to some old-timers, there's nothing to cast a shadow. Even there, cottonwoods, willows, and sycamores mark the watercourse of rivers and streams. Bur oaks, with their heavy green leaves and thick, corky bark that allows the trees to withstand prairie fires, find the open spaces hospitable. They've adapted to the sometimes arid conditions by casting down a four-foot taproot their first season of growth, which

Pasqueflower

firmly anchors the young tree while simultaneously finding the available moisture hidden in this dry inland sea.

Prairies are home to a variety of wildflowers, from tender pasqueflowers and bird's foot violets to black-eyed Susans and blazing stars. Insects, reptiles, amphibians, birds, rodents, and large grazing animals find habitat here, as well.

It is that relationship with grazing animals—and fire—that kept presettlement prairie constant, as they are discovering on the Konza. The large grazers helped to keep the biomass from crowding itself out; fire completed the job, returning nutrients to the soil in the form of ash.

Prairie fires were something to see, awesome in their scope and fury, and able to provide light to read by from a half mile away. The smoke could be seen from fifty miles and more across the open plains. Both benign and deadly, these fires preserved the prairie ecosystem, killing many encroaching saplings that would shade out the grasses if left to develop normally.

From earliest times, fire has been both friend and foe, even to human inhabitants; the burn I wait to help with at the Martha Lafite Thompson Nature Sanctuary will ensure the preservation of that small restored grassland. Native Americans started burns to herd bison for the hunt; some historians believe they also did it to preserve the prairie ecosystem. Early white settlers took advantage of the fuel potential of the plentiful grass to heat their homes, twisting stems and leaves into tight bundles that would keep a sod home warm. Laura Ingalls Wilder describes making fuel for heating and cooking by this method, as do many settlers' journals. (Where there was no wood to be had for construction, the prairie grasses with their thick mat of roots were a godsend. Most homes were soddies or earthen buildings cut from blocks of the soil itself in the absence of more traditional building materials. Some still stand, and among those preserved are snug homes of surprising charm and cleanliness. Some *were* hovels; others were inviting as a Hobbit's home.)

But the heat load contained in the dry grasses could as easily take life as preserve it, and although many prairie animals were apparently adapted to escape, many others died or were injured in wildfires. Sometimes, fear-crazed animals would turn suddenly and run back into the flames to die, and many nestlings too young to fly were lost to fire.

After a typically arid summer in the plains, the prairie was tinder dry. Wildfires raged across this region, traveling as fast as a horse could run—sometimes, tragically, faster. A painting by the early nineteenth-century artist George Catlin shows this firestorm in the prairie sky; Native Americans and their horses flee in panic before it.

The early settlers on the midwestern prairies also fought fire with fire by clean-burning a broad swath of land around their homes. If you've ever wondered why Americans have an almost pathological attachment to a neatly trimmed lawn, perhaps fear of fire might be the answer. Our tidy greenswards double as firebreaks.

Today, when we think of the original grasslands that waved for hundreds of miles over the midlands, we most often think of tallgrass, that rich mixture of towering grasses and sometimes even taller forbs. Tales of grass as tall as a horse's eye, grass that could hide a herd of bison from view are common. A settler's journal entry complains that the only way they could find the cattle in the tallgrass was to stand on horseback and watch for movement in the stems.

It's the tallgrass prairie I am most familiar with; it is most dramatic, most daunting—and most dangerous. Unless you're caught on the Great Plains without water. When walking in large stretches of these dense grasslands that reach far above my head I remember that I must keep to a path or take a compass with me. It is all too easy to become turned around here among the stems with no trees to cast long shadows. In places it is impossible to see the position of the sun overhead; my patch of sky is simply too small, pinched off between the stems. I carry a small brass compass with a built-in sundial, a dandy replica of one carried by Rogers Rangers in the 1760s. My friend Ed Wilde has found an original nineteenth-century compass housed in a finely polished walnut case that measures no larger than one and a half inches square. It looks very much like one that made the trek from St. Louis, Missouri, to Fort Clatsop, Oregon, with Lewis and Clark. But when you're in danger of becoming lost, any compass will do. A $2 job from the local discount store has gotten me out of more than one tallgrass maze.

At the site of the current Fort Osage, reconstructed on the original foundations of the fort William Clark designed in 1808, there is no prairie left: only the name of the nearby stream— Fire Prairie Creek—indicates there was virgin grassland any- where nearby. Like many other place names—Prairie du Chein, Prairie Home, Prairie Village—this one reflects a reality that has passed. But in the old accounts of the area there are many mentions of the richness of this prairie and the usefulness of the grasses in feeding the cattle of the settlement. Captain Clemson, the military commander of Fort Osage, wrote of being frus- trated when the young Osage men burned the prairie grasses (as was their habit), which the Fort had counted on to feed their livestock through the winter.

This small historic prairie found mention in the journals of many early explorers; the members of the Lewis and Clark Expedition of Discovery noted it on June 22, 1804, as they approached the spot they called Fort Point, later to become the site of Fort Osage. William Clark noted Fire Prairie in his diary (as did Patrick Gass and several others) and the night's camp near the site:

"We passed two large islands and an extensive prairie on the south, beginning with a rich low land, and rising to the distance of 70 or 80 feet of rolling clear country. . . . After coming 10½ miles we camped there on the south, opposite a large creek, called Fire-prairie river."

The naturalists John Bradbury and Thomas Nuttall, and the writer Henry Marie Brackenridge, along with a company of fur traders led by Manuel Lisa, passed through here in 1811 and remarked on the prairie's lush grasses.

Approaching the prairie and the fort, Bradbury noted the proliferation of bees, which were imported to America with the first settlers. On the entry for April 6, 1811, he remarks:

". . . bees have not been found westward of the Mississippi prior to the year 1797. They are now found as high up the Missouri as the Maha nation, having moved westward to the distance of 600 miles in fourteen years. Their extraordinary progress in these parts is probably owing to a portion of the country being prairie, and yielding therefore a succession of flowers during the whole summer, which is not the case in forests."

I thank these vanished prairies and our forebears as I spread honey on my biscuits. Who doesn't imagine bees as being among our original inhabitants?

Fire Prairie is gone—though the bees remain—and pieces of original prairie are few, and small, but there are a number of patches of reclaimed grasslands all across the Midwest, tiny corners of land planted to tallgrass as homeopathic reminders of what was. In my town, the Missouri Department of Conserva-

tion has joined with Dennis Carman (an environmentalist passing as an elementary art teacher) and with the kids of Westview
Elementary to re-create a bit of history in the school's front
yard. It is a teaching tool for the children (and the town) as well
as something of their very own. Not without its detractors from
the manicured-lawn school of thought, the prairie has nonetheless managed to survive various onslaughts, outgrow its adolescent awkwardness, and persevere as a reminder to the children
and to the community of how presettlement Missouri once
looked.

"How did you get started?" I asked. "What was the original idea?"

"We wanted to plant some trees, a windbreak or something. Bob Fluchel, then an education consultant for the Department of Conservation and an outdoor classroom specialist,
suggested a prairie, instead," Carman told me.

"We set up a five-year plan, and planned to try to get state
grants for each year, but just about the time we got it all together, funding for grants of this type completely dried up. It
turned out to be the best thing that could have happened; we
had to go to the community, do the research, and learn to do it
all ourselves. We got the seed from the Conservation Department and the kids planted it; we sent them out in long lines,
kids with coffee cans with holes punched in them. We filled the
cans with seeds and the kids sowed them as they walked.

"We worked with the EPA when we burned the prairie—an
important step in prairie maintenance, and we had to make a
burn plan—and the kids got an idea of how to work with government, how to go through channels, and all; it was a lot more
than just planting a bunch of seeds."

The continuing care of the prairie and its growing presence
make the project an ongoing one for each successive year's
class. Each year brings new surprises.

"We've seen fox, quail, and all kinds of birds; any time you
get those kinds of animals coming in to a created habitat you
know you're doing something right," Carman says.

The tiny patch of prairie has had far-reaching impact;

Charles Kuralt of CBS News came to Excelsior Springs to feature Carman, the kids, and the tallgrass in "School's In," an ongoing series on schools that work. This one does.

Other bits of native prairie have miraculously survived, the proliferation of croplands, riding mowers and herbicides notwithstanding. Railroad rights-of-way, highway edges and medians, and other such places still wave with mixed prairie grasses and wildflowers, giving the traveler a sense of place. *Walking* these bits of vegetative prehistory brings it home. Today, this particular bit of grassland looks deserted, a place that time mislaid somewhere on its relentless forward drive. The wind blows through the rough grasses, a whisper of sound that makes me strain for the words; it's as if Thornton Wilder's imaginary and resonant *Our Town* were plopped down here in northwest Missouri and the people who fill this old cemetery were trying to tell me something. As I walk among the stones, reading first one name, then another, I find the past a very real presence. It is a not uncomfortable sensation; the wind kisses my cheek like an elderly aunt; my scarf blows away from my face and I feel my father brush back my hair to see my childish ears.

I am not a visitor to cemeteries, not normally—not for the usual reasons, at any rate. I do not take flowers to my mother's grave; I brought them to her when she could smell their sweetness, instead. The dead live in my mind; there's nothing for me in these places but tactile history contained in the finely carved names and dates on the stones, the rough texture of lichen on limestone, and the blowing grasses. I glean someone else's past from these weathered gravestones and look for remnant plants that thrive in abandoned places.

Trenton Cemetery Prairie is such a place, saved by the very virtue of being a graveyard. Rough grasses obscure some of the old stones at the height of their summer's growth, but Trenton Cemetery is a monument to an earlier time. Established in 1830, its protected status resulted in one of the few parcels of native prairie remaining in the state, the human factor ironically—and incidentally—this time preserving the non-human. The Missouri Conservation Department maintains the area, protecting it from over-attention and weed-whackers, its preservation an accident no longer.

Trenton Cemetery is especially critical since so few parcels of original prairie north of the Missouri River remain; the richness of the soil has seen to that as most farms are cropped almost fenceline-to-fenceline. These patchwork remnants of ancestral prairie produce seed adapted to the northern Missouri climate, essential to reestablishing thriving ecosystems. Then, even reclaimed grasslands can contain the historic balance that made them strong enough to withstand fire and wind and grazing animals—everything, in fact, except a man with an iron plow. When we beat our swords into plowshares it seems we are still at war—with something.

Suggested Reading:

Brown, Lauren, *Audubon Society Nature Guide to Grasslands*, Alfred A. Knopf, New York, 1985.

Foster, Steven, and James A. Duke, *Peterson Field Guide Series: Eastern/Central Medicinal Plants*, Houghton Mifflin, Boston, 1990.

Kindscher, Kelly, *Edible Wild Plants of the Prairie: An Ethnobotanical Guide,* University Press of Kansas, Lawrence, 1987.

————, *Medicinal Wild Plants of the Prairie: An Ethnobotanical Guide*, University Press of Kansas, Lawrence, 1992.

Madson, John, *Where the Sky Began: Land of the Tallgrass Prairie*, Sierra Club Books, San Francisco, 1982.

Weaver, J. E., *Prairie Plants and Their Environment*, University of Nebraska Press, Lincoln and London, 1968.

• Seven •

Walks by Water

THE PARKING LOT was full when I arrived; I took the remaining spot near the dam, noting that the two other lots across the expanse of water were equally crowded. I had wanted solitude, a chance to walk by the lake in quiet observation, and almost turned away but for the living raft of geese halfway down the lake; that was what I came for. I could brave the gamut of humanity to reach the shore closest to them.

A walk down a paved path is a slow strobe of silence and voices, silence and voices on a lovely day like this. Bits of conversation enter my consciousness against my will, some comfortable, some angry, all enigmatic in such short snatches. Walkers pass me in ones and twos and entire families, both coming and going. At my slow pace, intended for observation, not exercise, even those coming up behind pass me quickly and move on, their voices dying into silence. But always, here on the path, another bubble of words wells up to distract me.

Amazing how many people I know, how many people know me. My "getaway" is a public one here in a state park only seven miles from my home, and conversation is a two-way street as long as I keep to the asphalt trail. But until I can reach the open meadow that butts up against the lake, the serpentine

155

path is the shortest distance between two points. The going is rough in the forest, the ground soft and mucky after weeks of rain and the undergrowth as closely spaced as the hairs on my head. I am wearing loafers rather than hiking shoes, and I stick to the path, chatting as though I were in a mall. Chatting—but reluctantly. This is not what I had in mind, not at all.

Encounter with wildness brings me to a different reality, one with a timetable at once more ancient and more immediate than my own. My day-to-day deadlines and responsibilities are all too invasive, all too present; I snatch at any excuse to leave them bobbing in my wake.

Field sketching is always handy. But it is not so much to sketch these wild things that I leave my world for theirs, rather to fill a hunger that has been with me always.

At first I am aware only of the drone of insects on this hot summer day, of flies and bees on an eternal quest for nectar. The sound is hypnotic, and the flowers nod somnolently under the weight of sound and the bodies of winged creatures. Helicopter dragonflies ply the shore, and an airborne gnat-ball rises and falls in antic unison. Hackberry butterflies land to taste my arm with their spring-loaded tongues, giving me the illusion of relationship, but it is my salt they are after. I might as well be a damp spot on the road.

There are hordes of these subtly colored butterflies. I send up clouds of them like dust when I walk; they flutter against my face and bare arms and I am delighted. I run and whoop like a kid, dancing with butterflies. A few moments later—when I

have regained my decorum—I meet a pair of fellow walkers on the path, a woman and her young daughter.

"Aren't they awful?" the woman asks, referring to the ubiquitous hackberries. "I hate the way they land all over you. They're nuisances."

But her little girl holds out her arm for the insects to land on, inspecting them closely. She meets my eyes and we smile like conspirators. Awful—if you think so.

This summer when we camped at Watkins Mill State Park, the tent was completely covered with butterflies when I returned from a walk; they rose with a soft battering of wings at my approach and landed again once I entered the tent. Their shadows on the white fabric were fascinating to watch, flickering shapes that made me feel as though we had set up camp underwater. A few hackberries entered with me, and that night as we readied for sleep, I could hear the soft whisper of wings against canvas.

As I approach the pond, blackbirds explode in a barrage of disapproval, asserting dominion with a show of red epaulets and martial song. Dressed in discreet drab, their mates hover and dart anxiously, lacing together the pond's shores with the fine, nervous thread of flight—weaving a territorial cat's cradle of their own.

I am the intruder here. There's no mistaking that. Ownership by law and deed mean nothing when the landscape is platted along a more ancient measure. The surveyor's rod belongs to each species that inhabits my land and is used according to instinctive order. The overlapping empires of bird and fish and bullfrog make no room for me. I am a trespasser on my own land, and the primeval boundaries, once transgressed, are redrawn with great show and sound.

Red-winged blackbirds *are* territorial creatures, but in a communal way. Where there is prime habitat there may be many breeding pairs present, their nests hidden amongst the cattails and tall reeds. The nests are spaced just so, according to acceptable distances. Here on my pond there are only two pairs, but they make up for their paucity of numbers with saber-rattling sound. I must retreat a quarter of a mile before they'll let it be and return to their beautiful song: "ok-a-leee."

Only the fish ignore me. It is as though we inhabit a parallel universe; they couldn't care less. We are separated by a molecule-thick layer of surface tension, me above, the fish, inviolate, below; I am no threat. They strike at cottonwood fluff and insect wing. Still unsatisfied, they avidly approach the pebble I toss into the water, then turn aside when they find it is not, after all, food. It is the only sign that they have reacted to forces set in motion outside their watery milieu.

Once in a while a veritable Loch Ness monster of a carp arrows through the water, writing its name in the emphatic calligraphy of its linear wake. At the other end of the pond from where I am—always at the other end—something silver flashes and arcs, then drops back into the water. Some hungry fish defies the laws of gravity and makes for a moment as though it will fly.

A huge lunker lunges shoreward time and again after some invisible morsel as though to take to the land on its errand if need be. I imagine some antediluvian fish finding sudden plenty at the shore, a smorgasbord of insect fare unavailable under water, and forging into amphiby.

The bullfrogs, one step up the evolutionary escalator into the world of air breathers, take note only when I approach too near—and clam up. Come closer still and they vault into the pond propelled by samurai thighs, only to reappear at water's edge a few feet away, imagining themselves invisible. In minutes the big frogs resume the claiming of territory with deep, booming grunts.

Smaller green frogs explode into the air at my approach, their sudden high-pitched cries of distress as startling to me as my sudden appearance is to them. The chorus frogs that fill early spring evenings with sound do not find a home here; they are too small to utilize these populous waters. Instead they choose small fishless ponds and sloughs, to cry out for a mate, to lay their eggs, and then to disappear into the woods.

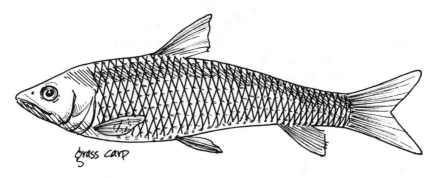

grass carp

A pile of sunning turtles scatter like an explosion of Frisbees at my approach. I scribble a quick sketch, laughing. After a decent interval they up-periscope, resurfacing to float for a while before diving again into invisibility, this time deliberately and without the sudden splash.

The redwings, on the other hand, remain on the alert for the better part of an hour. They are most exquisitely attuned to perceived menace and nurse a grudge like the Hatfields and McCoys.

Near the water's edge I see great blue herons and little blues, green herons, black-crowned night herons, and their cousins, the egrets.

The herons find these small quiet places to be fine habitat. They are protected and uncrowded here. Fish and frogs in abundance offer plentiful food. I find their tracks pressed into the mud; they wade the shallows or toss back a shining silver morsel, swallowing hard.

I watch them—when I can get close enough without startling the cautious birds into flight—walking slowly, deliberately in the shallow water as though to stir up small fish. Their knees appear to bend backward and it seems as though the herons should be awkward. They are not. They are dignity incarnate.

On another day, late in the autumn after a hard cold snap when the pond has frozen twice, I come up over the hill to find I've scared up a great blue heron feeding in the narrow ribbon of water near the shore. It rises silently and circles off over the trees on huge silent wings. I can't believe it's still here fishing in my icy pond this late in the year, and I stand to watch it oar its way slowly against the sunset-stained clouds until I can no longer find its pterodactyl shape among the bare limbs.

The mammals are the most cautious—and the most aware; our close kinship gives them that. They recognize and avoid us, seeing threat. They choose the nocturnal hours, or those ambiguous slivers of time between dusk and dark; my eyes are tuned to daylight. I find their tracks in the mud at water's edge— nothing more. Only rarely do I surprise a deer or raccoon on its rounds; more rarely still do I see a ghost-pale coyote. They fade silently away as though I had only imagined the encounter and leave me, always, wanting more. To wildlife I am always *other*, trapped in an existential loneliness, a homesickness I can never overcome.

A walk by water is not always so focused on the natural. Last summer someone found the trees on our dam inconvenient for easy casting and butchered them with a hatchet. Limbs have been hacked off like battleground amputations with no thought given to anything but getting them out of the way. Certainly there was no concern for aesthetics—or ownership. One tree is left with almost no limbs on one side, to a height of some twelve feet.

I was furious when I found them, hot as a blast furnace. They are a pair of beautiful oaks, a white oak and a young bur oak, the latter with thick, winged, corky stems. Their limbs were severed and dumped unceremoniously behind the dam along with the beer cans and bait containers I too often discover. I raged and paced for an hour.

Then, as so often is the case, as time passed I ruefully found I gravitated to the spot, drawn by a shady expanse between the trees, an unobstructed view, a spot from which to sketch and observe. But I will not thank the vandals. That would be too much.

A river runs through my small town, a river that is at once lovely and degraded—and occasionally dangerous. It is bordered by a park, a paved walkway, and old-growth forest. If it were not for the junk dumped there by people upstream and by those who use the park, it could be a small Eden. And wherever there is an Eden, there is a snake. This one was more in the form of a few anxious and overly neat people who wanted to see the river's gravel bars dredged, the river "cleaned up," dead wood and streamside vegetation cut away, and—yes—the snakes killed or chased away. It was a recipe for disaster as far as the health of the stream was concerned.

I called in the Department of Conservation's team to advise me on what the river *actually* needed, and was told that it was in far better health, overall, than neighboring streams. Water was clearer, aquatic life more diverse, streamside vegetation in good shape. Gravel bars act as filters for silt and pollutants; vegetation helps slow floodwaters. All we were advised to do was to clean up the man-made debris and plant trees to help stop erosion.

Interested citizens formed a group to fight overcontrol of the river and to take care of the necessary cleanup; the Friends of Fishing River, which cleans up the stream on a loose twice-yearly schedule, was born.

When fears of flooding (and of water snakes) surfaced again, the city, spurred by concerned citizens, investigated damming or dredging the river. The Corps of Engineers was called in and a preliminary investigation into feasibility was launched. A public hearing stirred more response from those opposed to attempting to control the river than from those in favor, and with good reason. "Control" would be a costly Band-Aid, one with more problems than solutions—one that neither we nor the river could afford.

I called the Corps for a map of the river and found that the expected high-water marks of a 50-year flood, a 100-year flood, and even a 500-year flood were expected only to have affected another ten feet of a single parking lot in town.

In 1993, the year of high water, the best predictions of the Corps as they concerned my town were inadequate. After five hours of downpour, a flood unprecedented in recent memory and unanticipated by prediction ripped through the downtown area. An eight-foot wall of water moving at an estimated forty miles per hour took out homes and businesses, bridges and roads. Businesses that had never before been affected by flooding had basements full of water; our City Hall's two lower floors were drowned. Our new police station was flooded. If I were going by the map, I would judge this to be a thousand-year flood.

My town was built on a flood plain, and while only the older section of town is affected by disastrous flooding, it still causes serious problems throughout the area.

Damming the river, a prohibitively expensive solution, or worse yet, exacerbating flood problems by grading gravel bars and removing bankside vegetation, are not answers. Flood insurance or letting the river do what it naturally will and adjusting ourselves to suit seems our best bet. We aim for a greenbelt system closest to the river and pray the water will never hit these levels again.

The Friends of Fishing River is no longer a lonely little band of ragtag volunteers. The Missouri Department of Conservation has founded an organization of loosely knit Stream Teams, of which we are a member. Through that organization we have joined the National River Network, out of Portland, Oregon, and the Adopt-a-Stream Foundation in Everett, Washington. These organizations offer information and support for protecting not only rivers and streams, but all wetlands; membership is nominal and the information is invaluable.

What I have learned, more than anything else, is that nature knows what it is about. Seasonal fluctuations in water levels we know as flooding are natural; the concept of flood is, in fact, a human one, born of our tendency to build where we should not, to live where it is unwise to live.

In Missouri, there is a long history of such human interaction with floodwaters. Long before this area was declared "frontier" by whites, the Osage tribes had divided themselves in half, calling themselves the Little Osage and the Great Osage. It had nothing to do with physical stature; the Osage peoples as a whole were very tall and well built, often over six and a half feet. Legend has it, however, that a great flood nearly wiped out the tribe in their ancestral camping grounds near the Osage River. Ever after that event, one band camped on the riverbanks for convenience and the availability of water and game (the Little Osage) while another—the Great Osage—took to the high bluffs for protection. That way, the entire tribe could never be wiped out by flood.

Here in Excelsior Springs, the town was built up around mineral water springs that emptied into the Fishing River. It was an economic decision meant to take advantage of the health benefits attributed to the waters, and—while it lasted (and when it didn't flood)—the decision was a good one. There are more naturally occurring mineral water types here than any- where else in the world except Baden-Baden, Germany. During its heyday, Excelsior Springs was host to such luminaries (and ne'er-do-wells) as the New York Giants, Al Capone, Franklin Delano Roosevelt, and Harry S Truman, who stayed at the Elms Hotel the night presidential victory was incorrectly declared for Thomas Dewey. Wide sidewalks were jammed with visitors; trains from Chicago and Kansas City arrived several times daily; the place was booming.

At the recent public hearing a technician with the Corps of Engineers looked out at the assembled townsfolk and said, "I've looked over your town, and I can tell the deterioration of your downtown area was due to the fear of flooding—am I right?"

He was not, in spite of everything. In 1955 the American Medical Association declared that mineral waters were ineffec- tive in treating health problems. In a double blow, a story in *Life* magazine purportedly exposed medical fraud by one of the clin- ics (the reporter pretended to have an illness and then pre- tended to be cured), effectively killing the mineral water busi- ness on which the town was built. The bathhouses, clinics, and hotels that had served hundreds of thousands closed. The doc- tors moved elsewhere, and the people employed in service industries—the bathhouse attendants, masseurs, waiters and waitresses, laundresses, and rooming house owners—found themselves out of work. The town became a bedroom community, dependent on a commute to the city.

Flood *is* impressive here, as it is anywhere; it can be devastating to those businesses still in its path. What it is *not* is the reason for our decline. What small town original business district didn't suffer during the '70s and '80s and with the advent of discount stores and fast-food joints on their perimeters? And when that town's *raison d'être* is mineral water when the public well goes dry, decline is inevitable.

The waters of the Fishing River provided an indelible visual aid to the words "flash flood." In less than forty-five minutes the river had risen twenty feet and more, inundating much of the downtown area and punishing the undersides of the major highway bridges with battering rams made of uprooted trees. Smaller bridges leading to side streets, to small businesses and the few houses left in the floodplain, were underwater; one was left with a hole the size of a Cadillac in its roadway. The park where I walk each morning was an anomaly, a rapidly moving lake; the footbridge was ripped from its foundation and flung downstream, its stone supports sheared off by the force of the water.

It may have been the general exhaustion after a night of storms; it may have been sadness that so much was changed, so much was lost, but my tiredness was infused with depression. I could barely drag myself out to survey the damage; I wanted to sleep.

But instead I found film and headed out to the walking path, the path that had so invited friendly conversation and a gentle kind of communal exercise. The high-water mark was at a sobering four feet or so above my head as I walked; to live beside this torrent must have been terrifying. I found debris so far overhead that I could not believe the trees had not bent down to receive it—but they were too big around to have yielded in that way. I discovered that all too often I was open-mouthed and gawking at what the water had done—and how quickly it had done its business and gone. "My *God*," I repeated, over and over. "My *God*."

But no matter how changed things are, no matter what is destroyed, there are always things to see, to discover, once beyond the awe and fear. Now that the flood had receded from the park, I found a huge gravel bar washed from the confines of the river across the greensward to the path and beyond. It looked like a beach in Maine, rocks of all colors and shapes smoothed in their long association with water, a mosaic of limestone and chert, jasper and quartzite. There were rocks of nearly solid aggregate fossil, unlike anything from our immediate vicinity. There was a tiny bugle of horn coral. There was iron-rich hematite, and a chunk of claystone as big as a kid's wagon, washed downstream with the rest.

Arrowhead hunters, always on the alert for signals from the past, were out in force. One man had found a primitive stone axe; another picked up a spear point. I discovered what may be a scraper. Beneath a pile of smaller, rounded stones I unearthed a very large, very old vertebra—of what, I couldn't begin to tell you. It was black with age and smelled faintly of river mud.

Downstream, there was more evidence of the incredible power of water; a logjam of trees was piled ten feet high against one of the oaks, but that wasn't what was unusual—these piles were everywhere. *This* particular logjam was stark and golden with peeled trees, their bark removed as slickly as a lumber mill could have done it, by their tumbling and scraping in the flood. No, more smoothly; there was no sign of mechanical scraping. The wood smelled rank, unpleasant; not at all what I expected on seeing the pale, polished wood—there was a sycamore stench that gave away the identity of these flayed logs.

Farther down the path, one of the large trees had been almost completely undermined by backwash. The current had dug a deep pit on the down-current side and I wondered if the tree would stand until the hole could be refilled—*if* it were refilled. In his rich floodplain garden, my cousin's three young fruit trees, twenty feet tall and just beginning to bear well, were swept from the ground, leaning crazily as though to point the direction of the departing flood.

It was hardly necessary. Everything read as a visual aid to the force of water currents: the muddy wave pattern that overlaid the grass in thick umber undulations; the interwoven leaves packed into the wire matrix of a chain-link fence; the direction of debris on the sides of all the trees and bushes in the park. By the time I reached the big shelter house at the east edge of the park I could read the clear message left by the backwash; the bank was almost undercut there, and the shelter itself filled with a slick, greasy gray mud that smelled of methane. Huge picnic tables, ten feet long, had become rafts that floated away down the river.

As I walked the path—carefully, carefully, the skim of mud made footing treacherous—I began to notice the death toll. Here, a young crappie had been run over by one of the first bicycles to brave the mud-covered path; there, a bluegill had had its eyes pecked out by an opportunistic bird. Midnight-black crows were everywhere, croaking sepulchrally like stereotypical undertakers. They'd come for the feast, attracted by the bright flash of tiny fish in the grass where the moving water had receded, leaving them without habitat. There were minnows—shiners and darters; bluegill and catfish fry; tiny bass; and huge, soft, gray-green bullfrog tadpoles. One by one, I picked them up and threw them back in the water. Live ones, dead ones, it didn't matter; I returned them to the creek as though under an imperative. A tiny, elderly woman wearing a shower cap and boots joined me. We bent and chased the little fish; her pitching arm was as good as mine, and she talked to herself as she lobbed handful after handful of squirming fry back to the water. A young boy and his mother enlisted in the brigade, and soon we were all catching fish and returning them to the river.

The crayfish beat us to some of them; this is their element, and they'd come from their muddy burrows to ply the protein-rich flood pools. I reached for a small fish in a shallow backwater and suddenly realized it was swimming sideways. No, not swimming; it was being carried by one of the largest crawdads I'd ever seen. If I were in the mood for Cajun instead of rescue, I'd have found a container for the big crayfish and made a meal of them.

By the time I returned home, muddy and stinking of river water, my mood was mixed. Incredibly sobering, the effects of the flood were also deeply stirring. If it had not been for the human suffering involved, I would have been excited, jazzed by the raw power of nature. "My God," my instinctive reaction had been. "An act of God," the insurance agents will call it. Perhaps we are correct; there is something about such occurrences that are beyond human, and although I don't believe in a vindictive deity, still such power renders me awestruck and humbled. It's an appropriate reaction.

The Missouri River in flood is enormous, dwarfing the flash floods that scour smaller tributaries like the Fishing River. Like a great inland sea grinding against its ancestral banks, the big river makes an impressive showing. As we walk along the edge, an edge only recently exposed after weeks of inundation under moving coffee-brown water, we are astounded by the thickness

Missouri River at
La Benita — mud is
extremely thick, like
potter's clay, since the flood.
Wm. Clark described the bluffs
nearby, as well as the wild
berries and "muskeeturs."

of layers of muddy silt deposits. Some are three to five feet deep, piled in stair steps that mark the timeline of receding floodwater. They are like quicksand, still soft underneath, and footing is chancy.

This area had been cut off for days as the river coursed across the highway. As it did in many other places, the water chewed its way through the roadbed—here, only partway. On highways 13, I-635, and 54 near Jefferson City, Missouri's capital, the concrete roadbeds looked like breached dams. There was nothing left. The highway 13 bridge at Lexington, an old structure to begin with, is said to have moved nearly a foot downstream. This unscheduled side trip left it out of commission for the foreseeable future; it stood in the way of the river and was not strong enough to prevail; the highway leading to it had simply disappeared, washed halfway to St. Louis.

An island now rises downstream from the 291 highway bridge, newly reopened after water inundated the approach roads. Here the river took back its former braided channel, splitting and surrounding a patch of trees that now stands midstream instead of bankside.

A sawyer moved violently up and down in the still rapidly moving water, the jagged trunk of a great tree caught in the mud of the riverbottom. Its precursors have been responsible for the many riverboats lost to these dangerous logs, visible or hidden just beneath the water's surface. More treacherous still are the planters, trees that have buried themselves below the surface, transplanted in the mud. Whitewater turbulence marks their position; in the dark they'd be impossible to see.

This was the highest the river has been in recent memory. I saw the 1951 flood from the hood of my father's old car; it spread from bluff to bluff and took millions of dollars worth of real estate with it, millions of tons of topsoil. I could barely breathe, looking at it. I held tightly to my father's hand, not knowing if I was frightened or excited by the power below us. I do know I was drawn to it; I wanted to get closer, to the water's edge if I could. I wanted to look out across the sheet of moving water that carried whole trees, dead cows, rafts of boards that were once someone's home, and I wanted to do it at eye level.

He held me back, of course, made me stay with the car, high above the river valley near Sugar Creek. But I've never forgotten the immensity of that sight.

The flood of '93 rivaled that earlier event, in damage if not in breadth (totals will not be in for some time). The levees and dams and holding lakes of the Corps of Engineers kept the river in check in some areas; from aerial photos I can see that the flood covered less acreage than it did in '51. There is speculation, however, that keeping the river within these artificial bounds also forced it higher and faster, like water in a sluice gate. The small town of Parkville, just north of Kansas City, flooded deeper than it ever had before, as did many others. The river was not able to spread out naturally over a wide area, which might have slowed it somewhat, and so had a force unprecedented in recent memory. But even with the levees, the Missouri managed to reclaim much of its former floodplain.

The river took more than its own. In the small town of Hardin, just east of here, it dredged coffins and vaults from the town cemetery, which is located more than two miles from the river—or where the river had been for years, at any rate. Great concrete vaults, watertight as battleships, floated off to the east, and of the thousand or so caskets affected, only a hundred and forty-some have been recovered at this writing. Identification of remains, some of which are said to date back to 1810, is a nightmare.

It is painful to talk to the survivors. Parents laid lovingly to rest are gone as surely as if evicted to wander the streets. Tiny coffins that held infants and children, visited often and wreathed with flowers, have disappeared downriver.

A kind of black humor developed out of the situation. One man who had coffins wash up in his yard was quoted as saying, "I saw people I hadn't seen in twenty years." Others talked about the folks finally getting to take that river cruise. But the humor is a mask for the pain.

Hardin residents, like those in Missouri City and dozens of

After the second flood the road was even more damaged than before.

other small river towns, saw their homes disappear beneath the angry brown water and stay there for weeks; the only access was by rowboat. Schools, businesses, roads, and sidewalks disappeared. Pets were left behind in the rush and for weeks the news was full of stories of people trying to rescue them. The Humane Society; the Red Cross; the Salvation Army; the National Guard: all were constant presences in flooded areas.

Loss to crops and to wildlife was incalculable. Cooley Lake, a Missouri Department of Conservation wildlife refuge and an old oxbow of the river, broke from its bounds and rejoined the

parent stream, taking the nests and young of thousands of summer birds with it. Deer, foxes, coyotes, rabbits, and others were displaced or drowned.

The Mississippi River was as wild as the Missouri. On her way home from the east, Jeanne Wilde reported that Fort de Chartres, a restored fur-trade-era fort, was only a diamond shape in a lake; the top of the palisade fence was all that remained visible. Hermann, Washington, St. Charles, and even parts of old St. Louis were affected, along with many other historic towns up and down the river. Tiny Ste. Genevieve, a

French town dating from the 1700s, barely survived the flood by mounting an unprecedented sandbagging campaign that drew history-minded volunteers from all over the nation. The town survived, but at a dollar figure that far exceeded its entire annual budget.

A friend's home, last seen in early July, was then surrounded by corn that reached high enough to tickle the eaves; only the roof was visible. After the flood the house was alone in a browned desert of dead stubble and silt that spread over a thousand acres. Vegetation can't survive the lack of oxygen and sunlight. The scorched-earth look stretched for miles; it was as though Agent Orange had been sprayed indiscriminately along the floodplains of the Midwest. Oxygen-starved soil, compacted and waterlogged, still strangles the roots of even mature trees; whether the thick fringe of trees that normally borders the river will survive is questionable.

In Missouri City, homes that were inundated for weeks now looked like a war zone, crumbling, piled with debris and stained with a half-dozen watermarks. Metal buildings stood with their siding ripped crazily loose and folded back upon itself, graphic illustrations of the power of the current. Those who remembered the charm of the sleepy little river town were sobered and speechless by the sight.

We were not the only spectators drawn to the receding river. Beyond the cars of the curious were more great blue herons, white herons, and cattle egrets than I'd ever seen in one place. Thirty or more great blues circled low over the pools; keeping count of such moving targets was difficult. They waded the shallows of remnant flood pools or moved from point to point with measured wingbeats as though mapping the distance between fishing holes, gleaning the river fish trapped there.

The day's walk beside the shrinking river stirred memories; the smell of mud tickled my nose, a scent both pleasurable and slightly acrid. Mixed in was a smell of death—or perhaps only methane.

There's something about scent that triggers memory like nothing else, and not surprisingly: Only forty-one molecules of

a given substance are enough to trigger the olfactory receptor, and these molecules are everywhere. They have a direct path to our brain, and scent triggers an immediate emotional response if we associate it with something from our past; it circumnavigates logic and goes right for long-term memory. We are capable of differentiating between a long series of scents as they come into contact with the scent receptor at the top of our nasal passages at the astounding rate of three per second. We respond to each in a few milliseconds.

And whether that scent is a bouquet of carnations or a river in flood, for me the effect is the same. It's as though I had stepped into a time machine and was standing again on the hood of the old Willys, holding tight to my father's hand. As I looked out across the devastation wreaked by this latest flood, I wished a hand to hold offered the same comfort.

Wetlands are a magnet that attracts all the wildlife on the continent. In summer, especially, when other water sources dwindle and dry, these places ensure the continuation of life. Red-winged blackbirds are everywhere; the yellow-headed variety is less common. The American bittern resembles an imma-

ture green heron, and in fact they are related. Bitterns are comical looking when they assume an upright pose to blend into the
background of shadow-mottled reeds. They almost pull it off,
too, but for those wild yellow eyes glaring back at me, and only
when this bird assumes camouflage mode does it become un-
mistakably distinctive.

   My friend Pete Rucker has a bittern in his care; a wildlife
agent brought it in for him to rehabilitate. The bird is angry to be
so caged, and as I look beneath the old terrycloth towel that

protects its privacy, it lowers its head, fluffs the feathers of its shoulders and back, and lets out a most emphatic sound, halfway between a hiss and a growl, clacking its big beak in my face. The bird—larger and more impressive in these close quarters than I would have imagined in the outdoors—is an enigma; it doesn't appear to be injured, but it doesn't fly.

"We don't know what's wrong with him, really," says Pete. "He's skinny as a rail."

When I explode into laughter at the pun—a rail is yet another bird—Pete looks gratified. "Well, thank goodness. Nobody else got the joke. They just looked at me like I was nuts."

Exotic wood storks and flamingos find southern wetlands to their liking; pelicans fill beaks and bellies nearby. Ducks and geese, rails, cormorants, grebes, and sandhill cranes—and the varied and beautiful heron clan—are all denizens of this world where land and water meet.

Turtles and frogs ply the waters or bask, drowsy-eyed, in the sun. Mussels and freshwater clams stud the mud just below the water's surface like nuts in a fruitcake, and sly crayfish scuttle backward to imagined safety at my approach. Snails prove their ancient pedigree by way of the fossil record—they've hardly changed a bit. Fish of many kinds arrow the water's surface or move wraithlike in the dark waters; an athletic and

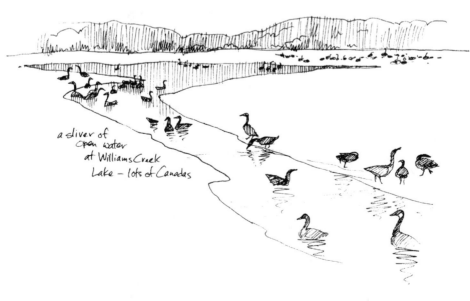

a sliver of
open water
at Williams Creek
Lake — lots of Canadas

enthusiastic feeder defies the laws of gravity to leap after its insect prey.

The air is dense with insect sound. Dragonflies and damselflies mate in odd-shaped hoops; the male grasps the female just behind the head. Occasionally they will take flight still locked in amorous embrace. Mud daubers visit the shore to stock up on building materials, and a Shriners' convention of butterflies is attracted to the minerals held in the mud.

Raccoons and coyotes visit the wetlands for the well-stocked supermarket of foods. The heart-shaped tracks of deer embroider the shoreline, and all sorts of mammals find life in the water.

Wild plants and flowers abound, from the face-like monkeyflower to the carnivorous pitcher plants and sundews in acidic bogs. Wild rice, cattails, and arrowhead were all important food plants for the Native Americans. This is fertile territory, and ancient—a key part of the puzzle that is our nation's ecosystem; to merely catalog the life-forms present would take volumes.

Once thought of as dangerous, insect-ridden places to be tamed at all costs, now wetlands are beginning to come into their own. We are realizing their importance to wildlife; we are discovering their beauty and diversity for ourselves.

Wetlands assume many forms, from an oasis in the desert to lakes and ponds, from small to sea-like. Oxbows are left where a river changed its course overnight. There are marshes, saltwater and fresh. Sloughs, swamps, bogs, and sedge meadows enter the equation. Floodplains act as giant sieves for rivers and creeks on temporary leave from their banks.

The concept of "flood" is a human one; the fluctuations of water levels in spring and fall are essential for the life and health of the biosystem. It is our tendency to build or farm in the floodplains that raises the question of flood damage. In the more ancient plan, land and water both benefit. Intermittent flooding nourishes the lowlands with rich new topsoil. As the water spreads out, flowing through the vegetation, which slows its raging currents, it is cleansed of silt. When it resumes its former banks, the river is refreshed; the slowing action of the floodplain prevents an overload of fresh water into coastal estuaries.

These estuaries are important breeding grounds for much of our nation's wildlife, and fine habitat for a variety of water-fowl. Upset the natural balance—even by exchanging fresh for salt water—and the place is ruined for these inhabitants; many will die.

Net loss in the past fifty years has been staggering; nation-wide, 50 percent of historical wetlands are already gone. In my state the figure is closer to 90 percent, according to the Missouri Department of Conservation. Like a drop of water in a hot skillet, our wetlands are shrinking as human development competes for prime space. In many areas, privately owned rural wetlands fall victim to their own fertility when they are converted to cropland.

It's not all human intervention that reduces the overall acreage of these existing wildlife magnets, though. Drying and flooding is a natural part of the process, and advocates shouldn't despair over short-term loss. Over the long term, the nature of our shallower wetlands is to phase themselves out through the process of eutrophication. Lush plant growth dies and falls to the bottom, decaying to form rich mud. As the process continues, the water becomes ever shallower until one day the pools fill in. The former wetland becomes meadow.

According to the original blueprint, however, dying wetlands are replaced by new ones. Change on nature's timetable allows a period for wildlife to adapt. When we accelerate the process, there's no way to compensate the loss quickly enough; we bankrupt our future.

There is hope for the survival of wetlands. We are becoming aware of their value—that's half the battle. Organizations like the Audubon Society and the Nature Conservancy are working to preserve them for the future. And here and there states are joining hands with the Federal Corps of Engineers to buy some

of these oases of prime habitat, beginning the process of protecting, reclaiming, or flooding intentionally what a few years
ago was dammed and dried—and dying.

Life and water are one. The liquid stuff sloshes in our cells,
rushes through our veins, keeps eyes and mucous membranes
moist and epidermis from drying to a papery husk like a snake's
shed skin. We can go only short times without water to drink; it
keeps the system operating smoothly like oil in an internal com-
bustion engine. The draw is as much instinctive as conscious.

I migrate to water like a Canada goose; no matter where I
walk—in the woods, across a meadow—I find myself drawn to
the silvery, reflective stuff, the motion, the life. Even on a winter day when the lake is locked in ice but for a narrow channel,
the water is the thing.

I can see the geese from a long distance; I had wondered,
when I arrived to find the broad expanse of lake opaque and
stilled by its icy armor, if there would be any geese at all. But
just beyond the trailhead they are sprinkled like pepper on the
gray-white lake. As I near, I can tell that a narrow ribbon of open
water remains, and that the geese pop in and out of it or bob on
the surface, dark corks that have found their wild voices.

The sound makes the hair on my arms stand up. The rise
and fall of the fine gabbling and honking touches a place I
sometimes forget is there. But as soon as I sort out the sound
from the others that fill this winter day, I am alert, head lifted,
eyes searching for the source.

I can't wait to get close. The path seems longer than ever,
and more populous. Too many people, too many sounds come
between me and these big birds, between me and peace. But at
last I come out of the woods at the second meadow, the one
closest to the strip of living water, and turn off toward the lake.
The grass is pale and dead. Leaves curl back upon themselves in
graceful helixes, but the stems point out the direction of the
prevailing winds. On this whole hillside, not a single plant has
chosen its own way. Everything bends before the wind.

The meadow is surprisingly dry, though it was blanketed by

a crust of ice-covered snow less than a week ago. I move stealthily through it, moving slowly so as not to frighten the geese. They gabble uneasily, beginning to oar invisibly away from the shore with webbed feet, and I freeze in place, pretending to be interested in something else. The geese resume their slow progress, up and down the strip of water, up on the edge of the ice and back into the lake again.

Again and again we repeat this ballet—me moving, geese leaving; me freezing in place and the geese returning—until I reach a young tree not twenty feet from the edge of the water. The grass is thick at its base, and appears dry; I sit and find it comfortable. In this position I am less threatening, less obviously human, and the geese appear to forget I am there. They float slowly back toward me, talking amongst themselves.

The homely conversation of the geese crowds out most other sounds—real or imagined—in my head, and the exchange I've played over and over in my imagination falls still at last. I fancy the company of these creatures, comfortable with one another and becoming comfortable with me as I sit on the pale, thick mat of grasses. The wind is light, only occasionally ruffling the leaves or combing the lion-colored grasses.

Some of the geese stretch and preen, spreading black wings like sails to catch the air. But instead they only shake them briskly as though to rid them of dust, then fold them once again to form a neat package close to their bodies.

A corps of geese step to the edge of the ice; they plunk into the lake, one by one, a comically ungainly moment for creatures of such consummate grace in the air or on the water. Now a new group takes ground duty, pacing slowly, magisterially into the sun's glare.

To look into the sun that reflects on the mirror of the ice is painful, but when I close my eyes sunlight gently kisses my lids and cheeks. How can it be so warm in early February? I am lost in drowsy contemplation until a tight squadron of ducks flies silently overhead, light-colored against the sky, then turns and startles me with a rush of wings at my left shoulder. The sound is loud and strange, as though a jet flew low just over the lake.

Why were they so silent before? They circle and turn as though to land among the geese nearest the shore, think better of it, and move to a less populous area of open water and splash down to disappear among the dark shapes in the distance. A hawk whistles against his hunger overhead. Had he hoped for a meal of fresh duck?

The mallards have broken my reverie, and I rise to explore along the lake's edge. The soft earth of the bank has given way, sheared off, and fallen into the water. I can see the thick, tangled mat of roots that held the grasses tight as long as the earth itself held steady. The soil is heavy with moisture; its own weight pulled it down, succumbing to inevitable gravity.

Something walks by habit along the lakeshore; a steady three feet from the bank a narrow path faithfully follows each small cove and peninsula as though scribed there, using the shoreline as a measure. This path, indented in the thick meadow grasses, is damp with hoarded moisture. I walk beside it rather than in it; each time I step into its narrow groove my feet sink in the mud beneath the stems.

The last creature to walk this path had cloven hooves, one of a herd of white-tailed deer that find safety in this state park. But here and there where the grass is thinned, I find the hand-like tracks of raccoons. And if this occasional proof of their passage were not enough, the lakeshore tells the tale. The watchful creatures have found the muddy bank and its treasury of edibles in an eighteen-inch strip of open water between the bank and the ice. The ice itself is opaque as a piece of paper, but this small strip of water is glass clear. I can see every blade of grass, every pebble, every track and mussel shell below its surface.

The raccoons don't need to see their prey, however. They feel for it beneath the chilly water, sensitive paws like a surgeon's fingers, probing the mud for snails and mussels. I find the empty shells at the wrack line and know the coons have eaten well.

Bits of goosedown along the high-water mark are evidence of what keeps these big birds from freezing in the winter. Soft, fine, without a central vein or rachis, this is the same delicate fluff that fills my down comforter and keeps me warm as a Canada goose on winter nights. Other feathers nearby are different; the short, watertight breast and body feathers that protect the big birds' undersides have down only at their bases.

The geese are disturbed by something real or imagined; their voices rise in decibels and frequency, then die back to the occasional honk and a comfortable chuffing. But finally, someone ups the ante; their voices become louder and louder and a whole fleet of them takes wing. Another follows, and another, until I imagine the lake will empty in a heartbeat. It does not. Only about half the flock lifts off over the trees, heading northwest; the other half decides, apparently, to hold the fort in the rapidly chilling air.

But not for long. The appointed departure time is announced by some instinctive voice mail, and another group takes to the air, circles, and heads into the east. The last of the geese rise from the water with a clatter and fly directly overhead with a rush of wings and a gabble of shouts that die away in the distance. The wind, suddenly from the north, reminds me I need to take off as well, and I head for home, filled with sound and silence.

Suggested Reading:

Abbey, Edward, *Down the River*, E. P. Dutton, New York, 1982.
Beasley, Conger, Jr., *Sundancers and River Demons*, University of Arkansas Press, Fayetteville, Arkansas and London, 1990.
Zwinger, Ann Haymond, *A Conscious Stillness*, Harper & Row, New York, 1982.
————, *Run, River, Run*, Harper & Row, New York, 1975.

• Eight •

Desert Rat

THERE IS SOMETHING SEDUCTIVE about the new. The unknown has always held its appeal; we are a people genetically founded in exploration. The explorer and the pioneer are part of our personal and national mythology. Our imaginations are fueled by possibility (and intrigued by the *im*possible); it's the nature of the beast. The fact that the route to the West has already been discovered, the highest mountain climbed, the broadest desert crossed has nothing to do with our personal rambles.

It is a distinctly American trait to want to discover for ourselves. Perhaps that's why so many of us take to the road each year, and why outfitters still make a living in this technological and sedentary world. If we are not actively out there *doing* it, we want to read about it, get our gear together, fantasize, get ready, put ourselves into the picture. Half preparation, half wishful thinking, it is nonetheless very American.

My sister had lived for years in the desert Southwest, always describing the mountains, the sky, and the desert in glorious and dramatic terms in an attempt to lure me onto an airplane for a visit. I had read Ann Zwinger's powerful evocations of desert, and Ed Abbey's *Desert Solitaire*, which made me see the landscape in my mind. Barry Lopez's *Desert Notes* cinched my fascination. I set aside my fear of flight, and the trip became reality.

Reality, but still a mystery. When empiric knowledge is gleaned only from a few short days, later research notwithstanding, I can only really tell you what I know, what I saw, and what it was to be a "stranger in a strange land."

The predominant color that remains in my memory is red. Redstone formations rising from the desert floor like shapes from some fantastic dream. Red marbles, eroded from the pockmarked formations and matching the holes in the rock. Red Aztec sandstone mountains lying against the horizon, great sleeping forms that never wake to the light of day. Red sand, eroding slowly from these mountains, drifting and filling the spaces between rock outcrops with soft, glittering, dust-fine particles. Rivers, red with these particles, moving and opaque. Even the shadows are red.

I know there is more to this desert landscape than redness. I have my photos to prove it. There are black and white and tan mountains. There are green, snow-topped mountains. There are buffs and grays and violets and blues. There are the thousand colors of wildflowers in a desert springtime. There are even subtle, desert-dry greens and rich, glowing jades, and in the washes where the sparse rainwater collects and sinks, willows and cottonwoods glow like stained glass in the backlight. There is a rainbow of colors, but in my mind I see always that rich, terra-cotta red. Valley of Fire; Redrock Canyon; Bowl of Fire; the names by which the desert is known evoke the color. They speak a truth I remember.

Desert. The word sounds empty, forsaken—worthless. Off-road vehicles tear through the sand without a thought—what can they hurt? Sealed tight in air-conditioned cars, we speed through in our hurry to get anywhere else but this arid vastness. At midday, nothing moves but the phantom waves of heat. But beyond the bright lights and frenetic activity of unsleeping Las Vegas is a world full of *life*. Fragile and rugged, delicate and enduring, the life of the desert is like a treasure to be discovered, bit by bit, as an archaeologist uncovers a secret world.

It was not always desert. These Aztec sandstone formations were once the bottom of an inland sea. Fossils attest to this different ecosystem, a marine environment that teemed with aquatic life.

As in my own Midwest, limestone—like sandstone, a sedimentary rock formed in prehistoric seas—is common in the caliche caprocks and in the loose gravel of the desert floor. A natural form of calcium carbonate or $CaCO_3$, caliche is the limey cement that holds these caprocks together. The sparse rainwater of the desert has leached it from the limestone, but the super-dry climate prevents it from soaking deeply into the soil. There isn't time. Rapid evaporation causes the dissolved minerals to precipitate as a white crust at subsoil level. Leached lime has filled the interstices between the rocks, cementing them in place in a hard white matrix, as though someone had come in with a million trucksful of Portland to hold the desert landscape in place. I find caliche pebbles, small nodules among the loose rocks of the desert floor.

Ancient Lake Chemehuevi, an Ice Age lake that contributed much of this rock, was thought to be larger than Lake Mead and Lake Mojave combined. The fossil record attests to its boundaries, and my nephew delighted in finding the recrystallized remains of marine creatures halfway up a mountain when he was a boy. My sister insists that after a desert rain the air still smells of the sea and a faint tang of fish.

In the long, slow progress of geologic years, seas retreated and lakes evaporated back into themselves—or their lava dams were breached, emptying them suddenly as a bathtub. Over time, weather patterns changed and rock forms eroded, leaving the fanciful sandstone shapes exposed and towering over the former sea floor.

Cross-bedding of geologic forms, great layers of rock in a jumble of slanting patterns that suggest movement, are evidence of just that. Some of these rock forms, geologists tell us, are the solidified remains of ancient sand dunes, frozen in motion and in time. Once the waters retreated, silicaceous sandstone was exposed to the elements. It eroded to create a desert of blowing dunes; we can see in the rocky striations where the sands layered and dunes merged, cemented by time and pressure into the immobility of stone.

Much of this red sandstone is marked with the long spill lines of dark-colored desert varnish. Oxides of iron and manganese, these streaks of dramatic varnish are caused by the evaporation of mineral-bearing solutions that come to the surface of the stone. They look, instead, as though someone had poured buckets of ebony stain over the cliffs.

Surfaces with untold years' accretion of this varnish acquire a dull patina, as though polished. At certain angles in the strong slant of desert light, whole cliffs gleam in the sun, reflecting the intense blue of the desert sky. Such boldness is a

challenge to the artist; I painted the landscape in bright striations of blue sky, blue-black cliff, and redstone, and it recalls a
specific place and time to me.

Even here, back among the mazes in the rock, there is the
touch of human handiwork; ancient artists have preceded me
by many hundreds of years. The Anasazi peoples left their mark
on the varnished redstone, those cryptic petroglyphs that defy
casual interpretation scratched through the black deposits.
There are suns, lightning bolts, and antelopes—a natural history
of the prehistoric Southwest; I strain to read the messages in the
stone.

The fingerprints of ancient volcanoes are also clear on this
land; Tony Hillerman's Navajo detectives would need no dusting to see them. Strike-slip faulting is visible, pointing to ancient
volcanic cones that have sheared into parts. Although eroded by
wind and time, the fault lines are unmistakable. Here and there,
the cone shape of a long-dormant volcano itself still looms in
the distance.

Ancient alluvial fans and terraces hint at the action of more
water than I can imagine in this arid place, marking the deltas of
long-gone rivers or the power of flash flood, an unexpected
threat in a landscape you must never take for granted. Spring
thaw in the mountains or a sudden flash flood still sends a rush
and roar of water through the streets of Las Vegas, trapping
people in their cars and drowning someone every few years. In
the desert, it is never a good idea to camp at the bottom of an
arroyo. An unexpected rainstorm in the foothills can turn the
gully to gullywasher.

Scorching sun coupled with an aridity that robs the body of
moisture in minutes make a Spartan landscape—but the native
plants and animals have evolved to fit.

In all this rocky dryness I hadn't expected so much vegetation; adapted to the harsh environment, it simply grows more
slowly with the lack of water or develops complex survival
techniques. These plants are far hardier than ones that grow in
temperate zones, as are most things that overcome adversity—
be they plants, animals, or humans. Hardy, they in fact possess a

lovely delicacy that seems impossible in these desert surroundings. Beavertail cactus, or *Opuntia basilaris* (a close relative of the *O. humifusa* I know at home), has beautiful, translucent magenta flowers. Pygmy barrel cactus, fishhook, and strawberry hedgehog cactus have flowers of surpassing delicacy for such cruelly armored plants. Showy sunray *(Enceliopsis argophylla)* rises like the phoenix, not from its ashes but from the detritus of dead growth of seasons past, until it teeters aloft on a column of dry leaves. In the higher elevations, larger plants like cholla, yucca, and even Joshua trees seem to thrive.

Many of these desert plants are succulents, hoarding their own supply of moisture within thick, fleshy leaves. They provide moisture also to the denizens of the desert, and you'll often see some creature munching a cactus pad to get at the water it holds. People have survived the desert in the same way, learning from the landscape what it takes to stay alive.

When the sparse rains fall the desert blushes with brief, tender color. A carpet of oriental lushness lovely as a Kilim rug transforms the landscape—for a short few days.

Living decorations, black widow spiders hang from low shrubs at my sister's Nevada home; like many desert creatures, they hunt at night. In the flashlight's beam they glisten as though lacquered, flashing the red hourglass that is their caste mark.

"What are you doing out there?" my husband calls to me.

"Um, nothing, dear."

This is a man whose favorite pastime is to scare himself; he's a prime candidate for horror movies old and new.

"This (or that, or the other) can *kill* you," he delights in warning me—and anyone who will listen. A favorite quote of his is from another desert dweller, Don Juan of the Carlos Casteneda books, ostensibly aimed at Casteneda: "Your body loves to be scared." His does, too. And while I appreciate the concern, I don't share the paranoia; I keep on sketching.

Black widows are not the only spiders of the desert, of course. Among the crew of smaller arachnids are the great, hairy tarantulas. We watched in fascination as a huge, dark

shape ascended a tall white stucco building and speculated on
the reaction of those whose balcony opened onto the desert far
below.

Contrary to childhood's fears of "banana spiders," so-
called because they sometimes hitchhike from the southern
hemisphere on a bunch of bananas, native North American
tarantulas are no more poisonous to humans than a bee or a
wasp. Up to two and one-half inches long, the male has longer
legs than the female, as well as more well-developed pedipalps,
those mitten-like appendages that wave just under a spider's
chin—if a spider has such a thing. No wonder so many people
keep tarantulas for pets; females live up to thirty-five years in
captivity, making pet funerals a far distant possibility.

The male desert tarantula tries to stay close to the female,
aggressively pursuing her wherever she goes. If not in possession of a mate, the normally nocturnal hunter wanders in the
pale light of dusk or dawn looking for one, hiding by day in
abandoned holes or under rocks.

The tarantula hawk is not a hawk at all, but a species of
wasp that makes these spiders its prey. It stings the hapless
arachnid between the legs, then lays eggs on the body, burying
the spider for a repast of fresh protein for the hatchlings. I

wonder how they make connections at all, since tarantula hawks presumably fly by day like the rest of their kin.

Like childhood's cartoons, the roadrunner and the coyote populate this arid land; at night, golf course oases become the opportunistic coyote's hunting grounds. Long-legged jackrabbits and kangaroo rats had best watch their backs. But they, too, are adapted to their niche; they're *fast*. The coyote misses more often than he succeeds.

Both the coyote and the jackrabbit use those big ears for more than hearing, though I watch as they swivel their sonar devices for news of one another. These are naturally evolved air conditioners as well, dissipating heat from large veins just beneath the surface. In the strong backlight the jackrabbit's ears glow as though signalling me to stop. I do, and watch while it returns my stare, then bounds off into the sagebrush.

The brown, crow-sized roadrunner *is* fast, though not so fast as his cartoon alter ego. No matter how close we get, it runs ahead rather than taking to the air; it apparently prefers walking to flying—as do I. According to the *Audubon Society Field Guide to North American Birds* it can easily outdistance a man, bobbing and feinting in and out of cactus thickets. With its odd, syncopated walk, jerking its tail back and forth and up and down, it appears to be dancing to music I can't hear. It paces the small gravel railroad-bed-turned-road that clings to the loose, rubbly incline of the mountain's edge, hotfooting it before us without fear—unless that dark, upraised crest on its head signals alarm. The roadrunner finds plenty to eat in this harsh environment, dining on lizards and snakes, mice, scorpions, vinegarones, and any number of insects.

My sister tells me she was frightened to move to the desert, for fear of poisonous scorpions. "Don't ever put on your shoes in the morning without shaking them out first," she was told. Presumably that might be true if you slept out under the stars, but in twenty years of desert life she's seen only two. I discovered none on my brief visit, and have seen more scorpions in Missouri than she has in "scorpion country."

The giant desert hairy scorpion, up to five and one-half

inches long, is impressive as the devil, but not as poisonous as you'd expect. These nocturnal hunters use their stingers to kill prey, but their poison is more deadly to spiders and insects than to people; most will cause only a painful swelling. The *centruroides* species, common to Arizona, is, however, poisonous and sometimes fatal.

Vinegarones, in case you wondered, are non-poisonous scorpion-wannabes. Many people mistake them for the scorpion's lobster-shaped body, and although they have no toxins they can deliver a heck of a pinch. Thelyphonidae family members, also called "vinegarroons" or whipscorpions, get their names from the strong vinegar-scented acid they emit when disturbed.

A queue of magnificent *Ovis canadensis mexicana* or desert bighorns stand at the crest of a hill, watching the humans below intently; they are shy creatures with little use for people—usually, my sister tells me. In the Lake Mead/Boulder City region, they may come into the park to eat and drink; she's had them approach closely enough that she could see the shapes of their irises. Like all goat-family members, these are horizontal rather than vertical like a cat's.

This particular group of bighorns is a mating band (rams and ewes spend most of the year in separation). Here are females, hornless young, and one apparently successful ram with a massive set of horns. He has been able to stand off challengers, literally butting heads over his harem of desirable females. No wonder the skulls of bighorn sheep are heavy as armor.

Bighorns need more water than other desert species, normally drinking at least once daily—though under adverse conditions they can go without for up to eight days. Springs and rock sinks are magnets, as they are for all desert life, and the big sheep's cloven hooves and natural agility let them get to the most remote water sources.

These hooves are flint hard at the edges, with a resilient undersurface roughened for good clinging and climbing capabilities. A concave hollow at the tip of each hoof gives this creature the ability to grip the most minute foothold, a ball and socket fitting that saves lives in this rugged country.

Desert bighorns are smaller than the northern species, smaller and more streamlined. Usually about fifty inches long from nose to tail-tip, they weigh up to two hundred pounds; Rocky Mountain bighorns may outweigh them by another hundred. Their heavy, curving horns are still impressive. Made of keratin, these grow from a living horn core. Annual rings, indentations I can see even from this distance, show the big male to be well over ten years old.

Although they must have a broad range, bighorns are adapted to take advantage of seasonal browse; they find plenty to eat if they make it a movable feast. Tender grasses that sprout after a desert rain are popular, but the leathery leaves of desert shrubs, cactus, and jojoba nuts are all eaten as well.

Cañon wrens fill the echoing sandstone labyrinths with descant notes as pure and cool as springwater. The bighorns

Cañon
Wren

look on, impassive, oblivious to the little birds. Both have adapted to the harsh environs and can be found throughout the desert lands.

As territorial here as anywhere, mockingbirds scold and sing, chasing anyone or anything they view as an intruder in their chosen stronghold. The sweet sounds of mourning doves bring my mind back home; who would have thought to meet them here in such numbers? Gambel's quail are a common sight in some areas of the desert Southwest; my sister finds them occasional visitors in her backyard. They are the very embodiment of the stereotypical quail, with gray-brown bodies, black faces, brown crowns—and those upright, teardrop-shaped feathers sticking up like exclamation points.

Desert tortoises that have thrived here for thousands of years now face the stress of human encroachment—humans and their domestic livestock—and that stress takes its toll. The tortoises struggle to survive within a desert no longer deserted.

Numbers decline; shells become brittle; average size has shrunk by 10 percent in the last four decades. Researchers discovered to their surprise that these creatures crave bones and calcareous rocks in the absence of the calcium-rich desert plants that are their preferred foods. In whatever form they can get it, tortoises require a great deal of this mineral to produce their shells and to make eggs strong enough to incubate. They are driven to eating rocks; caliche is handy.

A recent respiratory infection has decimated tortoise numbers to the point where this ancient reptile was added to the endangered species list in August 1989, and it wasn't a moment too soon. Desert developers are now required to survey the area for tortoises; if found they must move them to a new habitat before beginning to build. It's hardly the perfect solution; the stress of capture and moving to an unfamiliar habitat may be almost as difficult to adjust to as development itself.

Nevadans are fond of their animals; a growing environmental movement looks out for their welfare. It's a complex issue befitting this complex ecosystem. Mustangs have bred in such numbers they are occasionally a problem; in order to protect them and their environment, they are sometimes rounded up and adopted, some say a controversial solution.

In Red Rock Canyon, burros have the right-of-way—but burros are as non-indigenous as the mustangs, brought here by miners of the last century. In some areas they have so degraded habitat that survival is difficult for the home boys. Bighorns, Sonoran white-tailed and desert mule deer, peccaries, and pronghorns compete for the same habitat, the same water supplies. Still, like the wild horses of the desert Southwest, burros have carved a place for themselves in our affections. They seem a part of this desert landscape, as much at home as a Gila monster.

"The beggars! They're not so cute when they're in your face," my brother-in-law says as my sister sits there, laughing. "We went up to the canyon to sketch, and took a picnic with us. I had the window down, and the next thing I know this huge, woolly head is in the car with me. Then another one pokes its head in next to the first. Those things have *big* teeth, and they were practically in my lap."

My sister adds, "I thought they were great. Of course, I was safely on the other side of the car!"

"I yelled at her to give me something to feed them," Rich said. "Here I am trapped between the back of the seat and the steering wheel, with no place to go. I couldn't even get at the ignition. She hands me an apple, the burro chomps down on it and bites it in half. The second burro goes for the other half, and while they're distracted I get the car started and ease it out of there.

"I never saw such big teeth in my life," he says with a faraway look.

It's a picture I wish I hadn't missed—but it points to the dangers of mistaking wild animals for tame. Like bears, like raccoons, these burros are unpredictable. When you come between them and food, anything can happen; Rich was lucky just to lose an apple.

In the desert, scents are exotic, heady—clean. Creosote

bush and sagebrush combine with the bone-dry whiff of the air itself. I breathe deep to fill my lungs with it, as though this incense could purify me—a sweetgrass and sage bundle burned in a ceremony of passage. Bare of flowers now in the fall, creosote explodes into bright yellow after spring rains, but the scent is still as fresh and head-clearing. If I suddenly awoke to find myself here in the dark I'd recognize it instantly.

On a recent visit to St. Louis we discovered the desert biosphere at the Missouri Botanical Gardens. I had expected to see the cactus, creosote bush, and palo verde that would recall Nevada; I didn't expect the rush of memory carried by the scent. The desert was here, under glass, a perfume held aloft in this immense crystal container.

Dr. John MacDougal, curator of the Desert House, says the scent is natural, the emanations from the plants themselves. There are huge ponytail palms and columnar cacti that have been here since the 1904 World's Fair, held in St. Louis. Creosote bush, aloe, desert spoon, and yucca add their spice to this captive atmosphere. A computer readout sent to me by Chris Dietrich, plant recorder at the gardens, shows 509 plants currently in the Desert House, from Agavaceae to Zygophyllaceae—with plenty of Cactaceae thrown in; no wonder it smells of the Southwest.

There are several essentials to remember when walking in the desert: Carry water, carry water, carry water. Incidentals like "don't pick a cactus bouquet" (it's illegal and painful) and "don't play with the rattlesnakes" go almost without saying. Water is the single most important survival tool in the desert; we dehydrate more quickly in this dry heat than we imagine, and death by heatstroke in a land where temperatures can reach 120 degrees plus is not the most pleasant end. The old expression "it makes my blood boil" rings uncomfortably true here. It may not actually reach the boiling point, but it feels like it when core temperatures rise far above our normal 98.6 degrees.

Sensible clothing is a must, as well. Sandals may feel cooler for a while, but that hot sand on bare toes can be painful, as is a cactus spine in your foot. Take along a wide-brimmed hat if you'll be out for long; sunburn is a distinct possibility, especially if you are unused to the intensity of desert light. Sunscreen is a good idea; try to find the gel kind and you won't feel quite as much like a well-basted Thanksgiving turkey. Or take along a long-sleeved shirt to protect your arms from sunburn. Wear sunglasses if you are sensitive to light.

Don't try to go too far unless you are an experienced desert rambler; it's a lot longer walk *back* to your car or camp than it was getting there. In the desert distances increase exponentially with heat and fatigue—or seem to. Better to take a series of short exploratory walks than a long expedition unless you're an old desert rat like Ed Abbey.

You may want to time your visit to coincide with sunrise or sunset. Not only is the desert spectacular at these times, but it is also more hospitable—to humans and desert natives alike. You'll see far more active wildlife before the oven-like heat drives them into hiding.

Of course, you can also time your walks to the kinder seasons. I enjoyed October in Nevada; the weather was perfect. At its hottest it was only in the low 90s, and as my sister had always insisted, "It's a dry heat." That means, near as I can measure the complex scientific computations, that you can still breathe. Here in the Midwest when temperatures near the century mark and humidity is at its worst, we are parboiled; gills would be a handy adjunct to filter the wet, steamy air. The weather bureau's comfort index says "forget it." And we do. Until the temperature soars over 105 or so, dry heat seems to ameliorate that miserable feeling.

Night in the desert can still be quite chilly; if you plan a short walk then, take along a sweater—and remember that other creatures are also more active. Watch where you step.

Anyplace you go has its caveats; we are all responsible for our own well-being, and common sense is a precious commodity. Use it in the desert and you'll never forget the experience.

The road to the Valley of Fire took us past some spectacular scenery. Basin and range spread out before us in ranks, bluing in the distance to a rich cobalt. Lake Mead, spectacular and controversial body of water that it is, was an unbelievable sight, plugging up the canyons in the midst of desert. Giant Hoover Dam, at one time considered the eighth wonder of the world, makes human life in the desert possible—in such numbers, anyway—providing water and hydroelectric power for Glitter City, Henderson, and other towns that have sprung up nearby. It drowns some of the loveliest of historic desert waterways, but the sea of blue it forms has a beauty all its own.

Gulls seemed oddly out of place on this desert lake; expectations beat out logic every time until you get the chance to think—or better yet, to see for yourself and then ask why. A large body of water with the Pacific Ocean not so far away—equals seagulls.

Desert pavement, as it is called, forms a mosaic in the sweep of country between mountainous outcroppings. These strewn rocks of red and black and white blanket the ground, oddly similar in size and shape where the finer sands in between have blown away. My nephew searched this rocky rubble as a child to bring his mother bits of raw opal and amethyst.

As we neared the canyon I was taken with the brushy clumps of gray-green vegetation dotting the landscape into diminishing distance. Voluptuous folds of red earth mounded softly together, slumping into a deep ravine where the shadows were midnight colored. Where the edge of a hillside met the sky, vegetation caught the light and turned pale as wheat.

Gnarled fingers of bright red rock stretched upward, gesturing at something far overhead. I couldn't help but look where they pointed, and what I saw was rich blue sky and white clouds and the daylight moon suspended above us. I could see why my sister was so taken by this place, and we played in the desert like kids, exploring between the great rocks and examining minute leaves on plants more sparing with their energy than those at home.

"That's enough, you two," Rich insisted. "You haven't seen anything yet."

"But I have. This is gorgeous."

"Nope; let's go. The canyon isn't far from here."

He was right. We entered a cut between two immense Mojave sandstone formations and found ourselves in another world, a world of elastic shapes frozen in time, a world of magic and meaning. Here, the red stone formed huge stacks as though a pile of dishes big as whales were about to crash to the floor. They were held in place by only a slender column of sandstone.

The planes of the rock were jumbled as though there had been an upheaval; but these, too, were the remains of ancient dunes formed over millennia of changing winds and turned to solid rock, cemented in place by pressure and by the iron within the rock—the source of that red color.

The rock is not entirely solid, however. Sandstone is relatively soft, and easily shaped by wind and water. That statement doesn't begin to touch the truth, that overriding sense of a master sculptor at work, a Michelangelo of natural forms. Here, it appeared to have bubbled up into a huge, rounded shape about to boil over an invisible pot, complete with the strings of stuff that appeared to drip from the edges. Round holes like air pockets in bubbling, molten rock completed the picture.

In other places the forms were angular, hard-edged, and striated with lines as through scribed with a ruler. How could they have been so different from the earlier formations? What made the difference just a few yards down the canyon?

No rock face is without its planes and lines, caverns and tiny holes. These latter appear carved from the rock with a melon-ball cutter; the marble-sized stones that came from the holes litter the sand. Each orb is abrasive, irregular, a bead not made by human hands; I imaging the attempt to return each rocky ball to its proper socket, and shake my head at such impossibility.

Wind and water are the more dramatic actors, working with broad Shakespearean gestures, but the patient lichen etches its way into the stone as well, making rock into dust. Bright gold-green, turquoise, and black lichens pry away at the grains of sand, trying to undo the work of the more active sculptors; trying, and succeeding, though at a pace I am un-equipped to monitor. I have only a few days. This would take millennia.

The lichen attests to the relative purity of the air here; these prehistoric plants will not thrive in a polluted atmosphere. When the lichen disappears it is long past time to stop the nuclear testing still going on in Nevada, past time for much stronger regulations on the chemical plants that seem to sprout in this land we too often mistake for empty and useless. An explosion that cracked the walls of my sister's home, broke all the windows, and ripped the door off the hinges seemed to make hardly a ripple in the larger world; people in Henderson are still dealing with damage, years after the fact. I ask myself whether anyone bothers to monitor the humble bellwethers of lichen and stone and hope the answer is yes.

We walked between the towering rock shapes as though through a cathedral, hushed, stepping softly so as not to disturb—what? I didn't know whether to look up at the soaring buttresses of stone, or deep into the earth to find a natural well of crystal water reflecting a sapphire sky.

Domes of rock were underfoot, and between them basins of dust-fine red sand like symbolic pools in a Zen garden. I found the tracks of another human and was startled to remember that this was a public park, so profound had been the silence. The only sounds were a hawk overhead and the sweet descant trill of the wren echoing off the walls.

When we came upon petroglyphs pecked into the dark desert varnish 600 to 3,000 years ago or more, I felt for a moment as though that explained the footsteps I had seen. Surely the Anasazi to whom these markings are attributed had just passed this way. If I walked quietly enough, quickly enough, perhaps I could catch up.

I traced the cryptic shapes with my fingers; rain clouds, man shapes, zigzag marking that must mean lightning—it would appear these prehistoric desert dwellers called for rain in this arid landscape. Here, a bighorn sheep, simple and symbolic, practically leapt off the dark desert varnish; were these early

ones bent on communication—with me, with one another, with the gods? Was it worship or incantation—or did they discern a difference?

An excavation near Tule Springs has revealed a bit more about the earlier desert dwellers, perhaps the Anasazi, perhaps another people. Among other things, it appears they were red-haired.

Valley of Fire State Park is large enough to contain all my questions. Approximately 36,800 acres made up of eroded dune formations, canyons, rubbly slopes, open sweeps of desert, synclines, and anticlines catch the full gamut of desert weather, from 0 degrees on the coldest winter days to 120—hot enough, if not to fry an egg, certainly to fry my brain if I stay out too long.

"We give warnings in the summer. Hikers need to be aware of the danger of dehydration," the ranger tells me. "Haven't lost anybody lately, though." The twinkle in his eye tells me he's kidding, but I watch the sky for the graceful shapes of turkey vultures just the same.

They are here, along with the black, croaking ravens, red-tailed hawks, cañon and cactus wrens, and the occasional roadrunner. Coyotes, big-eared kit foxes, badgers, bobcats, and ringtail or miner's cats are common; bighorns less so, but present, nonetheless. The desert is not deserted; in its fashion it is as populous as any landscape on earth—perhaps more than my more familiar territory where the pressure of too many humans per square mile stresses wildlife to the limit. I had expected an empty landscape, as silent as the stones. Instead I find the desert an active and complex ecosystem, a walk through time and timelessness.

Suggested Reading:

Abbey, Edward, *Desert Solitaire*, Ballantine Books, New York, 1985.

————, *A Voice Crying in the Wilderness (Vox Clamantis in Deserto): Notes from a Secret Journal*, St. Martin's Press, New York, 1989.

Lopez, Barry, *Desert Notes*, Sheed and Ward, Kansas City, Kansas, 1976.

Zwinger, Ann Haymond, *A Desert Country near the Sea: A Natural History of the Cape Region of Baja California*, Harper & Row, New York, 1983.

————, *The Mysterious Lands*, E. P. Dutton, New York, 1989.

The Sierra Club Guides to the National Parks: Desert Southwest, Stewart, Tabori and Chang, New York, 1984.

• Nine •

A Resonant Place:
New England Seacoast

FROM RICH SALT MARSHES where the sea dances in an endless pas de deux with the land to the bony, volcanic outcroppings that jut into the ocean, the coast of Maine carries its own brand of magic; it is home at last to the imaginings of a lifetime.

What is it about the coast of New England? Many of us born in the heartland, who never saw the Atlantic or heard its crashing waves, are nonetheless drawn there as if to the primordial soup of our origins. As a teenager, when other kids were enthralled with chopped and channeled Chevies and T-birds, my best friend Roberta and I were dreaming of clipper ships, learning the names of the rigging and hearing the creak of tarred hemp ropes in the ears of imagination, feeling the swell of the sea under our feet and tasting the tang of salt on our lips. We wanted to see Mystic Seaport, Cape Cod, the coast of Maine; we wanted to live it. Granted, the imagination of a teenage girl is a powerful thing, but it was a fascination that has stayed with both of us for over three decades. When I got the chance to go, to actually see the eastern seaboard, I grabbed it like the brass ring at a carnival.

Airplane travel is generic; you are locked in a tin pocket of pressurized air that looks pretty much like every other plane you've ever been in, regardless of destination. When you actually touch down to find the world beneath your feet so changed, so different from the place you left, it takes a while to adjust. The automobile trip from the Portland airport to Port Clyde, 100 miles north up the coast, allowed time for decompression.

We eased into strangeness; the coast road, where it ran just inland, helped. The hills and valleys that bordered the small highway were not that different from the hills and valleys of Missouri; many of the same trees grew here, and the small towns were as small towns almost anywhere, and I was frustrated by the need to get to Port Clyde in a timely manner. We passed up a hundred tempting walks. It was when I caught a glimpse of the ocean that my excitement level shifted into overdrive, and I ragged our poor guide with as many questions as an inquisitive five-year-old. I had, after all, a lifetime's wonderings to satisfy. It was as though I expected to get to know this place in a two-hour drive; I wanted to be briefed on everything. "What's that? Where's the ocean from here? Are there rocks on the beach where we're going, or sand? Tell me about the tides. Will we see breakers? Is that a salt marsh? What grows there? Are there great blue herons? Egrets? Do you see moose where you live? Will we hear loons? Is that Mount Katahdin?"

It wasn't, but she was most patient, and answered all the questions my mind and eyes could generate. The rest had to wait for our arrival, which turned out to be almost too late in the evening to explore. We took a brief walk to a nearby mudflat to pay our respects to the sea, and returned to the old hotel. Tired from the long preparations, the flight, and the drive, we watched the sun sink into an incandescent ocean from the hotel's balcony while swifts returned to their nests under the eaves. They peered from the daubed mud apartments and complained of our presence on the narrow second-story porch. It felt good to see these little birds, as common at home as they are in Maine; for all my curiosity, I was glad for similarities as well as differences. I had only enough energy left for a quick sketch of a small head watching me from the bowl-like nest.

Because I only had eight days, because I had always wanted to be here, exactly where I found myself, sleep was out of the question—except in brief spurts. It was not only that I was too excited to waste time in unconsciousness; it wasn't that the sounds of the place kept me awake with their strangeness— though strange they were. It was that I wanted to wring every moment out of my venture, see everything I could, experience as much of the Atlantic seacoast as possible. Each morning I rose before the sun, took my shower while the coffee perked, and burst out the door like a kid to see the Maine I had only read about. It was exotic, a storied place that heretofore had existed only in my mind, in books, and in the haunting paint- ings of artists from Winslow Homer to Andrew Wyeth. I knew what to expect—and I had no idea what to expect. But the yellow brick road led to the sea.

Evenings, my husband and I would head out together. After a long day's teaching, the time alone with him was a delight. I saw the world through his eyes or enjoyed the pleasure of show- ing him the things I had discovered on my own that morning. Our explorations—alone, together—became an immediate habit.

The first morning I stayed close to town, rambling the narrow, winding streets that led, each of them, to the ocean. A path paralleled the rocky coast, stringing backyards together. This tiny public thoroughfare was used by nearly everyone, it seemed, though that first day I felt like a voyeur, peering into people's gardens and admiring flowers that seemed as foreign as the coast itself. Some I knew, some I didn't, but even those I was familiar with seemed oddly different from the same species at home. Perhaps it was only the abundant coastal moisture that made them so large and prolific that they seemed exotic. Even the geraniums that decorated almost every dooryard seemed somehow unusual, if only in their ubiquitous presence. Noticing the stacks of lobster pots and overturned and weathering dories beside each house, I told my husband with a laugh that perhaps Maine zoning ordinances required such things.

The old hotel perched on an incline only a half block from the ocean; the general store hugged the shore; the homes and boathouses and fishing docks wrapped themselves around the wrack line; and the sight and scent and sound of the sea were everywhere. There were more gulls than I'd ever seen in my life, in sheer numbers and varieties, wheeling, soaring, riding thermals, coming in for landings, laughing, yelping, hawking, kowkowing. I liked the sound of their harsh cries. They reminded me of crows or ravens, but with a poignant edge that twisted my emotions.

Lest you imagine that we must have no gulls so far inland in Missouri, think again. These opportunistic birds find plenty to feed on here, as they did in Nevada—flying up the Mississippi, hanging left at the Missouri River, and investigating every respectable-sized body of water between here and Wyoming. On a recent walk by Williams Creek Lake not seven miles from my home, Harris and I watched as seven huge white gulls wheeled against bare trees still gray with winter. The birds mirrored the pale, upright branches of the sycamore trees, swirling like bits of paper in the wind. As we made our way through the brush to the bank we could see the dark wing-tips and orange bills that marked them as herring gulls.

Still, we have nothing to compare to the proliferation of *Laridae* on the coast of Maine. On that first morning I saw enough herring gulls to feel as though I'd never seen them at all. Laughing gulls skittered amongst the larger birds; the occasional odd-man-out of a glaucous gull made a sometime appearance. The slow wingbeats of a black-backed gull brought this bird almost in my face, so intent was it on prey. Common and increasing in numbers and range, according to Peterson, still I saw only a few.

I am no expert birder, especially of these unfamiliar species. But I could tell there were more gulls here, whirling about the feast with abandon or keeping to themselves far out to sea, than I could identify without a crash course from Audubon himself. I tried to sort them out, tell which was which, but the possibilities were too many and my binoculars half a conti-

nent away. Great and lesser black-backed gulls, ring-billed gulls, black-legged kittiwakes, laughing gulls, Bonaparte's gulls—I was frustrated by my brief time and my ignorance, all too aware I'd only just get started before we'd have to leave. I gave it up and lost myself in their voices, seacoast incarnate.

In an hour of fog and early sunrise, I watched as a gull appeared like a ghost from the pearlescent atmosphere. It rose high overhead, then dropped something repeatedly on the concrete jetty nearby.

"What is it doing?" I asked one of the fishermen who readied his gear for the day. "Same as me, ma'am; fishing. That's how the old devil gets at his meal. He catches one of those hard-shelled critters and drops it on the rocks to crack it open. Pretty smart, eh?"

Smarter than me, anyway. I was embarrassed to have asked; it should have been obvious, and after an hour or so, it was. The gulls sailplane on the wind and dive for prey, dining on a variety of fresh seafood: tiny orange fiddler crabs and mussels and dogwinkles. Their remains littered the rocks and jetties along the shore, emptied of edibles. The sunset color of the crab's shell retains its freshness for a long time; I tucked one into my pocket, and after four years in the Midwest it remains the same.

It's an incredibly active place, this rocky coastline where earth and sea converge. Because of the range of habitats, most of New England's wildlife can be seen here at one time or another, either in migration or as permanent residents. The gulls are a constant, but many other birds are common here. This is one of our great flyways; millions of birds pass along the eastern coast twice each year. In that it is similar to my own Midwest and the Central and Mississippi flyways.

Ducks and geese, seabirds, and shorebirds convene along the coast, the great blue heron stalking the shallows of a protected cove at low tide, the cormorant disappearing silently beneath the waves to stay under an inordinately long time before bobbing back to the surface. These birds, the great cormorants as well as the double-crested cormorants I see at home, have feathers that become quite waterlogged—unlike the glistening, repellent plumage of waterfowl. With that feature and their ability to express the air from the lungs, they are able to dive deep after prey and stay submerged longer than I can imagine possible. When they surface, they often perch on a rock or piling, wings outstretched to dry like an anhinga.

Comical shorebirds danced with the waves, skittering in and out with the edge of the seafoam, looking for food. Dunlins, sandpipers, and plovers inhabit these beaches; I was startled to find a killdeer among them until I checked my field guide. I had imagined them quintessentially midwestern, but these common birds not only inhabit my own area but are found sea to sea from Canada to Mexico.

We walked along the cove in the light of a rising moon, listening to night sounds, and at last heard the loons. The sound raised the hairs on my arms and a quick moisture in my eyes;

embarrassed, baffled, I rubbed away the tears. "Listen," I said. "Loons." We stood for long moments, waiting for the sound; waiting for the tears again.

These are common loons here along the coast this night; they call to proclaim their territory, to protect the nest. "A yodel-like laugh," Golden's *Birds of North America* calls this evocative sound that carries with it such a freight of emotion. That description hardly fits what I feel when I hear them, what so many others feel. It is an eerie sound, the sound of the north—the sound of strangeness.

The mating colors of these common loons are more spectacular than their winter garb of soft brown—the better to find an accepting mate impressed by this display of dapper black and white. The red-throated loons also found along the coast are not so dramatically dressed for the season, but the ruddy throat patch adds a touch of color to their subtle grays and browns. The red-throat's call is more quack than quaver, and I'd never have known they were related if it weren't for the bird's shape and the loon-like way it sits low in the water.

Birders congregate in estuaries and along the rocky points, armed with binoculars; with luck they may see an Atlantic puffin in full mating mufti, its orange and black and yellow beak filled with small silvery fish. A student gave me a photo he had taken of a puffin at the Audubon sanctuary a few miles up the coast, its harlequin profile arresting as a carved African mask.

The rising and falling ocean is a mysterious presence along the coast, inexorable. I had not spent enough time near such a body of water to be familiar with the ramifications of the tides. When we arrived, low tide had left the little town tottering on stilts, long-legged jetties and huge seawalls exposed to show their cargo of barnacles and seaweed. Boats were moored to sliding contraptions to allow them to rise or fall with water that kept its own timeless timetable. The cove was drawn with long, calligraphic fingers of water as the ocean pulled back into itself, and everything that the water had gathered was exposed, for a while, by the pull of the moon. Life itself kept the tide's hours, escaping back into the depths or hiding in tidepools or under rocks to wait for the return of the sea.

Is it always so foggy along the coast, or was it typical of June? It's the kind of question a visitor asks when, in home territory, fog is an anomaly, not the norm. Night after night foghorns wailed disconsolately into the darkness from every point along the coast, warning of stony reefs or a granite peninsula hidden beneath high tide and screened by the thick draperies of fog. The sound was mournful and evocative; I lay in my bed, unable to sleep with the moan of the horns in my ears.

Once manned, the ubiquitous seacoast lighthouse is now automated, as are the foghorns. They are no less exotic, though I'll admit I'd prefer to think the stalwarts that once watched from these lights or walked the beaches in foul weather are still out there; I've read too much Henry Beston not to miss that. When I came upon a bronze plaque embedded in a stone wall that reads "Land's End, A.D. 1906" I wondered who put it there, and who had read those words that seem to mean so much. At land's end is both magic and tragedy.

The shoreline along Penobscot Bay is a quickfooted jaunt among ocean-rounded stones that would as soon throw you into the surf as allow you to walk on them. Obsidian-black, these rocks are polished to a high gloss, big as stacked basketballs and offering as uncertain footing. I hopped from one to the next, trying to land on a larger rock that seemed more firmly seated among the smaller stones that loosely mortared it in place. This was a good place to twist an ankle, and a long way back to town. I tottered along the beach like a novice tightrope walker, but managed to stay upright. Returning to the safer footing of the grass or the small coast road, the better part of valor, was not a viable option as far as I was concerned. I had two precious hours before my class, and I wasn't about to waste it in cautious exploration among the wildflowers. It was land's end I'd flown halfway across the continent to see.

Bending for a closer look between these rounded stones, I noticed a thick accretion of seaweed. Among the wiry threads

and rococo shapes were thousands of tiny barnacles, clinging tightly to their chosen spot. The sun came out as I sketched, and I discovered that not only do these young barnacles attach themselves in cracks and on the protected side of the rocks—as does the bladder wrack and other seaweeds—but they are just past the sun line as well, ensconced safely in shade.

Bladder wrack may not be the proper name for this brown, forked seaweed; it's a name given to me by an old seaman. The *Peterson Field Guide to the Atlantic Seashore* names this rockweed, a *Fucus* species that includes a spiral form as well as one with fine filaments. *Fucus versiculosus* is the only rockweed with air bladders, which appear in pairs near the tips of the fronds. I pinched them to make them pop, and the strong scent of ocean rose from the rockweed.

Some seaweeds were long and filamentous; others were bright green and leafy as a spring garden. Still others on this stretch of beach were horsetail fringes that looked as though they belonged in an aquarium. Some rocks were bare of seaweed and polished as tumbled gemstones; others only a few feet away had a thick, woolly coat of green-brown stuff. But under their growth of seaweed they looked as smoothly polished as the nearby rocks. Elsewhere, a mixed salad of seaweed chose seemingly random spots to form thick colonies—though if I had been here longer I could have learned to see the reason behind the apparent randomness.

Just down from these rounded, polished beach stones I discovered Marshall Point Light, a lighthouse on its way to becoming a museum. The light itself, like the others, is now automated, but the lighthouse keeper's house was in the process of restoration. White-cedar shingles replaced those that had become too weatherbeaten, shining like gold in the strong, thin

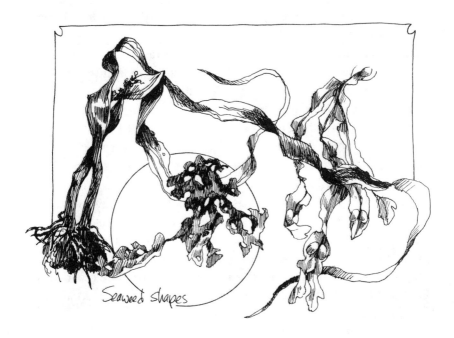

Seaweed shapes

sunlight. Dressed in reflective white paint, the old house gleamed against evergreens that rose black as ink behind the house. The effect, with the clear blue sky, was startling.

Long grasses blew in the incessant sea wind, and wild-flowers made an undulating calico of color in the pale green of the grass. From the edge of the sea, the vista was imposing. The jumble of rocks on the shore arranged themselves in zones of color and form. Nearest the sea they were larger, smoother, and almost purple in the shadows; closer to the house they appeared nearly white.

The light itself was reached by a sturdy catwalk, painted white like the lighthouse keeper's home—like the lighthouse itself. Gulls as white as the buildings soared overhead, croaking and kow-kowing. Quintessentially New England, it was as though I had stepped into the midst of a picture postcard and found myself delighted to be there, a postcard that narrowly escaped the cliché by its immediacy, its reality. I suppose all clichés begin with a basic, immutable truth; here one was, and I loved it.

Soft blue islands and peninsulas are just darker than the morning's fog; their distance informs their color. The blue becomes grayer and darkens near the granite rocks of the shore. Red lettering—5 MPH—and a red stripe on a gray schooner moored just offshore are the only bits of color when the fog is thick and the air is muffled.

Balsam fir is incense on the air; the scent of the ocean itself is at once iodine and salt, familiar and inexpressibly exotic. Seaweed adds its strange tang, as do the drying tidepools and the bits of a gull's dinner washed up on the rock, a fishy smell not as unpleasant as it sounds. At the small wharf where sailors ready their boats and wait upon the tides, the air is strong with gasoline and the medicinal scent of creosote. Like the scent of railroad ties that supported the long lines of tangled tracks near my childhood home and the cough syrup of Pinex and honey my mother concocted when I was young, the aroma carries its baggage of memory and emotion. I couldn't walk often enough beside this small wharf; its scents and sights are a magnet.

The nearby rocks entice me to sketch them, to explore along the shoreline. A small boat is moored, upside down, in a patch of sand between rocks that once were molten. Volcanic granite still bears the voluptuous lines of arrested motion, flowing in stasis toward the sea. Bits of mica glitter in the pale sun that breaks through the fog, a wan light that gains strength as it claims dominion over the airborne moisture. Colors are still muted in the morning light, but the sun catches the edge of a tangle of seaweed that drapes itself over the granite, shining through the wrack as through stained glass, a piercing, acid green against the gray-blue of the far shore. The broad expanse of stone itself gleams in the light, a bald pate of pinkish granite. Far out on the point, a piling rises from the rock, wrapped round with a frayed hawser; someone must tie up here when the tide rises.

Just beyond this broad granite dome, the stone changes shape again, a trickster formation that is now jumbled, now polished, now strung out in long rock fingers of black and white that inch toward the sea only in my imagination. Tide-

pools are caught in the interstices, and I explore the stones, leaping from one to another to see what awaits the incoming tide. The cobalt and violet shells of blue mussels are startlingly bright under the salt water, and bits of bivalves and spiral-shelled creatures are smoothed by the sand and waves, carved into fantastic shapes. A student brings me a sea-polished violet mussel, studded with tiny barnacles and wrapped about with the bleached remains of a seaweed's resolute holdfast; it is a sculpture from the sea, and I wrap it in tissue and tuck it into a disposable coffee container in my suitcase. It is Maine in a Styrofoam cup and I am determined to make it home with its delicate, powerful beauty intact.

In this fecund season, welcome after the long cold, wildflowers fringe the coastline with showy abandon. Nearby, rocky hillsides are veiled with soft color like my mother's Sunday hat. Lady's slipper orchids are common. In June, every roadside and bit of rough ground is dressed with the tall, showy spikes of lupine in pastel hues. Pink, purple, violet; the colors are lovely in the midday sun. Palmate, grayish green leaves are the perfect foil. *Lupinus perinnis* was once thought to leave the soil barren, "wolfing" up the nutrients, hence the name derived from "lupus." But in fact like all pea-family members it enhances fertility by fixing atmospheric nitrogen in the soil—and in a form useful to other plants.

Among these great drifts of pastel color, I discovered a favorite wildflower of the eastern seacoast—the orange hawkweed, a hairy little plant that looks like a cheerful bouquet of dandelions on a tall, thready stem. Like the dandelion, *Hieracium aurantiacum* is also considered a weed by New England farmers, it grows with such enthusiasm, spreading quickly from leafy runners. But unlike that familiar garden plant, hawkweeds come in orange as well as yellow. Someone tells me this is Indian paintbrush, but if it is, it is different from the plant that bears that name at home—clear evidence of the reason for Latin binomials. Common names are all too slippery, referring to one plant here and another in the next state.

Near the salt marshes, bunchberry spreads low-growing

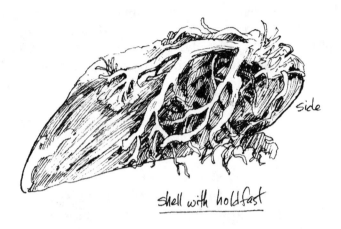

side

shell with holdfast

top

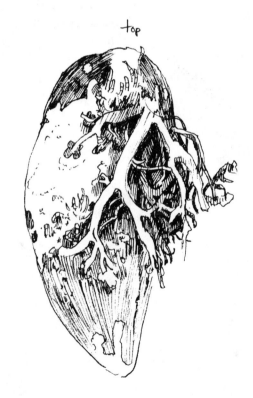

leaves and waxy white flowers; in the fall, their place will be taken by the bright red berries.

A bit farther down the road, someone has dammed a small creek to form a tiny pond—or perhaps it is natural here among the granite rocks. It is lovely, its surface a mosaic of the round leaves of water lily and fringed with knee-deep ferns and spikes of blue flag. I would imagine this the loveliest time to visit Maine if I hadn't seen so many pictures of cranberry bogs in autumn with the lichen-encrusted rocks fringed about with tawny grasses and blood-red leaves. Next time.

Birch trunks stand ghostlike against the dark foliage of the evergreens beside this small coastal highway. The granitic out-croppings that bound the highway cut remind me of home, but with a flavor of somewhere else, somewhere harder and more rugged. Northwest Missouri limestone mellows and flakes, sculpted by water and weather to voluptuous shapes. These rocks look as young and angular as when they were formed by fire deep within; gentling granite takes longer.

Pine, balsam fir, and gray and yellow birch play counterpoint to one another in a chiaroscuro exchange of light and
dark. I tried to capture the effect in my sketchbook, but the
attempt was frustrated by the complexity of the image and by
swarms of blackflies and mosquitoes, just hatched after a particularly wet early spring. They were *wicked*, as they say in
these parts—which means bad, good, or abundant, depending
on circumstance. These were both bad and abundant, and
everywhere I paused to sketch it was necessary to stop what I
was doing to wave my arms madly or blow the biting insects off
my face. Someone told me Avon's Skin So Soft was the panacea
of choice in these parts, but the blackflies didn't believe in
commercials; they bit right through it, and through the deet I
resorted to as well. A too-hospitable habitat in the balsam forests that crowded up against the roads gave the mosquitoes a
running start. Each depression in the soil held its half bucket of
water after the rains; each half bucket was an incubator to thousands of mosquito larvae, and when they hatched they were
hungry. I was fair game, along with every other tender-skinned
outlander in the state.

If their bites weren't so irritating, blackflies would be interesting. Fortunately, I was not among those badly affected by
them; some people are prone to infection or allergic reaction.
My bites were itchy inconveniences and no more. But the little
flies' propensity to bite at the hairline makes them particularly
irksome; it gave me the willies. Bats do not fly in your hair,
contrary to the old wives' tale; blackflies do, and if an insect-
eating bat wanted to follow them I would have been grateful for
the assistance.

As the rising sun chased the fog out to sea, I came across a
tiny clearing in the woods that was etched with fleeting sun-
beams drawn out between the trees. The effect was evocative as
a note of music. Where the sunlight struck thigh-high ferns the
color was bright primavera green; back in the woods the light
was still pale blue, soft as watered silk.

Rivers drain water as richly colored as strong tea from these
coniferous forests; at first I couldn't understand the strong tan-

nic color of the water, unbelievable to one used to rivers either transparent as lead crystal or mud brown with erosion. *Clear* brown water did not scan. But I climbed down to put a hand into it to find it both transparent and dark as the richest amber.

Heavily glaciated areas like this northeastern corner of America are home to most of the country's bogs and the glacier-formed ponds called kettles. Cold and anaerobic, these are not the rich, soupy waters of home, full of life and action. The bog is much less complex in its community of life forms, but insects here had best watch out. If there are fewer fish and frogs to get them, the plants will take up the slack; carnivorous sundews and pitcher plants flourish. Leatherleaf, Labrador tea, cranberry, and bog rosemary, shrubs that appreciate this acidic habitat, are common.

It's a different operation at work, different by far from midwestern waters; here in the North the water is both too chilled to enable the chemical process of decomposition to proceed normally and too acidic in pH to cooperate in any case; it's a perfect preservative, a cold-water pickle. When plants fall into the water, they form a thick tangle of mostly undecayed matter called peat. Rather than becoming a meadow and deciduous forest in due course, as most small bodies of water do in the process called eutrophication, this cold-water habitat eventually becomes a peat bog. These bogs preserve things as diverse as ancient plant seeds, woolly mammoths, and human artifacts, and they dye the water hereabouts with the characteristic brown. They are simply not hospitable to bacteria and other agents of decomposition. That's why the water is so achingly clear—and why the bogs support a quite different community of plants and animals.

Where the rivers drain these peatlands, they take on the same transparent russet hue as the bogs. As they empty into the sea there is an endless exchange of fresh water for salt, an endless exchange of clear water for tea.

I hadn't realized how far the tide reaches up these small streams and rivers; there must be times when you don't know if they're coming or going when the tide pushes them back against their headwaters and salt water mixes with fresh. From the small bridge that crossed the anonymous amber river, pink granite boulders big as sleeping dinosaurs lay half submerged in the water. A soft fringe of salt hay provided a counterpoint to their bony, skull-like shapes. When these rivers reach the sea, their waters carve U-shaped valleys that open windows on the ocean. Broad tideflats eventually form, sometimes studded with islands that bristle with evergreens. I looked out over such a scene just at sunset, wishing I could be on the small island that gazed endlessly out to sea; wishing I could stay forever to see the changing seasons and the weathering of granite headlands.

The tidal flats here are scribed with a thousand calligraphic rivulets that catch the light in this place that is neither fully land nor sea. I was fascinated by the patterns drawn by the water, intricately interwoven lines etched in silver like an illuminated manuscript—trying to capture their sense on paper. The long perspective of the tide flats and the braided lines of the water were a complex Book of Kells and more beautiful by far, transiently scribed with earth and light, gull feathers and moving water.

In this cove, islands of rock jutted from the water; they retreated into the distance as though walking into the ocean, hoping to disappear into the sea. Someone had built a small cottage by the shore, nearly lost in the thick salt hay. The white building glowed softly against the shadowed hills across the inlet, and I wondered what it was like to live there, looking from those lighted windows and listening for the loons.

This ecosystem was as foreign to me as anything I've ever seen. In California, and elsewhere on the eastern seaboard as well, the ocean beats relentlessly against the rock; the rock stands firm as though refusing to be bested. It was this dramatic confrontation of rock and water I had expected to see. (Although how I reconciled in my mind the image of rugged breakers and peaceful seacoast towns I can't imagine. There must be protected coves to allow human settlement to take root.) This gentle exchange of liquid—salt for fresh, fresh for salt—created an unexpectedly soft landscape of tall green grasses, thick and pure and unmixed as lawn. There was something somehow sensual and moving about this endless exchange—something that spoke of continuity, changelessness in a world too willing to change.

I was wrong, of course. Such surface impressions are bound to be romantic and wrongheaded, after a lifetime's mooning over the Maine coast like a girl with a crush on landscape. This rugged and prolific explosion of life appears impervious to harm, immune to humankind's abuses. It is not. The seacoast is threatened as is environment everywhere. There is simply too much pressure—and too much that is unnatural.

Our impact is inescapable. A charming cove surrounded on three sides by a small New England town looks the perfect nineteenth-century fishing village. I imagine the inhabitants able to step from their doors and into the ubiquitous dory, bringing home enough from the sea that laps at their doorstep to feed themselves for a week. Instead a sign near the town's pier warns against eating anything caught from these polluted waters; the town sewer empties into the bay. Nearby, plastic pop-can rings and Styrofoam food containers tangle together with nylon fishing line. Seabirds get caught in the debris, wrapping rings and line around their beaks and starving; wrapping them around wings or feet, rendering them unable to move. Here, too, medical waste washes up on the beaches. Oil spills are a constant threat to coastline and the wildlife that finds it home. Industry empties its waste into rivers that flow to the sea as though that great receptacle could handle anything we throw its way, and unchecked growth threatens eventually to make all but officially protected areas as crowded as any city.

In this birder's delight, this naturalist's haven, the impact of our use and abuse is as present as anywhere. The beauty and charm are still here; the magic remains—but it must be cherished and protected in order to last.

The trip back to the plane was an anticlimax. I had learned what it was like to walk the seacoast. To be trapped in a car, listening to human voices instead of the voice of the ocean, racing to catch a plane after long, slow walks along the rocky beach, was beyond letdown; I felt like I was leaving home. As the sun caught the tilting expanse of ocean when the plane curled back over the land, I watched from the tiny, scratched window until I could no longer see the coast. All too short, still this trip provided me with a lifetime's memories of rambles well taken. I won't forget. A walk along the Maine coast is an exploration along a timeless frontier between land and sea that carries a cargo of genetic memory. The iodine scent of surf and the incense of balsam fir are laced together with gull-voice foghorn-moan, an intricate bundle of sensation that unwraps itself slowly in the mind over time.

Suggested Reading:

Gosner, Kenneth L., *Peterson Field Guides: Atlantic Seashore*, Houghton Mifflin, Boston, 1978.

Niering, William A., *The Audubon Society Nature Guides: Wetlands*, Alfred A. Knopf, New York, 1985.

Rails to Trails

THE AIR IS curiously still this spring day, with a silence broken only by the voices of small songbirds and the occasional racket of a nearby flock of Canada geese. The quiet only holds outside my head; inside, memory brings the steady *whooshhh-hh—whooshhh-hh-h* of a steam engine laboring up the incline, echoing the puffs of my breath as I climb the steep hill.

The big steam-powered locomotives of my youth were running as they were meant to when that sound punctuated the air. For me it means I've been too long on level ground; I am out of shape for climbing. Limestone outcroppings form a barrier against easy access and the only way up is hand over hand. The forest has taken over the hillside; underbrush is both thick and thorny. Once I reach the old railroad bed, though, the going is easier. It was graded close to a hundred years ago and remained busy as a cat during my town's heyday before being abandoned to the trees.

The ties are gone now; the rails were salvaged years ago, to reappear in auto bodies and steel buildings and girders. There is nothing to suggest that this was ever a railroad but the anomaly of heavy concrete bridges in the woods, the strangely level ribbon of ground winding through the forest, and, at its end, the pair of small, neat brick stations, now a print shop and the school district's offices.

It's odd to walk where trains once owned the right-of-way, and to walk in perfect safety—or as safe as it gets in the woods, with only the natural dangers of a turned ankle or falling branch to threaten. But still I feel my indrawn breath held in subdued excitement, just knowing where I am. And what was here.

Titmice and chickadees whistle in the trees, their tinwhistle voices much quieter than the locomotive's. In the evening and early morning, wild turkeys and white-tailed deer leave their safe haven among the trees to feed in the lowlands in front of the monastery. David has watched his cat play hide-and-seek with a young deer, dodging and chasing like a pair of kittens. But by full day the deer have retreated to the forest, hiding among the invisible trestles, wrapped in the green silence of the woods. We see no sign of them but their heart-shaped tracks and beadlike droppings.

Here in David's woods, mayapples bloom in profusion where iron and creosoted ties and tamped gravel once crunched underfoot. Spreading outward in huge colonies, the plants blanket the ground like a convention of elves with green umbrellas.

These are particularly healthy specimens, perhaps fifteen to eighteen inches tall. Waxy white flowers with six to nine petals droop beneath the deeply cut leaves of those plants with a double stem; their scent is fresh, sweet, and strong. My friend Joy Smith has climbed here with me to dig some from David's property. She has a horticulturist's touch; if anyone can make these grow in a backyard, Joy can.

My grandmother made jelly from the fruit of the mayapple, which she (and many of the older hillfolk) called mandrake. It is not, in fact, related to the poisonous European mandrake, but the root is similar—and only the fully ripe yellow-green fruit is edible. The seeds, roots, leaves, and green fruits act as a strong cathartic.

Gauging proper ripeness is never a problem for me; by the

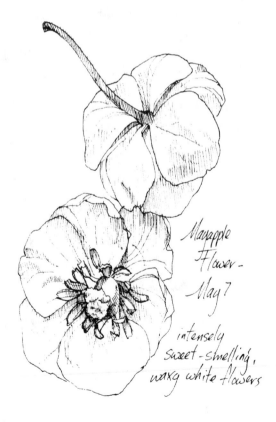

Mayapple
Flower -
May?

intensely
sweet-smelling,
waxy white flowers

time I remember to look for the fruits, the foxes, mice, and raccoons have found them. One of the common names for this wild edible is raccoon-berry (along with ground lemon and Indian apple), which reflects its popularity with humans and animals alike.

Turkey vultures spin lazily overhead, their bare red heads catching the sun. Joy's husband, Tom, who has joined us, sits beside a big oak tree, smoking and watching them. A slow-talking southerner who is comfortable in the forest, Tom towers over ''Miss Joy,'' and holds the sack for her finds. I point her to those that have the best chance of surviving transplant.

I'd never suggest digging plants from the wild; too many are scarce or threatened and difficult to grow. But this is David's property and in this forest of little green umbrellas it's hard to

believe a few plants would be missed. I make my small speech and subside into helping.

Fragrant sumac dots the spaces between the trees, its tight French-knotted flowers and sweet-smelling twigs the only clear clues to identification this early in the season. The scent prickles in my nose and I call to Joy to let her smell the tender, bruised bark. The greenish gold flowers appear with the leaves or even before; later, these will become hairy red fruits and identification will be easy.

This plant was widely used by the Native Americans; in 1590, Harriot Virginia Indians were said to use "Dyes of divers kindes. There is Shoemake well knowen, and used in England for blacke. . . . The inhabitants use them only for the dyeing of hayre; and colouring of their faces, and Mantles made of Deare skinnes; and also for the dying of Rushes to make artificiall workes withal in the Matts and Baskettes."

A later reference by Gerard-Johnson states that "leaves of Sumach boyled in wine and drunken, do stop the laske, the inordinate course of womens sickness, and all other inordinate issues of bloud. The seed of Sumach eaten in sauces with meat, stoppeth all manner of fluxes of the belly, the bloudy flix, and all other issues, especially the whites of women. The decoction of the leaves maketh haires blacke, and is put into stooles to fume upward into the bodies of those that have the Dysenterie, and is to be given to them also to drinke. The leaves made into an ointment or plaister with honey and vinegar, staith the spreading nature of Gangrenes."

Quite a pharmacological repertoire for a single plant, and not the only properties it is reputedly endowed with. *Medicinal and Other Uses of North American Plants: A Historical Survey with Special Reference to the Eastern Indian Tribes*, by Charlotte Erichsen-Brown, contains five closely spaced pages of documented uses of the sumacs dating from 1070 A.D. to 1976. And while the *Peterson Field Guide to Edible Wild Plants* doesn't specifically mention fragrant sumac (*Rhus aromatica*), the other members of the clan (excluding only poison sumac, or

Rhus vernix, the white-berried plant) are all mentioned for their edible properties as a lemony drink.

As we pass these useful plants—along with spring beauty's fading leaves and hidden tubers, healing plantain, acorns strewn beneath the oaks, and the last of the morel mushrooms—I am reminded that we have lost more than the intricate web of railroads that once took us anywhere we could imagine and find the fare for. We have lost our intimate and interlocking connection with the earth itself. How many of us could survive in the wild, finding food and medicinals, dyestuffs, and even the makings of our cookware and clothing among the trees and grasslands?

A new friend, Ruth Ann Cleveland, is an herbalist. She concocts a healing salve from plantain, comfrey, spearmint, and other healing plants, and although I accepted her small jar of sweet-smelling green stuff as a curiosity, I find it indispensable for everything from itches and sunburn to dry skin. A naturalist's hands tend to work under harsh conditions and mine usually reflect that; now they are as smooth and soft as they've been in years. Ruth Ann is reforging a connection to the land, and I find the links of that chain to be strong and good.

The undergrowth is sparse up here on the hill; perhaps the underlying ridge of limestone or the railroad bed's base of gravel a few inches below the accretion of new soil have something to do with it. Perhaps it is only the shade of the thick trees that have taken over since the trains departed that keep down competing growth. The ground is still crisp with a deep layer of fallen leaves, and we play like children, tossing double handfuls up into the air to watch them blow in the wind that comes, at last, from the south.

The evidence of the trees suggests that it must be many years since the railroad was abandoned. Most are middle-aged with a generous understory of saplings. A few, however, seem far too well developed, as big around as a bushel basket in the abandoned right-of-way, and seventy years old at least. Did the train just skirt them, whistling past their already well-developed trunks? It is impossible to tell exactly where the tracks were with only the broken swath of level ground to point the general direction.

Between Excelsior Springs and Liberty—and from there into Kansas City, the nearest big city—I can find the signs that tell me this was once the busy Interurban Railroad. Here is a culvert over a little stream; there is a deep cut between two hills, a deep hollow with a broad, flat bottom. Some of these cuts have been used as private landfills, and they are tangled with rolls of barbed wire, old washing machines, and the remains of someone's roof.

In the years between 1880, the town's founding, and the 1950s, when the health benefits of mineral waters were discounted by an article in the *Saturday Evening Post*, this railroad was constantly in use. Thousands of health seekers came to take the waters; those who served them came in their wake. Tourists, the curious, the famous, and the infamous rode the Interurban. Harry Truman was staying at the historic Elms

Hotel, just a block from the small depot, when the news came that he had lost the election to Thomas Dewey. Reports of his political "death" were greatly exaggerated; our local museum still displays the photo of Truman holding up the newspaper and smiling that canary-eating grin.

Franklin Delano Roosevelt stayed here, as did the New York Giants—and Al Capone. Railroads moved them all, the great and the not-so-great.

They moved me, too, as a child; a place in my mind still echoes with their magic and with the wail of whistles blown away in the wind. My house was set squarely between two sets of railroad tracks. Since I didn't know which side of the tracks I lived on, I had the distinct feeling that I could do anything I imagined myself capable of without benefit of society's smile or censure. It was a good way to grow up.

The closest rails, a half block from my home, were a magnet. I spent hours sitting beside the tracks, watching the trains come and go, waving wistfully at the engineer and the brakeman in the big red caboose. I could imagine myself riding the rails, hopping a freight as my father had done during the Great Depression. I wondered what it was like for my family when it was necessary for Dad to sweep grains of wheat from between the boards of the big boxcars to feed my mother and sister. I wondered what it was to be hungry and to stay that way.

There were the other passengers as well, the paying gentry, the ones for whom the trains were the most elegant mode of travel, with their linen tablecloths and flowers on the table. All the glamour of rails passed by at the end of my street, brightly lit as a feast-day cake. I wanted to go wherever it was those finely dressed people in the fancy dining cars were headed. Once in a while someone would meet my gaze from a train window and smile or wave and I'd want to run after them: "Take me with you."

It wasn't that I had an unhappy childhood, that there was something I needed to get away from. It was more that near the railroads the days—and nights—seemed always filled with possibility, mystery. There was always the question of what was on the other side of the hill, what was around the bend and across state lines. When I heard the whistle—or the deep-throated rumble of iron against steel and the echoing boom of new trains being made up in the railyard—I knew someone was going to find the answers to a piece of that mystery. Someone's possibility would become reality.

I lay awake on hot summer nights, imagining the long line of railcars leaving the outskirts of Kansas City and bending out across the plains, a moving ribbon of light under velvet prairie skies laboring up the mountains, winding between the steep passes, leaving a long, plaintive whistle behind them to tempt me after them. In my mind the trains always went west, to openness.

Just after World War II my young life intersected with those of a wonderful variety of travelers. GIs heading home, tramps, hobos all seemed to find my backyard and my mother's hearty soups, stews, and noodles. They'd do a bit of work in exchange for a meal, then hop the next train and move on. As they ate, I'd ply them with questions about where they came from and where they were headed, of what the land was like there. I heard tales of the New England seacoast and the desert Southwest, of Germany and Japan and the great expanse of ocean. It was a priceless education—and it was a time I can't imagine returning. No one trusts their child with strangers now. No one can. I sat with these strange men—some ragged, some still smartly uniformed—and listened for as long as they'd talk to me. My mother never seemed concerned, never felt the need to supervise every moment. I felt safe, perfectly so; I was. Safe, and full of dreams and stories, tales from the men who passed for an hour or two through my life, making my imagination richer with the remnants of them.

Later, I got to ride one of those great silver trains myself, though by the 1960s they were powered by diesel and not steam. I was eighteen; my mother had just died after a long illness. I had been her nurse and companion for years, and my aunt, who lived in California, knew I'd need a change of scene. She bought me a train ticket west.

It was exactly what I needed. The years of walking wistfully beside the tracks—listening ear to rail like a TV Indian or flattening an endless procession of copper pennies beneath the iron wheels—were finally over. The west; the railroad; there was a ticket in my name waiting at the depot, and I was ready.

It was as though magic had reached back through the years to yank me along with it. Trains go where highways do not, clinging to the sides of mountains, tunneling through like great mechanical moles. They sway underfoot like the ocean; their breath is loud and the sounds of metal-on-metal hypnotic. They are dreams, hitched steel-on-steel.

This particular train had an observation car. I lived there from Missouri to California, scarcely coming down to eat, absorbing everything until my eyes ached with the strain. The vistas that stretched into the distance were wonderful; the mountains that crowded the train, confining it in its narrow silver line, were wild and rugged; big horn sheep watched us pass. The wide desert night was lit with a billion stars. I don't remember sleeping.

My husband tells of tamping ties for sixty cents a day near Kincaid, Kansas, as a young man. They used long steel bars to compact the gravel under the heavy wooden ties, so these supports wouldn't shift under the weight of the trains. They followed the gandy dancers, the legendary men who aligned the miles of new track using only steel rods, a rhythmic chant, and the muscles of arms and backs and legs. Now machines have taken their place and the backbreaking labor of tamping and alignment is done by diesel power.

Today, many miles of these tracks are abandoned. Their trestles still span rivers tumbling impossibly far below, their tunnels still arrow through mountainsides, but the wail and rumble of trains are gone. In many places, new sounds—bicycle tires crunching on gravel, the laughter of children, and the steady footsteps of hikers—have replaced them, thanks in great part to the Rails-to-Trails Conservancy, a non-profit organization based in Washington, D.C. Under the National Trails System Act, when a railroad abandons a section of track, the state or communities through which it runs can petition to keep that section under public ownership. There are some 526 rail-trails already in use nationwide, and more being converted all the time.

The Rails-to-Trails Conservancy helps expedite the change, monitoring sections of line about to be abandoned and helping towns and cities with the mounds of paperwork necessary for the conversion. It is a perfect use for these abandoned corridors, once part of the largest rail system in the world with more than 300,000 miles of track—and it all began in the Midwest.

In 1963, the late naturalist May Theilgaard Watts suggested this use of an abandoned right-of-way on the outskirts of Chicago. In a letter to the editor of the *Chicago Tribune*, she wrote, "We are human beings. We are able to walk upright on two feet. We need a footpath. Right now there is a chance for Chicago and its suburbs to have a footpath, a long one." Built on the firm foundation of one woman's words, the Illinois Prairie Path came into being. It took twenty years, but fifty-five miles of trail are now open to hikers, bicyclists, and wheelchair users.

That's one of the fine things about rail conversions: They are accessible. Long, slow grades meant to ease the passage of thousands of tons of steel, coal, wheat, and passengers also mean easy walking and pleasant cycling—and a place where the wheelchair-bound can enjoy the outdoors like anyone else. No wonder rail-to-trail conversion is gaining in popularity. As more than 2,000 miles of rail are abandoned each year, we users eye the line and see walkers disappearing into the distance, watching for scissor-tailed flycatchers. The railroads pass through every type of habitat in the United States; the trails preserve and showcase the remains of prime landscape, both wilderness and urban.

Yet it can get hairy, depending on who owns the land—the railroads, the government, or private owners. The conversion of railroads to public trails has not always been smooth.

In Missouri, a long section of the Missouri-Kansas-Texas, or MKT, railbed was to be abandoned, and the Missouri Department of Natural Resources joined with other interested parties to take it over as a long, thin state park—the Katy Trail. The plan to remove the rails and turn the corridor over to hikers and bicyclists met with enthusiastic response from many quarters, from those who simply like the exercise to advocates of environment and wilderness.

The plan, however, was not without its outspoken detractors; there were even a few death threats bandied about from one side of the debate to the other. Landowners through whose property the railbed passed accused the state of unconstitutional land-grabbing; they were concerned about littering, vandalism, liability, and trespassing. They fought—in some cases, hard—to keep the trail from happening.

But one reason for the public-ownership provision is that the dwindling resources of natural gas and oil, the changing fortunes of the shipping industry, and their effects on the economic balance may cause the railroads to come back. Rail-banking makes good sense; the Certificate of Interim Trail Use allows for putting the corridors back into their original use if need be. The logic is that if these abandoned railroads are still open—and under public ownership—it won't be necessary to re-buy the land from perhaps reluctant private owners. The Interstate Commerce Commission debated for years over the question before deciding on this solution.

Where the railroads owned their rights-of-way outright, conversion to trails does not create a legal problem; they simply sell what they own, outright and fee-simple. The Katy Trail, however, was made up largely of easements through private property. Landowners were quick to file a lawsuit that went all the way to the Supreme Court.

"When the DNR filed the Certificate of Interim Trail Use on the Katy, then Governor John Ashcroft asked the legislature for a statement of good faith toward its management and maintenance," said Jim Denny, now historian for the Missouri Department of Natural Resources. "They okayed hiring a manager for the park, a couple of rangers, and a couple of jeeps. That's when opposition really heated up."

"Landowners accused us of land-grabbing; the lawsuit was

filed in Missouri courts, but since this was an issue concerning the Interstate Commerce Commission, it quickly became apparent that it had to go to the Supreme Court. It took two years to grind through the federal system," Denny continued.

"A similar case, heard just before the Katy's, was decided in favor of the trail, and set a precedent for such use. We got the okay—but there are still a few people dead set against it. You know, it's funny, though—in one little town where opponents were most outspoken, most of the detractors are now members of the Katy Trail Bicycling and Social Club."

The deciding factor in the trail's finally becoming a reality was a massive influx of private funds from the late Edward "Ted" D. Jones, a stockbroker. He insured the Katy's rebirth when he gave the money to secure the right-of-way; the railroad had been asking a million dollars. Jones offered $200,000 and his offer was accepted.

Once the Supreme Court decision was in place and legalities had been addressed, a five-mile section of trail was opened in April 1990, from Rocheport to Huntsdale. Shortly afterward, an additional section linked up McBaine. In October of that year the Highway 40 to Marthasville section was completed. A second Jones donation is providing much of the funding for the conversion, and his widow is still very much committed to the project. Katy Trail State Park Superintendent John Balkenbush tells me the Department of Natural Resources is aiming at a late '93 or early '94 completion date.

This historic railroad was the first to enter Indian Territory from Missouri after the Civil War; it carried settlers and equipment from Missouri throughout Oklahoma and Texas. The Katy Trail conversion is among the most scenic in the nation, snaking along beside the historic Missouri River on one side and spectacular Burlington limestone and dolomite sandstone bluffs on the other. These bluffs are impressive reminders of a prehistoric sea that lapped shores higher, even, than the 200- to 300-foot reach of the rocky, convoluted cliffs. Early explorers including Lewis and Clark, trappers and traders, naturalists John Bradbury, Thomas Nuttall, and John James Audubon—and other river rats—noted the river and its bluffs in their journals and accounts; they are impossible to ignore.

When the Katy Trail is done, it will be the longest rails-to-trails conversion in America, 233 miles connecting the small towns of Machens in the east and Clinton in the west—and much of Missouri's history in between. The eastern leg, from St. Charles to Marthasville, takes you through Defiance, where Daniel Boone spent his last years, and by a number of the salt licks that appear in over eighty Missouri place names—including Boone's Lick.

Most of the white bluffs that hem in the muddy Missouri are made up of calcareous limestone, but towering St. Peter sandstone bluffs near Augusta are silicate reminders of the old Klondike quarry, where the white quartz sandstone was ground for glass.

Missouri's Rhineland borders the river for many miles; small, neat, and picturesque German-American towns lie in the folds of hills, surrounded by vineyards. Early settlers chose this rich country for its resemblance to their homeland and its wine country. The wine industry still flourishes here, and Augusta's Mount Pleasant Wine Company took top honors with a 1986 vintage port; their 1987 Jour de la Victoire Ice Wine won a silver medal, the highest award given to an American ice wine in international competition.

Now the many vineyards along the trail offer wine tastings and the little towns offer bed and breakfast and antiques to further tempt you off the trail. At the trailheads, you will find restrooms, drinking water, and parking. Some restrooms are porta-potties, but other facilities are in restored railroad depots, heated in winter and with a bit more historic interest than "Hernando's Hideaway."

The section of the Katy Trail that runs from Jefferson City to Franklin is the most spectacular. Here, the bluffs are made up of fossil-rich limestone. Missouri's state fossil, the buglike crinoid, appears in abundance. Lewis and Clark Cave, on private property just below the much larger Boone Cave, is marked with a sign; the spot is said to be one of the explorers' overnight camps near the mouth of Moniteau Creek. A cryptic pictograph, one of the few remaining bits of evidence of Native American occupancy in these parts, is visible above the cave; William Clark sketched it in his journal, and the Moniteau County Historical Society uses Clark's sketch as a logo.

Bob Dyer, an old friend who is also an author, songwriter, and historian, reports that he distinctly remembers seeing the pictograph, but that the last time he was there he stared at the stone for half an hour without making it out. Many of these remnants of an earlier culture were lost to the effects of weather—or vandals. But perhaps the light just wasn't right.

"It's a little confusing, the notes in Lewis and Clark's journals and the river as it is today. When you go to find a specific place, you have to remember that the river has changed; even the places where creeks enter the river may have changed. Also, there were two creeks with the same name; Lewis and Clark referred to the Moniteau and the Little Moniteau," Dyer reminded me.

"But on June 7, 1804, they ate near the Moniteau, at present-day Rocheport; this creek probably stayed put because it's right between two lines of bluffs."

"Doesn't Moniteau mean Great Spirit?" I asked.

"Well, sort of. I think it's more in the sense of the fact that

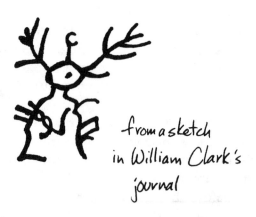

from a sketch in William Clark's journal

the Indians believed there was spirit—manito—in everything. There were tree manitos and rock manitos, but everything had manito. Since they were all part of the Great Spirit, I guess you could say the word means that; Moniteau is the French spelling. I don't even think it's a local word; it was Algonquin, maybe from up around the Great Lakes."

In Clark's own words in his journal of June 5, 1804, we find: "Passed a projecting rock on which was painted a figure and a Creek at 2m. above Called Little Manitou Creek, from the Painted rock this Creek 20 yds wide."

It's still hard to tell where the pictograph's location might be—if, indeed, it still exists. It might be at the place mentioned, for on June 7 Clark noted that the expedition "Set out early passed the head of the Island opposit which we Camped last night, and braekfast at the Mouth of a large Creek. . . . called big Monitou. . . . a Short distance above the mouth of the Creek, is Several Courious paintings and carving on the projecting rock of Limestone. . . . We landed at this Inscription and found it a Den of Rattle Snakes."

There were once thousands of these pictographs on the rocks throughout the Midwest. Many were lost to the railroad itself, when the corridor was blasted through the rocks. But when you see one, it is as exciting as though you were the original discoverer.

Near Franklin, the original town of which was lost to flood in the 1820s, you can see a marker that may keep its place in the pages of history as the beginning of the Santa Fe Trail. Dyer penned a song about Franklin and its place in history; he was active "in a behind-the-scenes kind of way," as he puts it, in the effort to keep the Katy Trail available and its history alive.

The trail conversion has turned around more than one small Missouri town. Where empty storefronts once looked disconsolately out on streets almost as abandoned, now shops, bed and breakfasts, cafes, and bicycle rental shops stand. Some of the Katy's most ardent detractors now bike its lovely curves to see the big river shining in the sun.

Although biking the trail is probably the most popular

mode of transportation, for a naturalist the locomotion of long muscles is more satisfying. This narrow corridor through three of Missouri's natural divisions—Ozark Border, Big Rivers, and Osage Plains—offers a view of reclaimed wilderness, rich farmland, and historic townships not visible from any highway. I don't like to miss a thing.

For now, eagles are visible in winter at close range; they find the nearby Missouri River excellent for hunting, though they don't care much for the close proximity of trail users and may retreat somewhat from the press of human neighbors. George Kassler, chief park naturalist, tells me he has gotten within a hundred feet of the big birds on many occasions.

"In fact there's a great deal of diversity in bird life from one end to the other of the trail," Kassler says. "Since the trail cuts through some beautiful farmland and remnant prairie at the

western end as well as pretty dense woods further east, you're likely to see about anything, including huge flocks of cardinals. Then again, sometimes you don't see anything at all.

"There are turkeys, turkey vultures, and geese. In fact, along the stretch of trail just west of Jefferson City, you can hardly walk in winter without scaring a goose or two from the bluffs."

"I had heard they nested there in summer," I said. "Pretty clever; they keep the goslings safe from predators by finding such inaccessible places. I guess the young ones don't leave the nest until they can fly down to the river; pretty good example of adaptive behavior."

"Yep, and the fact that we see them in winter, too, means that they don't give it up. They know where home is."

Mammals are visible along the trail, too. Deer, raccoons, ground squirrels, coyotes, foxes, and others cross from cover to cover or hunt the more isolated stretches.

"We see 'Missouri Bison' from the trail corridor, too," joked Kassler. "Where it cuts through farmland there are a lot of cattle. But really, if you use your imagination, you can see bison instead of cows, prairies instead of meadows. There are a few remnant prairies along the trail, too.

"Wildflowers are everywhere. Right now, because of a particularly wet spring and early summer, they're especially abundant; usually by June we see a little break before the late summer and fall explosion of color. Flowers are sometimes a little barren outside of the wooded areas," Kassler told me, "but this year they're all over the place."

"What about the kinds of things you often see along railroad rights-of-way—plants that haven't survived elsewhere because we've mowed them down or poisoned them as weeds?" I asked.

These places often act as wild gardens where anomalies flourish. Plants out of their normal element, brought here by the passing trains, may grow undisturbed. Native wildflowers thrive in these long, skinny ribbons of habitat, particularly along seldom-used lines where herbicide-spraying programs have been abandoned. Where these lines have been converted to trails, habitat will remain protected.

"We see a lot of diversity," Kassler answered. "In fact, the remnants of prairie are probably there because of fires that were started by the sparks from the old engines. It takes fire to really maintain a healthy prairie.

"There's all kinds of natural diversity here. We get black snakes, racers, ribbon snakes, copperheads, and other reptiles along the trail. In fact, that's one of our biggest problems; people run them down with their bike tires, either deliberately because they hate snakes—*all* snakes—or accidentally, because they're not looking where they're going."

These cold-blooded creatures seek the warm gravel of the trail. Our irrational fear of snakes becomes their downfall, as does the strange quirk that makes some humans kill anything they're capable of killing.

In most cases, snakes are harmless. Even copperheads have never caused a death in Missouri, though I'd rather not go through the pain and swelling of a bite. The best way to avoid injury is to avoid the snake, not kill it.

"We need to work hard to maintain the natural environment here," said Kassler. "The park only averages 100 feet across. It's a narrow ribbon of habitat bordered by private property—often farmland—on both sides. Even the river and the bluffs are out of the park's boundaries, but within those confines we have a great deal of wildlife, either nesting, hunting, or just passing through. Most snakes are harmless; we need for people to leave them alone, let them be for others to see.

"We hate to have to resort to reminding people that they're breaking the law and are subject to prosecution if they're caught killing anything—or picking or digging plants or flowers, as far as that goes. The plants can't maintain a healthy supply of seed if they're not left to develop naturally."

A few years of unintentional abuse by well-meaning people and there won't be anything left to see but the sky and the bluffs and the river. Along such a narrow corridor, this becomes a critical concern, because the Katy Trail gets a lot of visitors—

250,000 in 1992, people from twelve countries and forty states. If each one picked a single flower before it had a chance to set seed, that flower would disappear in short order.

These rails-to-trails corridors are precious. They take us to places that modern roads can't. Today where river bluffs or rough country present a problem, we just avoid the "scenic route" and move the highway. The old roadbeds preserve an environment—and a time—that lets us look backward to how it once was. Over 100 years ago, a president of the MKT Railroad looked down a long stretch of track and said, "The Katy's future never looked brighter!" Although he may not have envisioned quite the scene we find today with a long gravel trail disappearing into the blue summer distance, his words are still true.

Author's note: The flood of the summer of '93 affected great stretches of the Katy Trail as well as the little river towns along its length. Most of the towns will rebuild their flooded sections and the Katy will be back as well.

Suggested Reading:

Johnson, Cathy, and Patti DeLano, *Missouri off the Beaten Path* (2nd Edition), Globe Pequot Press, Old Saybrook, Connecticut, 1993.

Masterson, V. V., *The Katy Railroad and the Last Frontier*, University of Missouri Press, Columbia, 1988 (first published in 1952).

Ogburn, Charlton, *Railroads: The Great American Adventure*, National Geographic Society, Washington, D.C., 1977.

Winterich, Julie, and Karen-Lee Ryan, *500 Great Rail-Trails: A Directory of Multi-Use Paths Created from Abandoned Railroads*, Rails-to-Trails Conservancy, Living Planet Press, Los Angeles and Washington, D.C., 1993.

Or write: Rails-to-Trails Conservancy, 1400 Sixteenth Street NW, Washington, D.C. 20036.

Eleven

Nightwatch

IT HAS BEEN CLOUDY, it seems, for months, with some form of precipitation falling from the sky most days of a long, wet week. Sleet and wet snowflakes as big as origami birds, deep drifts, and freezing drizzle were a winter-long smorgasbord of meteorological show-and-tell. Sunshine was difficult to come by. Now in April the rain has been nearly incessant and I feel as though my skin must be pasty white with lack of sunlight; perhaps I'll go blind as a cavefish. Day after day is shrouded in lumpy gray cloud cover or a seamless fog. Glowering thunderheads mutter with low growls that explode into cannonfire. Nights have been as cloudy, starless; "dark," as my father would say, "as the inside of a cow." Presumably, that's about as dark as it gets.

For months weathermen have remarked on the dearth of sunny days, and records fall, day by day, like dominoes—if not literally then certainly in wry conversations in the small cafe in my town where farmers gather when it's too wet for most chores.

"Think we'll ever get a plow in the ground this year?"

"Dunno; my cattle are up to their knees in mud. Darned near lost a calf down the hollow. Poor little thing just sunk right in like quicksand. Couldn't move. It was up to its nose when I found it, with its mama bawlin' nearby.''

The ground *is* soft with moisture, though not quite quicksand in most places. Even under a thick cover of newly green grass it gives noticeably underfoot and we joke about not needing an air mattress when we camp *this* year. The ground is plenty soft enough. Moles in their eternal underground night have honeycombed it with their tunnels; I feel them collapse under my weight and compensate for the sudden change in footing.

This week, after more rain on top of the copious amounts we've already had, the ground is both mushy and audible. I walk out into the night and hear a light splash when I step, a soft sucking at my shoes when I lift my feet. I sink in slightly at each step, and remember the drought of a few years back when walking this same stretch of grass was like treading on marbles and rocks, as though the earth itself would throw me like a bronco. This night the ground is soft and wet and spongy, and feels as though I could sink into it like that calf.

Sounds in the profound quiet of the night are present nonetheless. If I listen I can hear the moisture gather at the terminal tips of limbs and drop to the ground, and I can't tell if it is raining, again, or if this rainlike sound is merely an echo. After months of precipitation, I hear it in my sleep.

The smell of earth is far different now, too. In drought there was a tang of dust, a faintly burned odor. Now a rich, fertile scent rises from the soil itself, as if all it would take was a day of sun and we'd be up to our knees in vegetation. Microscopic actinomycetes in the newly warmed soil give off that lovely plowed-field scent that wakens memories of home and childhood and salads made by well-loved, gnarled hands. My grandmother's garden—big as a field in her backyard—smell like that when ground was broken after an April rain. My own small plot is as redolent, waiting for the rain to end so I can seed the rich, black earth.

Odd how you notice more when there is little light to see by. Other senses take over; we become receptors of a different set of messages, messages both cryptic and intriguing. If we let ourselves we can be as aware of our surroundings as though we could see them clearly; perhaps more so. When our show-off sense of sight is dimmed, our skin seems particularly aware of sensory stimuli. As our largest organ it is well supplied with nerve endings suited to the task. I feel the least breeze and can tell an immediate difference in temperature as I walk downhill into the rising cool of a hollow.

Delightfully unfamiliar, the night is another country. I walk through its dark hours like a tunnel, smelling new scents, feeling its caress, listening to its music. It is a habitat all its own, claimed by a different set of birds and mammals than the daylight hours—unless the normal diurnal creatures are disturbed. Sometimes when I walk in the dark I am startled by a sudden chitter and loud whir of wings; some sleeping songbird has been wakened by my passing, and it explodes from its roost with great energy and muttered imprecation.

It takes a different approach to walk at night, a readiness to suspend the familiar for the unknown, an adventurousness, if only on a minor scale. There is a slight sense of danger; what you don't know *can* hurt you, and there is a need for ordinary care to be extended to take into consideration the fact that your eyes are not as reliable now as during the day.

George Hiser, our local conservation agent, was reminded of that truth not long ago, and in unpleasant fashion. He and a friend had been out trying to get a turkey to gobble in response to a mimicked barred owl's call, and walking back in the growing dusk in sneakers and shorts, he was bitten by a copperhead.

"It got me just below the inside of the left ankle; I had to have stepped right over him without seeing a thing," Hiser told me.

The swelling was quick and emphatic, and George spent a day in the hospital telling everyone: "It was my fault; I *know* better than that." He hates to see an irrational fear of snakes result in wholesale slaughter of these beneficial reptiles. Even pit vipers have their place in Hiser's cosmos.

Fortunately, copperhead bites are more painful than ulti-

mately dangerous; they are the least toxic of Missouri's pit vipers. Of the 100 to 200 people bitten each year in my state, no human deaths have ever been recorded. Still, it's wise to *try* to watch where you're going or go properly dressed for snake country. The elk-skin leggings my friend Ed wears while trekking look hot for a summer's walk, but they'd certainly help prevent snakebite.

When I walk at night I cultivate a different gait. Mindful of invisible bumps and potholes that may be distorted by deep shadow, I ready my natural shock absorbers to receive them, keeping knees looser and slightly bent. My more normal, purposeful walk of the sighted hours is of use only where streetlights give me a hint of my surroundings. My usual absent-minded ramble that gets me from here to there while my thoughts take wing in the daytime is awakened, alert to any change in ground surface or slant. In the woods, I walk with a stick, ready to fend off branches that slap at my face. I compensate for my diminished capabilities with close attention to the more subtle hints dropped by my surroundings. It isn't hard.

It also isn't second nature, not anymore. Since the first cave dwellers discovered that fire offered not only heat but light, we have preferred to spend our time where we can see what we're doing. There are fewer surprises that way. Fewer surprises, but fewer opportunities for serendipity.

The hair rises on my arms, and the hackles on my neck. A quick thrill of shivers travels up my spine on invisible fingers, and I squint into the gloom as if by doing so the night would become less opaque.

What *is* that vague shadow over in the tall grass? What is that sound? Why do I feel something is watching me?

I feel it because it probably is. And probably it is benign, as startled by my presence in its nocturnal territory as I would be by a possum in the front parlor.

I seldom see deer in the daylight hours, though I know they are here. The big whitetails weave webs of tracks through the night, as active as the spiders that rebuild their webs for the hunt. As I walk, a loud nearby *snort!* makes me freeze in place. Halfway between a sneeze and a grunt, it is the alarm sound of a deer. It can see me far better than I can discern its shape camouflaged by darkness.

This night the ever-present clouds have at last broken up. Sometime after dark, sometime after the last round of hard lashing wind and the rapid clatter of hailstones, a window opened in the sky. There are stars overhead, glittering against the transparent dark.

Even so, light seems almost totally absent; it's the dark of the moon, and hours before the tiny sliver rises in any case, carrying with it a hint of its shadowy self. Still we can see where we're going well enough, once rods and cones in our eyes adjust themselves to the night. And there is that welcome starlight to see by, though it has traveled light-years to reach us.

Now color vision abates, and black and white sensitivities take up the slack; cones recede, rods advance. I can see not only my hand in front of my face, but the nightshadows we throw on the asphalt road through the park. The cat that hunts at the edge of the park, remembering wildness for all its closeness to the little Victorian neighborhood across the bridge, is far better equipped than I. With 130 million photoreceptors to my 120 million, it's ahead in the numbers game. But that's not its only advantage. In dim light my pupils expand to gather every bit of available light, as do the cat's—but feline pupils are capable of much greater relative expansion than mine. Its irises nearly disappear, swallowed up by dark pools of light-seeking pupil.

The sky glows with its own dim, tenuous light, emitting measurable luminosity. It's a combination of luminars that create this incandescence: the auroral glows, the scattered light of cosmic dust particles, the quick sparkle of a meteor shower, radiation from atmospheric gases in the ionosphere—and the lovely light of stars and nebulae. I can almost sense the pure light of space where the sun shines unobstructed between the planets beyond our own small darkness, throwing prickly shadow cones like the bristles of a Jimsonweed pod.

And the lake glows back, its surface still, mirror-like in the calm, suddenly windless night. Not a leaf moves; not the least wave disturbs the surface of the water, only a slow, gentle ripple as though the lake rocked itself to sleep, and I wonder in this year of storms if this luminescent tranquility will stay with us once daylight comes.

Be advised, if you imagine the countryside drowsing silently under the stars. It is not. Crickets pierce the air with

sound from spring until fall, boring their way into sleep. Whip-poorwills call all night long during mating season, and although it is a sound sweet to my ears—well loved by my mother and sought out on many a spring ride through a country night—still I am awake to hear it, smiling into the darkness. Sleep is not an option, and I may as well walk to see if I can get close enough to hear the whippoorwill's indrawn breath, sounding a faint *click* before each stanza of song.

These birds are ground dwellers, making their nests among the sticks and leaf litter. Small, weak feet make them ill-equipped for perching. If I do see a whippoorwill on a limb, it will most likely be aligned with the limb and resting its body on the wood, rather than jauntily crossways like most birds. So complete is their camouflage, a variegated mufti of spotted, gray-brown feathers, that even in daylight I've never found one sitting on a nest though I've walked miles through these Missouri woods.

Nighthawks boom in the cloudless night sky. Neither strictly nocturnal nor, in fact, hawks, these big relatives of the whippoorwill cry and circle overhead, and when they dive their wings make a startling *whooomp!* against the resistant air as though playing a wind instrument I cannot see. Distinctive shapes in the fading light—scimitar-winged hunters—make them easy to identify, flying much later than the chimney swifts that go off to bed in great dark clouds against the sunset.

At the edge of the forest, woodcocks call with a plaintive *peent*-ing sound meant to entice a mate. Unlike the nighthawk's great sonic boom, their wings make an odd "chippering" when diving. As I entered the woods on the way to the cabin, I startled one from its nest, and it rose with a great flutter of wings. Round as a chicken, the woodcock I have heard all these early spring nights looked amazingly awkward to have choreographed the impressive mating flights we watched from the edge of the meadow. These flights are unique, fascinating, spiraling high overhead in great, powerful loops. The woodcock then kamikazes downward at a startling speed, pulling up at the last possible moment. If I am lucky I can see the long, slender bill used to probe for earthworms silhouetted against the sky, like a darning needle sticking out of a pincushion.

Raccoons rattle through the leaves in search of food or argue over territory; I hear their shrieks and grunts and watch, bemused, from a safe distance. It wouldn't do to get in the middle of the fracas. These masked mammals, so clever and dexterous that we invariably imagine them as pets, are nonetheless occasional carriers of rabies. In a fight, no wild animal is harmless, no matter how cute.

This year there are fewer raccoons pacing the darkness. Disease in the form of canine distemper has decimated their numbers in my part of the country, and I miss their almost constant presence on my nocturnal rambles. The distemper epizootic is cyclic, Pete, my veterinarian, says. Those that are left will be immune for a while, and their offspring will share a lessened immunity; population will build back up. Then the whole event starts over.

Deer mice chew on the floor joists, a sound that bores into my sleep and calls me out for a brief turn around the walnut

grove. It is a noisy ramble in these hours I normally miss to a good night's sleep. Bobcats hunt in the night; foxes bark; coyotes set up an a cappella chorus and the young join in, weaving small falsetto voices above and through the wild symphony. And every dog in three counties hears the elusive, interesting sounds in the darkness and responds by telling its neighbor, full voiced and excited.

Among the cacophony of night sounds is the occasional deep-throated hoot of the great horned owl; once just at dusk my husband and I walked the path around Williams Creek Lake, listening for night voices. One seemed much closer than the others, but although we looked for the origin of the repeated hoots for a quarter of a mile, we could find nothing. The big bird had clammed up or sailed off on silent wings at our approach. Now we rounded a turn near a small bridge and looked up to see an odd sight—it was an owl I had never seen before. It had "ears" that stood up like a great horned owl's—not ears at all, nor horns, but merely feather tufts. But instead of the lighter-colored belly normal to most owl species, this one had a dark front. On closer inspection, I could not see the scaly yellow feet—and no wonder. Suddenly we realized that the owl intently observed us over its shoulder with its head turned completely aft. When it turned slowly to the fore again, eyes blinking independently of one another, I had the unnerving feeling that Linda Blair had sprouted feathers and we'd best summon an exorcist to the woods.

A more common sound than the great horned owl's syncopated call is the repeated *who-cooks-for-you, who-cooks-for-you-a-a-alllll* of the resident barred owls that seem to own midwestern woods. I seldom take a nocturnal walk without their aural accompaniment. Even in winter these big owls call to one another as they hunt, presumably reporting on their quadrant of the night.

Unlike most owl species, the barred owl has eyes as dark as the night itself. The stereotypical yellow glare of the owl I see in my mind does not apply, giving this Strigidae family member a far more approachable appearance than most. It is as though the family dog had sprouted feathers and turned to flight. I am not fooled by the owl's sweet face and bottomless eyes, however. In visiting Pete's wildlife rehabilitation facilities I've found the barred owl as adamant about protecting itself and its immediate territory as any other raptor. The big bird backs up its intent with slashing talons and a sharp, hooked beak. Designed to capture prey, these tools are as useful in discouraging my advances.

And advances are to be discouraged in any case. These are not pets. The inclination of humans to domesticate everything we come in contact with is as difficult to override as a computer command built into my hard drive, but it must be done if these creatures are to be returned to the wild. They have to take care of themselves, and it's sad to see an animal that has imprinted on human beings. It is lost, crippled, unable to find its way back to the instinctive and learned wariness and the wild skills that will keep it alive. Beth Howard, administrator at the Lakeside Nature Center in Kansas City's Swope Park, says that all you can do in that case is either re-create the natural fear of humanity with isolation or loud noises, or keep the animal in captivity for the rest of its life. It's not a happy choice.

Once in a great while I hear the tremulous call of a barn owl

at the edge of the forest. These once common night birds, ghostly in white plumage, are rare now that most of the old barns have disappeared, torn down or weathered slowly into the ground. The steel buildings that have replaced them, with tight-fitting doors and windows that offer no egress, are hardly welcoming to barn owls and other native denizens. Nest boxes provided for these displaced creatures have not been as effective as hoped, but a few have found use.

Much more common are the tiny screech owls. These pocket-sized raptors are regulars of this nocturnal habitat, but their voices could only be called a screech by one soured on the night. It is a sweet tremolo, repeated over several times before ending with a much lower, pulsating trill.

I have seen both red phase and gray phase screech owls in this corner of the Midwest, though the word "phase" may be a misnomer, according to some. Unlike the willow ptarmigan, which changes predictably from brown to white and back again depending on the season, these little owls may decide on a color scheme and stick with it for life, or switch at will, depending on where they live—and other factors known only to screech owls. Eastern screech owls may alternate red and gray phases, while western screechers choose between brown and gray with never a red in their wardrobe. In my area of the country an individual owl may not change at all, so I'm told.

Like long-eared and short-eared owls, screechers have tufts that stick up like a great-horned owl's feather "horns." These are no more ears than horns, but feathered "plumicorns," more decorative than functional.

Occasionally we see a long-eared owl or a tiny saw-whet, but most unusual by far was the huge snowy owl that made Resurrection Cemetery in nearby North Kansas City its temporary headquarters. For a season, birders traveled from several states to see it, and no wonder. It was a magnificent creature when it spread big white wings, as though a guardian angel had visited the cemetery to guide someone home.

The forest that surrounds my cabin is the perfect place for wildlife rehabilitation. Far from the road, there is little to disturb the patient. There are a variety of habitats nearby, ensuring an abundance of food, and water in the pond if the creek is dry. My modest 18 acres back up to 300 more, relatively unspoiled, unoccupied timber that crawls with mice and voles, raccoons, opossums, skunks, ground squirrels, and lizards—wildlife heaven. I can be here in less than ten minutes; closer to five if I'm lucky.

Many creatures have found a welcome here among those born on home territory. Wendy, a friend who is also involved in wildlife rehabilitation, released a raccoon and a Virginia opossum, both nocturnal species. Injured songbirds, once healed, find room among the trees. "Give me your tired, your poor, your . . ."

The Assassin—a great horned owl that had lost a confrontation with a Buick—didn't act tired at all when he arrived. He was *mad*, infused with an energy born of fury and fear. Named by Pete's children for his nasty disposition, he wasn't used to being transported in a carrying cage meant to hold the family cat, and the transition from the Ruckers' place to mine must have been unsettling. When released from the small carrier into the more spacious flight cage, he attacked, slashing Pete's face with talons an inch long and barely missing his eyes. A veterinarian must get used to these attacks on his person—but I can't imagine he'd ever be completely ready for them.

I learned an instant respect for the owl that went far beyond his impressive size—according to one source, the great horned owl is the largest of all American species except the great gray. Caged or not, hand-fed or not, this was no pet.

Pete left the owl in its cage with a supply of raw chicken and instructions for its care and feeding—and for my safety. When I opened the wire enclosure the next morning to offer a supply of water for bathing (owls get most of their needed moisture from their food), I was careful in the extreme. My husband distracted the owl's attention from the rear; I opened the door, hastily deposited the big pan, and beat it out of there as quickly as possible.

The owl was totally alert, totally focused even in repose. He sat in his flight cage at the edge of the trees, waiting to be released into this unfamiliar habitat, and seemed to be taking inventory. His head swiveled in response to the slightest sound that might signal prey, the most subtle scent that told him a faraway skunk might be available for the canny hunter. Squirrels, voles, small birds—his big eyes caught each movement. It is perfect habitat for owls.

An owl's eyes are, in fact, immense, big as a Susan B. Anthony dollar. They are larger than human eyes, protruding from the skull and encased in a sheath of bone. That's why an owl turns its head to follow movement; those big, tubular eyes have little room for the kind of muscles that allow our own eyes to swivel in their sockets. They are capable only of extremely limited eye movement, perhaps to fine-tune their focus. The owl's eyes are placed forward on its head (unlike those of most other birds, which are set to each side and designed for great peripheral vision, the better to counter an attack with evasive action). The eyes-front configuration gives the owl excellent binocular vision—like ours. What this means to the owl, of course, is that he can focus astoundingly well and that he can see what's in front of him in detail and dimension. These are the eyes of a hunter.

The Assassin's pupils are not controlled by light level alone, but contract and expand in an instant—sometimes, unnervingly, independently of each other. His night vision is superb; the owl has many more light-sensitive rods than we do, though to say he can see in total darkness is probably incorrect. If an owl seems to possess supernatural hunting skills under these circumstances, it is probably due to its acute hearing, able to focus on a single point with amazing accuracy. That dish-like face with its array of fine feathers directs sound to the eardrum just as the outer parts of our ears do; asymmetrical placement of the ears in the owl's skull make for great triangulation of auditory signals. Zap! The prey is in the crosshairs.

We planned to set the Assassin free at dusk on Monday; he had been with me two full days, and he would begin to lose tone in his flight muscles if he were caged much longer. Either

Pete would have to bring the jesses out and fly him amongst the closely spaced trees for exercise or we would let him go on his own.

In the oppressive heat, the owl's white throat patch vibrated rapidly as though he were panting—as in fact he was. I felt like doing the same as I sketched him from nearby. My studio with its electric fan was a mirage as tempting as a tall glass of iced tea with a slice of lemon and a sprig of mint. Sweat trickled down my forehead and into my eyes, but I hated to make the sudden move to wipe it away that would startle the owl. Setting discomfort aside, I had no intention of letting the opportunity escape; how often do we have the chance to be alone in the presence of wildness and to try to capture its essence on paper?

I thought that given enough time and silence in the midsummer heat the Assassin would drowse, allowing me to work at a leisurely pace as had the little screech owl I painted two years ago, and once he almost did. He was becoming used to me

by then, as long as I kept my distance and made no sudden moves; it was obvious I posed no threat. The lights dimmed in the big yellow eyes; they narrowed sleepily, the bottom lid rising to meet the top, and I expected to see the pale blue-white nictitating eyelid come up like a gauze curtain. If it did, I missed it; the pinkish lids with their fringe of lash-like feathers met, the neck settled into the shoulders, and the owl balanced himself for sleep. But a dog barked in the hills nearby, and after that he was again deadly focused and alert.

I wondered if the neighborhood dogs had found his cage the night before and harassed him. It was peaceful as the grave, from early morning until after dusk while I was present, but the other side of the clock was a mystery.

Night is indeed a different matter here in the country. Once when we stayed over at the cabin, a big dog with a eardrum-rattling voice treed a raccoon, keeping us awake until 2:00 A.M. After hours of this we gave up the hope that the dog would tire of his blood sport. With no way to deter him short of the hand axe, we packed up and left to find sleep in our own bed at home. Perhaps the racket doesn't bother the nocturnal owl—he punches the time clock when the sun goes down.

I waited for Pete and his wife, Nancy, and the kids to come out to release the Assassin after Andy's softball game, savoring the last of my time with the big owl—hating to see it end. Shadows crept up the east hill, engulfing cabin and cage. Whip-poorwills voiced their lament beyond the grove and I had begun to hope the Ruckers had decided to wait one more day.

But at last as darkness fell I heard the sounds of dogs on the road and the rattle of gravel, and saw headlights moving slowly down my rough drive.

Nancy had brought her visiting mother; both children were excited. We all crowded around the cage, trying to be quiet while Pete donned heavy leather gloves and unlocked the cage. He grabbed the Assassin's legs, lifting the big bird for what we expected to be the last time, showed him the chicken thigh I had placed atop the flight cage; held him high and let go, and the owl sailed off—straight down onto the path twenty feet away.

"We'll try it again," Pete said.

We had stepped back to give him room, and carefully, he recaptured the Assassin, raised him again, and let him go once more. The owl settled gracefully among the brush and weeds only slightly farther away, and a few feet off the path in the heavy brush.

"Damn! Stupid owl," Pete swore softly. "He flew two hundred feet at home just two days ago." He was disappointed that his charge had fared poorly, and was beginning to worry about the owl's ability to succeed on his own.

Sending Nancy to the truck to get a big towel to throw over the owl, Pete maneuvered again through the edge of the woods after the Assassin.

"Cut him off, Andy; go around in back of him."

I positioned myself beside the path when it looked as though *Bubo virginianus* might cut back toward the creek and the flight cage, and our blocking tactics must have worked. Pete recaptured the bird without incident, lifting him gently from beneath the towel.

"I don't think he likes this many people," five-year-old Leslie said.

And maybe she was right. Deciding to put the owl on top of the flight cage near his meal instead of tossing him up for another attempted takeoff, Pete and the family trooped back to their car.

"He'll fly if he wants to. If not he'll stay there till tomorrow, close to food," Pete reassured me.

Headlights marked the car's trajectory back up the hill, and I watched the dim shape of the Assassin as he waited, it seemed, for a sign. And when the lights were less than halfway up the drive he must have received it; when I looked back he was gone.

I checked the ground near the cage. Nothing. I walked around the path, but there was no sound. Not a hiss, not a bill clack. The Assassin had disappeared. And by morning, so had the chicken thigh.

I continued to leave offerings for two weeks after we released the big owl, and I watched for owl pellets near the cage
and on my walks, clues that my friend had eaten nearby. I found
nothing—at least not then. Owl pellets are a common artifact of
the woods. I often find them under a favorite roosting tree.
Dissecting them back at the cabin, where a magnifying glass and
good light are handy, I am able to get a picture of what these
owls eat—and of what else populates the woods. Mice, moles,
voles, and small birds all make up the owls' chosen cuisine; I
could have told if the Assassin had crunched up a chicken bone.
Digging through the pellets after these cryptic clues requires a
certain detachment and a bit of a cast-iron stomach.

Recently, just after a long ramble through the woods, a
friend called me at the cabin. It had been a productive walk, and
I had found several specimens, some desiccated, some fresh,
and all interesting.

"What are you up to?" David asked.

"You might not want to ask that just now."

"Why not?" he said, intrigued.

"I'm dissecting owl pellets," I told him. "That way I can
tell what they're eating."

"Owl pellets. Right." And with that we changed the subject, moving quickly on to other things. As a bishop in the
American Orthodox Church, regurgitated owl leavings are not
exactly his stock in trade—though the subject has made fine
fodder for later teasings. David loves to tell people what I do at
the cabin.

These bits of waste may be less than appetizing conversation, but they're fine and encyclopedic bits of natural information. Owl pellets, coyote droppings, and other organic leavings
can tell a lot about the diversity of the forest and its denizens—
and the state of their health, as well as what they're finding
nearby to eat. Nocturnal and crepuscular hunters—those creatures that inhabit the other side of the hourglass—keep their
secrets too well unless we are willing to take the clues we're
given. Coyote and fox droppings are often dried-out bits of fur,
filled, like the owl pellets, with bits of skull and bone. Some-

where there are still berries to eat; the purple-stained droppings of the birds attest to that. Raccoon scat may be thickly studded with persimmon seeds when I have yet to find a persimmon tree anywhere in the vicinity. No matter; it's there. The raccoons tell me so. All these nocturnal hunters leave plain evidence for me to read; it doesn't take a Sherlock.

Fort Scott National Historic Site in Fort Scott, Kansas, is an 1842 military post built to keep the peace on the Indian frontier. The buildings are set foursquare to one another across an expanse of buffalo grass; large, wooden, two-story edifices that seem somehow French with their second-story entrances, soaring flights of stairs, and broad porches. The authentically restored fort includes a hospital, officers' quarters, guardhouse, powder magazine, and museum. Once each year, a mountain man rendezvous is held on the grounds, beside a patch of tall-grass of the sort that once surrounded the fort.

I spent the night in a tipi there, unable to sleep in the strange surroundings. The embers in the firepit waned to a pulsating glow, and wisps of gray rose to the smoke hole overhead, half obscuring the stars; I lay on my back to find them in the tiny black hollow. We were staying in a friend's tipi, sharing this ancient lodging with two other couples, and what would have seemed strange at home was, in this lodgepole anomaly, perfectly natural.

At last the others drifted into sleep. My husband's even breathing beside me told me he was comfortable in these ancient surroundings; soft snores contained within the canvas walls said I was alone in my wakefulness.

Lights and shadows played across the canvas as the trees overhead leaned and danced in the wind. Crickets called into the cooling night, their slowing song a gauge to the dropping temperatures after a day of heat and rain. Cattle called uneasily in the distance, their voices rising and falling in syncopated cycles, a distinctly imported sound in this ancient setting. Overhead, a great horned owl called to its mate and was answered from a tree at the far end of the patch of prairie. The night sounds that came from the prairie grasses were hypnotic, but they did not make me drowsy; instead, they called me outside without my willing it. I sat for a while on the wooden trunk I had left outside the lodge; then, curiosity and a kind of restlessness I couldn't ignore took over. It was too strange, too exotic— too strangely familiar. I felt as though I were in a movie and soon the theme from *Dances with Wolves* would rise from the dark grasses. I couldn't sit still, and walked the camp, the compound, and the edge of the prairie.

In the coolness, the grasses themselves had a voice, a whisper of wind on stem and leaf that strangely magnified every sound. Here and there down the line of tents and lodges someone coughed or turned over in his bedroll, the human noises as timeless as the voices of the wind and the songs of the grass. A few fires still glowed before the camps; a log fell into the embers with a soft hiss and a scatter of orange sparks that danced up into the blackness. The smell of wood smoke wove itself into the night-scent of the tallgrass.

Alone with my thoughts and with these age-old scents and sounds, it was hard to believe I had driven here in a rented minivan, that a few hours ago we had shared a pizza a block or two away in the small Italian restaurant, laughing and joking and shooting straws at one another like teenagers. Now time had fallen away in the small hours of the night, focusing in on itself, its field of vision narrowed to a time that could have been 200 years ago or 2,000. Against the transparent darkness the shapes of the seed heads were startlingly clear, as though drawn in crisp ink lines. Even at night, even in darkness, the sky is the light-giver.

I prowled the line of buffalo grass between the tents, lost in the sense of the past, walking as silently as possible so as not to disturb the camp and watching the edge of the tall grass as though I expected a bison to appear, or an antelope; when a man emerged from his tent across the way I was startled as though suddenly awakened. I had fallen headlong into reverie like Alice through the looking glass, and thought perhaps I was dreaming, for the prairie at night is very different from the same place in the daytime—and a bed laid on buffalo grass is not a Beautyrest.

"It's beautiful, isn't it?" I asked him as he passed.

"Yes; are you all right?"

"It's just too much to sleep," I replied. "I don't want to miss it." He nodded understanding and moved on between the rows of canvas lodges and tents, long hair tied behind his neck, woolen capote and bare feet a sight from this country's past. It seemed fitting, in the small hours at the edge of the tallgrass.

Suggested Reading:

Johnson, Cathy, *Nocturnal Naturalist*, Globe Pequot Press, Old Saybrook, Connecticut, 1989.

Kappel-Smith, Diana, *Night Life: Nature from Dawn to Dusk*, Little, Brown & Co., Boston, 1990.

• T w e l v e •

The Local Wilderness

Broken Stones

The creekbed is a jumble of rocks and stones and pebbles—all sizes, all shapes. They are mortared together with a rough aggregate of smaller and smaller bits. Some have been ground to powder and I wonder that they don't set up like the portland cement they resemble, to become rock once again. With sufficient time—give or take a few million years—and the pressure exerted by subsequent layers, they probably will.

There are new smaller rocks in the making; the deep cold has split several of the limestone rocks in the creek into pieces with the dreadfully accurate chisel of a chill I can barely comprehend. They sit where they split, like Chinese puzzles dropped on the ground, their pieces asunder but still adjacent. How many years will it take of tumbling away down the creek, sanded by the water and by one another, until they are rounded and smoothed and not even God could find their puzzle mates?

Someone once said that life was like that—we are stones tossed together in a moving stream, wearing away one another's rough edges with our constant human contact. The metaphor is meant to be a positive one—we take on polish as our differences are worn away. But to me it speaks of loss of individuality, loss

of that special angularity of personality that makes us each unique. I *like* a difference of opinion, a new slant on our world view, a different accent that puts a spin on the same old words.

It's a wind-waving slackrope we walk here, I'll admit; individuality is both to be prized and played down. Individuality in the best sense of the word means the courage not to go blindly along with the herd, to be what we are, and to stand for what we know is right, what is brightest and best in our makeup. But we Americans pride ourselves on our pioneer mentality, our "rugged individualism." That mindset has taken us a long way down some wrong turns. One of the more unsettling of these is represented by the Uzi-toting survivalist who slips through the wilderness in nearly all parts of our country, waiting to inherit the land by virtue of being the last one left alive.

None of us is immune. Even those less extreme are subtly

influenced, imagining ourselves pitted against the elements in a contest with nature. Nature, of course, doesn't give a damn if we are even *here*, let alone who wins or loses. The concept doesn't apply. Our vestigial frontier mentality leads us to the idea of conquest and domination of nature; if anything is worn away, we want it to be the unpredictability, the sheer unconquerability of nature itself, not us—never us.

It isn't going to happen. Bill McKibben's well-taken points in *The End of Nature* notwithstanding, we are slated to lose that particular contest. Nature has certainly been changed and perhaps inalterably. The anonymous traveler who packed away the tenuous balance of nature in this rich Pandora's box must be appalled at the course we have set. In the Adirondacks, ice that formerly set up as hard and as amenable to travel as a superhighway by the onset of cold now remains soft and pithy far into the winter, the result of acid rain in the water. But even with our changes—inadvertent or otherwise—the balance falls to nature. It will not be controlled, not in any significant sense. Anyone who has ever faced down the awesome power of a tornado or seen the inexorable waters of a flood knows that. You don't stop the forces of wind and weather, climate and season; you don't even moderate them. *You* adjust. *You* bend. Or you are the one who is conquered.

If we choose to eradicate ourselves as we grind away at nature, so it goes. The planet—unless we blow it to smithereens—will recover without us in a few million patient years. And except for my own quite human desire to live forever and anon—or for my species to—I'm not sure that's such a bad idea.

I carry one of these winter-split rock puzzles carefully back to the cabin, holding pieces together as I go, and place it on the shelf by the door. But soon the bits fall to the deck as I go in and out, and like a relationship gone sour, I can no longer make the pieces fit. The sense has gone out of the stone.

Sometimes even the everyday realities become skewed by tragedy, by stress. What provided an unquestioned comfort is now seen through the unfocused eyes of a different perspective, unavoidable and painful.

A cotton wool fog is pulled down around our ears; the day has an air of unreality. What had seemed familiar and secure is today wrapped in a strange, claustrophobic closeness, and everything I knew is changed. Today as I walk through these accustomed woods I feel as disoriented as though I had wandered onto foreign soil. My mind is a mine field of emotion and I walk carefully to avoid being blown to bits. I can see no more than a few feet into the thick fog blanket that suffocates my hillside, though my eyes strain to see beyond the veil as if searching for a glimpse of the future. My thoughts are at once chaotic and strangely muffled. I imagine I can shake my head to clear it, but the attempt only reawakens the dull pain that sits just behind my eyes.

In my woods—my own safe woods where I've gone to seek a kind of perspective, a freshening of perception—there is the sound of artillery. I flinch as though struck, then duck to the ground as though a Scud missile streaked overhead. It is only the sound of limbs breaking under the weight of ice; the storm came and went over a period of days, coating everything with a deadly accretion of crystalline danger. I've made it here between onslaughts, driving gingerly over the hilly gravel road, maneuvering past cars that have lost their momentum and landed in the ditch at crazy angles as though bombed and deserted.

Again there is a crash, and another, and another, this time from the cabin itself. In the thin warmth—only slightly above freezing—the layer of ice lets go my metal roof, sliding down the long furrows to crash onto the deck. When I arrive I find these guided missiles halfway down their launching ramps, curving crazily toward the wooden platform as the combined effects of gravity and melt draw them downward. As the point of no return is reached, each lets go and hits the deck, shattering into glassy shards like war-zone windows.

I walk oblivious to the reality of my surroundings, oblivious to everything but the thoughts that rage through my brain. There has been too much loss, too much anxiety, too little sleep. My home in town seemed more like a prison than a fortress, and escape was imperative. But at last, in the alien chill of the ice storm, a different reality reasserts itself, a reality that lies far beyond the human. It is terrible and powerful, seductive and comforting.

Eventually, against all odds a deeper quiet fills my ears, laced beneath the crash of ice and limbs, gently crowding out my chaotic thoughts. The fog becomes more comforter than obstacle, wrapping me away from the world. The world—my small corner of it—shrinks to the area I can see through the vapor; details are sharply limned, and the bright, ornate crust of lichen catches my eye. I can't help but admire its endurance. The symbiotic relationship between the algae and fungus that work together to make this single entity is ancient, successful, and right. Algae works its alchemy of photosynthesis; fungi breaks down the rock to make nutrients, and the two, hand in vegetative hand, join to become lichen, that most primitive and hardy life form that thrives even on the Arctic circle—and perhaps on Mars itself.

There are tracks of deer in the dusting of snow that covers the icy crust; three-toed tracks of a covey of quail stitch across them in counter-rhythm. A squirrel, unaware of the conflict that rends the world I know, has dined on the flat table of a cut stump, leaving his litter behind him to return, inevitably, to soil. Another grasps my proffered bread in small, dexterous paws, his eyes large and dark; I think of my beautiful godchild Nora, whose bottomless eyes have always made me think of small wild animals; I can't help but laugh at the juxtaposition. When at last I leave the grove it is with a measure of peace, however transient; even in the face of pain and loss, nature has that to offer. It is not us; it is not human; it is completely, comfortingly other. And like the lichen, it endures.

Walking in your own backyard may seem too tame, too predictable at first consideration; how could peace—or adventure—be found in these mundane surroundings? We are used to thinking in terms of hiking through *wilderness*, and that is a

Mushroom remains on the old Osage orange stump — the squirrels' favored table

fine and pleasant thing, if all too rare. My backyard, on the other hand, is available to me on a moment's notice. What I see from my kitchen window is investigated in seconds, and a turn around the cabin's eighteen acres is a walk through mystery and delight; there is always something to discover. A walk needn't imply an expedition. It can be spontaneous as an errant thought and, in the best of worlds, should be.

It's a matter of keeping an open mind, and a set of eyes as fresh as a child's. And, in fact, sharing your rambles on occasion with a youngster is as good a way as any to cultivate that freshness.

Think about it. A child on a walk is full of questions. "What's that?" is one of the most common, and it's asked about everything from mushrooms to rocks to insects. A child's curiosity is universal; everything is fair game. Taking a young one along reminds you what it is to see—to really *see*—the world around you. And to care what's in it. If I can practice half that open-ended attitude, the world is a new and exciting place, even if it is right outside my back door. *Especially* if it is right outside my back door.

Not only is this local wilderness accessible, it is available any time of the day or night. What is old hat at noon is magic by moonlight. Season as well as time works its legerdemain; the view I've seen 5,000 times from my front porch is suddenly transformed by the fire of sunset glinting off an ice storm's crystal tracery.

It is a lesson hard learned by its very familiarity. And the lesson I detect is this: Never, never take the earth for granted, not any part of it. It is precious, essential—and threatened, even in these small, homely pieces.

Too often, it is as though we think it doesn't matter if it is already familiar to us. We appear to believe we needn't take care of that which is hemmed in by civilization, as though it's too late to care. But it is these very pocket-sized bits and pieces of wildness that can be most valuable to us on a day-to-day basis.

I live not three blocks from Isley Park Woods, an old-growth, presettlement forest that preserves a fragment of what

Missouri was like before Europeans arrived. Here are wild-flowers, from early spring beauties and bloodroot to autumn's haunting Indian pipes. Whippoorwills, barred owls, turkey vultures (and turkeys), white-tailed deer, woodchucks, squirrels, and many other creatures find this small wilderness home. It is a city park and a Missouri Natural Area—and it is under almost constant attack by those who have no idea what a natural area is.

"Well, what do we have to do to maintain it?" asked one well-meaning young man who wanted to pave a walking trail through the woods and open it up to increased human traffic.

"Leave it alone" is the best answer. Let it be natural. Let nature, as they say, take its course.

Our city fathers often put forward the same sorts of dubious improvements, planning to make paths, extend the walking trail, put in picnic tables, rake up the leaf litter, and cut the deadwood that makes nest holes for downy woodpeckers, bluebirds, and chickadees, as well as squirrels and raccoons. The plan is always to "clean up the park." I mount my soapbox at least twice a year to try to preserve this tiny place, a place for study and contemplation and peace. We can't take it for granted, not this place nor any other small remnant of nature.

Spring seemed to have gotten lost somewhere along the bleak corridors of winter, made a wrong turn and wandered, disoriented, way past its appointed time. We feel the longing in our veins, like a shortage of some vital nutrient. In a world long accustomed to the rigors of winter, it seemed as though spring's perennial message of life and rebirth would never arrive. But in hints and whispers and outright assertions, here, at last, it is.

The neighborhood park, with its natural area a reminder of presettlement landscape, calls from three blocks away. Even as I sit in front of my computer screen, I know it is there. My eyes wander toward the south window, where I can see the forest on the hill, and I am gone.

Trees still stand etched in stark calligraphy against the sky, or wear veils of softest, sheerest color. The willows respond first to the changing season, with a flush of red twigs or golden leaf buds that mask the contours of the hills. Then flowering redbud and the early wild plum begin to show their colors like street-corner gang members.

The showy redbud, *Cercis canadensis*, isn't red at all, but a kind of indescribable rose-fuchsia. It won't sport large heart-shaped leaves till later; now they are tiny and tender and red-green at the terminal ends of twigs, wearing protective coloring to prevent damage from the sun.

This is a slender tree of the understory, no more than forty feet tall. Here and there it has chosen a spot to congregate, tinting the forest hot pink. Filling in an abandoned tractor road, fringing an overgrown clearing, redbud makes late April days a study in beauty. By midsummer, branches will be fringed with thousands of green-bean-like pods among the leaves; for the adventurous among us, the fresh young pods are also edible, as are the flowers.

You may know redbud as Judas tree. According to legend the related Asian species, *Cercis siliquastum*, was the tree on which Judas Iscariot hanged himself—the pale white flowers blushed red, stained indelibly with blood.

Soft, gray catkins of pussy willow (*Salix discolor*) hatch like furry caterpillars from glossy, protective scales each spring. Their "cocoons" have shielded them well, but when we can't wait another minute, we bring the bud-laden switches inside in late winter to force a promise of spring. Young twigs are red-brown and smooth and appear almost polished; older twigs are dry and gray—I can empathize with them all too easily. Before long, male plants are dusty with yellow pollen, triggering the first of the year's sneezes for those so inclined.

Trout lilies are among the early wildflowers in the woods; their large, maroon-spotted basal leaves swim through intermittent breezes like their namesakes in an Ozark stream. Dogtooth violets, they are sometimes called—but they are neither violets nor conspicuously doggy. What they are is both shy and jaunty, nodding modestly on thready stems, petals back-turned like sailors' hats. According to my *Peterson's Field Guide to the*

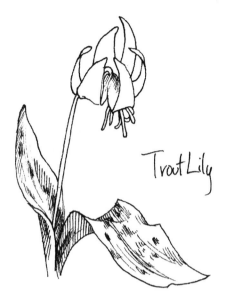

Trout Lily

Wildflowers, the white trout lily—*Erythronium albidum*—seldom has mottled leaves; that's the province of *Erythronium americanum*, the yellow trout lily or adder's tongue. But here in my part of the Midwest, the plants don't read—the early wildflower is both mottled, as if broken shade fell on the leaves, and flowered in pale, delicate, rose-tinged white.

Cut-leaved toothwort or *Dentaria laciniata* is a member of the mustard family; if you look closely you'll see the family resemblance in small flowers arrayed in a terminal cluster. Both Latin and common names refer to tooth-like projections on underground stems, but to me those small white flowers look decidedly molarish.

Mild weather and duly fallen rain bring serendipity: a sparse stand of edible morel mushrooms, the delectable *Morchella*. Where I live the woods and abandoned orchards are alive with would-be feasters, poaching gleefully on a particularly promising habitat. Who can blame them? That rich, earthy taste beckons across the years, stronger than memory. My friend Terri hopes for enough to make mushroom catsup, a condiment from our past, but if I find 'em, I fry 'em, and let cholesterol and catsup be damned.

Early spring heralds itself audibly, as well; the sleighbell voices of spring peepers ring from every farm pond and slough. A true chorus frog, *Hyla crucifer* is the tiny three-quarter-inch amphibian that makes this racket to call up a consort from the cold wintry mud, neither secretive nor silent in its mating. We all know what's on the *frog's* mind, but the sound still brings a catch to the throat as does the clamor of geese overhead.

Among the first insects to appear in early spring are the hibernators. Like bears, the tiny, blood-red spots of moving color—ladybug beetles (family Coccinellidae)—have slept in the soil overwinter. They're communal; I brush aside a comforter of fallen leaves to find thousands of them clustered together for warmth. Their unmistakable ladybug odor rises on the chilly air in a cloud.

These little predators, aphid eaters, all, are out on warm, late-winter days; by spring they are everywhere. Their voracious insect eating earned them their name in the Middle Ages when they rid the blessed grapevines of pests, thereby saving both the sacramental wines and the syllabub; they became known as ''Our Lady's Bugs'' from that day to this.

Red is not their only color; one fall I found a congregation of red, yellow, ashy-gray, and greenish ladybirds—and a few black with red spots for good measure, a confetti convention on their way to winter.

Another insect hibernator is the somber mourning cloak, *Nymphalis antiopa*, the first butterfly of spring. Unlike any other butterfly in our region, this one has hidden beneath tree

bark—or the shingles on my roof—to wait judiciously for hospitable weather.

A walk in almost any spring habitat save desert brings
that most welcome bird whose sudden caroling after the long
silence calls up the spring: the American robin. Even in the
desert the robin may pass through on its way to somewhere
else. We watch for the first robin on our lawns and at the edge
of the woods as if for spring itself; they often dance their odd,
head-cocked-then-duck-and-run ballet while snow is still on the
ground.

And in fact, deep in the woods a few of these relatives of
the hermit thrush may have wintered over, never going south at
all. Most of us never notice these winter robins unless we come
upon one of their roosts. These may contain thousands of the
creatures; it would be hard to miss them. I saw one disgruntled
individual in January in the park, emitting only an anxious—or
was it irritable?—*perp!*

When the ground thaws and robins hear the hidden move-
ments of earthworms underfoot we watch the feast with amuse-
ment. One fellow seemed so glad for the spring treat of fresh
worms that he stuffed himself as I do on Thanksgiving. It was
nearly impossible for him to swallow the huge night crawler he
had pulled protesting from the cold ground; his crop bulged
crookedly and he staggered lopsided as a drunk, a worm end
dangling from his beak. This well-loved bird had been hard at
work, eating and mating and raising his young; it looked as if he
was building up his strength for the prodigious task. A robin
may raise several broods; one is just fledged when the next one
hatches. And, the male is a bird for the nineties—he helps to
care for his young.

I don't need a computer to track the turning of the earth
toward the sun; the abacus beads of these spring signs are sufficient. I tick them off, one by one, with satisfaction.

What we call home is an accident of birth; what captures
our allegiance is ingrained, and although I fantasize about New
England or the Canadian woods, it is here where I live that has

first claim. I was born into these riverine hills more years ago than I care to track, a natal accident that suits me like no other. It is history—my own, my family's, the earth's—that keeps me here. History and natural history.

The Missouri River flows through my imagination; it has made its indelible channel there as well as on the land, where, from the air, you can still trace the complex braidings of the ancient riverbed. *Peketanoui*—River of the Big Canoes—catches the moon in its swath and cradles it in a sheet of silver light. It carves its way through layers of limestone and silt, and though reined in somewhat by dams and locks, still it goes its own way, patiently and inexorably fulfilling its own agenda. When it is time, when weeks of rain erase our wishful remnants of control, the river reclaims its own.

Huge catfish scour the riverbottom in search of food, their whisker-like barbels of more use than eyes in the silty murk. Blue cats upward of 300 pounds were caught here a century ago; a 100-pound fish is not uncommon today. Herons stalk the shallows, startling the air itself with pterodactyl croaks. Bald eagles fish the river—symbols incarnate. Broad beds of mussels tempt shell rustlers; legal musseling is allowed only in three areas, but mavericks go their outlaw ways like the frontiersmen before them.

Family legend has it that the Clark of my grandmother's maiden name came directly from William Clark, the famed explorer who with Meriwether Lewis helped to forge the white man's way west. I was never moved to investigate beyond legend until I discovered that both Lewis and Clark were naturalists, specifically commissioned by Thomas Jefferson to discover what plants and animals lived in the territories. The thought makes me smile, since the naturalist's trade is how I make my living, as does reading the explorers' accounts of a bend in the river not five minutes from where I write.

It's the rock as well as the river that captures my imagination. Here pale outcroppings of Pennsylvanian-era limestone poke through the glacial soil like an ancient, bony skeleton. It is 300 million years old, and it has much to tell the paleobiologist; a certain forensic knowledge extrapolates a tale of life and death at the bottom of a shallow inland sea that lapped above present-day Kansas City when this area was equatorial.

Small marine animals—ammonites, brachiopods, corals—are folded into the stone like nutmeats in a fruitcake. Bug-eyed trilobytes stare blind and noncommittal from the rock. As water levels fluctuated, bits of plant life were fossilized between layers of rock like ancient flowers pressed between the pages of my grandmother's field guide.

My corner of Missouri knew the mammoths and mastodons; their fossilized teeth are found nearby, and Meriwether Lewis reported his theories regarding these New World elephants to President Jefferson. Musk oxen grazed where bison would follow; sometimes I imagine their dark hair blowing in the long winter grasses of remnant prairie.

Stone that was once alive has a power in the mind. Animal, vegetable, or mineral? Here, there's no easy answer.

There was no Missouri River as we know it until some

15,000 years ago; the wall of ice of the last glacier pushed the waters before it as it advanced to form the present-day river. As the ice melted, vanquished slowly to the north, dust blew up against the face of the glacier and fell to earth, forming the loess hills where my cabin hides. Sometimes I find *loesskindchen*, "children of the loess"—small chubby stones that occasionally formed within the larger matrix. I grin with delight, knowing that some may have precipitated around a tiny bone or shark's tooth, but I leave the mystery intact. To find out is to crush a loesskindchen.

Glacial meltwater deposited rocks of a different sort, travelers from the north picked up and abandoned here by the wall of ice. Entombed in the ice, larger rocks and boulders moved with the glacier, scribing the limestone bedrock, to be jettisoned here like excess baggage along the Oregon Trail. Glacial erratics litter the landscape north of the Missouri, but it's litter of a magical sort. The Native American tribes used the largest of these monolithic chunks of quartzite and granite as landmarks and ceremonial sites. I picked up a smaller version on my way to the cabin, marking land of my own, though my ceremony is solitary and cerebral.

Calcareous limestone is soft, as stones go; susceptible to the action of water and wind. Missouri has more caves than any other state in the union—5,400 and counting—carved by great underground rivers into a maze of crystalline caverns and sinks. Not far from my cabin is a ledge of rock, scimitar-curved, suspended over the valley like a tent. It was used by Native Americans to provide cover on the long hunts up from the river; I find prehistoric smoke stains on the roof. There is no permanent stream here, only the seasonal action of meltwater and rain to patiently cut away the rock. Someday this open-mouthed cave will retreat into the hill and disappear, but for now I seek its shelter and wonder about those who went before. It is the same rock cave that held the campfire and deer print I found last year; I return to it when I can, as if on a pilgrimage.

Not all action is as slow as the wearing away of limestone. Here we have had volcanoes and earthquakes; in the St. Francois Mountains to the south—among the oldest mountains on the continent—ancient lava flows are sketched in graceful, art nouveau lines in the stone. At New Madrid, the fault that rang bells in Boston when last it danced a grand-scale fandango waits underfoot, poised to shift like a sleeping giant. I will feel it here, when it does. The possibility adds a certain piquancy to life and tends to discourage complacency. There's no doubt of its intentions; historical record is fresh; prehistory concurs, and synclines and anticlines written in limestone layers mark where the rock lifted and rucked. Today measurable activity occurs almost daily.

Geology forms and informs this land; the limestone that underlies this section of the country seems an odd enough reason to stay, but it's one of the best I can offer. The timeless nature of landscape gives me perspective on a scale that comforts as well as humbles—here before our advent, it will be here when we are gone.

It was the anomalous flash of white that lured me into the woods on a day almost too busy to breathe in—but too beautiful to waste. A bit of pale buff halfway up the hillside in the rapidly greening forest caught my eye like a signal flag, and after one too many phone calls I had to see what it was.

The shortest distance between two points is indeed a straight line, and within the bounds of possibility in this deep valley, I took that tack, crossing the creek and climbing up the rocks like an aging mountain goat. I kept my eye more or less on the goal, orienting myself by its odd color.

There is a small trace that bisects the hill a quarter of the way to the top, an ancient road well on its way to reclamation by the woods. It is visible mostly by the slant of the ground and the modest girth of the saplings in its way. It is used by deer and dogs and the occasional hunter wandering onto posted property.

It was the leavings of one of the latter I thought I saw on the path, a Styrofoam coffee cup crushed to a flattened bowl. But as I bent to pick it up I saw it was, instead, a turtle's shell, weathered white as ivory against the damp black earth. I lifted it carefully; the shell fragments were loose at the bony sutures that hold this hard armor together like a skull, and I wanted to take it with me. Realizing that the rest of the turtle—sans flesh—might still be there as well, I sat like a child on the soggy earth to gently tease the remains from the ground.

It was a job fit for an archaeologist. Translucent amber sections of tortoise shell lined the depression, flaked away from the hard white inner shell. Most were only slightly concave, but a few were V-shaped, the bits that covered the joining of flat plastron and upper shell. Beneath these I found first the lower section of plastron, then the hinged upper piece, like two mismatched panels of a Chinese ivory screen. The flatness of these two pieces told me this turtle had been female; the male has a concave plastron to allow him to stay mounted during intercourse—no easy matter if you and your mate are both shaped like salad bowls. Bow-legged bits of leg bone and tiny vertebrae and the delicate V of the lower jaw emerged from the soft soil, but only one fragment of skull remained—at least that I could find.

Last spring I had seen a female box turtle burrowing into

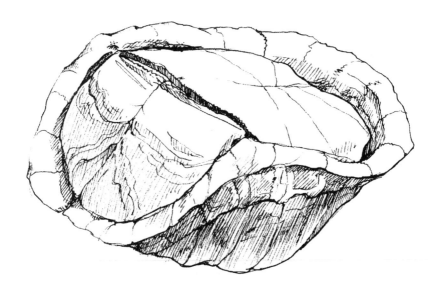

the soft, loose mound of an anthill nearby—the perfect place to lay her eggs with a minimum of effort, to the turtle's mind. I wondered if she had returned to hibernate in this remembered spot, then perished overwinter.

My friend Grady Manus has a pocket made from a box turtle's shell, an early Native American answer to the absence of built-in storage in clothing. It was a common custom on the frontier, and the first Europeans to walk my piece of Missouri borrowed the idea—or traded for these handy containers. In his job as administrator of Fort Osage, Grady wears his turtle-shell pocket suspended from his belt to show the wide-eyed school-children where he keeps his secrets. My shell is too beautiful as it is, a collection of fragments that once held the secret of life, instead.

This white shell reminds me that early spring is the best time for a walk in the woods, the best time to see the oddities uncovered by melting snow. I find the skulls of mystery birds and marmots, the white surfaces of artist's fungus primed for my instant scrimshaw.

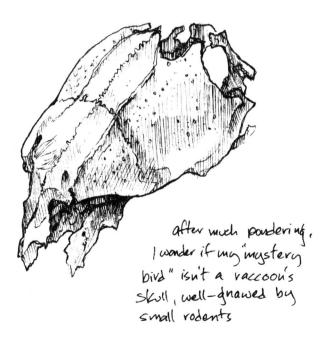

after much pondering, I wonder if my "mystery bird" isn't a raccoon's skull, well-gnawed by small rodents

But this day I found only leaves bleached by the long, white winter, snail shells studding the hillside, bits of white chert weathered from the rock, a bent branch covered with a mildew-like fungus that looked like a coat of white paint—and the peace that comes from taking off, lighting out, and leaving work and worries behind.

I look for anomalies in the woods, the things that catch your eye and plant their questions in your mind. This day I found them in the form of a turtle's shell and a sense of possibility in my own backyard.

Suggested Reading:

Johnson, Cathy, *The Naturalist's Path*, Walker, New York, 1991.

————, *One Square Mile: An Artist's Journal of the American Heartland*, Walker, New York, 1992.

Mitchell, John Hanson, *A Field Guide to Your Own Back Yard*, W. W. Norton, New York, 1985.